Siegel's
TORTS

Essay and Multiple-Choice Questions and Answers

Brian N. Siegel
J.D., Columbia Law School

and

Lazar Emanuel
J.D., Harvard Law School

ASPEN
PUBLISHERS

1185 Avenue of the Americas, New York, NY 10036
www.aspenpublishers.com

©1996, 1998 Aspen Publishers, Inc.

A WoltersKluwer Company

Printed in the United States of America.

ISBN 0-7355-4932-X

This book is intended as a general review of a legal subject. It is not intended as a source of advice for the solution of legal matters or problems. For advice on legal matters, the reader should consult an attorney.

2 3 4 5 6 7 8 9 0

About the Authors

Professor Brian N. Siegel received his *Juris Doctorate* from Columbia Law School, where he was designated a Harlan Fiske Stone Scholar for academic excellence. He is the author of *How to Succeed in Law School* and numerous works pertaining to preparation for the California Bar examination. Professor Siegel has taught as a member of the adjunct faculty at Pepperdine School of Law and Whittier College School of Law, as well as for the UCLA Extension Program.

Lazar Emanuel is a graduate of Harvard Law School. In 1950, he became a founding partner of the New York firm now known as Cowan, Liebowitz & Latman. From 1960 through 1971, he was president of Communications Industries Corp., multiple licensee of radio and television stations in the Northeast. Since 1987, he has served as Executive Vice President and General Counsel of Emanuel Publishing Corp. He has edited many of the publications in the Professor Series of study aids and in the Siegel's series of Essay and Multiple-Choice Question & Answer books.

Acknowledgment

The authors gratefully acknowledge the assistance of the California Committee of Bar Examiners which provided access to questions upon which many of the essay questions in this book are based.

Introduction

Although your grades are a significant factor in obtaining a summer internship or permanent position at a law firm, no formalized preparation for finals is offered at most law schools. Students, for the most part, are expected to fend for themselves in learning the exam-taking process. Ironically, law school exams ordinarily bear little correspondence to the teaching methods used by professors during the school year. They require you to spend most of your time briefing cases. Although many claim this is "great preparation" for issue-spotting on exams, it really isn't. Because you focus on one principle of law at a time, you don't get practice in relating one issue to another or in developing a picture of the entire course. When exams finally come, you're forced to make an abrupt 180-degree turn. Suddenly, you are asked to recognize, define and discuss a variety of issues buried within a single multi-issue fact pattern. In most schools, you are then asked to select among a number of possible answers, all of which look inviting but only one of which is right.

The comprehensive course outline you've created so diligently and with such pain, means little if you're unable to apply its contents on your final exams. There is a vast difference between reading opinions in which the legal principles are clearly stated, and applying those same principles to hypothetical exams and multiple choice questions.

The purpose of this book is to help you bridge the gap between memorizing a rule of law and **understanding how to use it** in the context of an exam. After an initial overview describing the exam writing process, you will be presented with a large number of hypotheticals which test your ability to write analytical essays and to pick the right answers to multiple-choice questions. **Do them — all of them!** Then review the suggested answers which follow. You'll find that the key to superior grades lies in applying your knowledge through questions and answers, not rote memory.

In the sample answers (both to the essays and to the multiple choice), you will notice references to *Emanuel* on *Torts* (General Edition). The reference tells you where in the outline to find the relevant discussion. Thus, a reference to "Ch. 12–VI(B)(5)(a)" means Chapter 12, section (Roman numeral) VI, capital letter B within that section, number 5, paragraph a. This notation is perhaps less convenient than page numbers, but it helps us keep the reference constant from one edition of a book to the next.

GOOD LUCK !

Table of Contents

Preparing Effectively for Essay Examinations

Essay Questions

Essay Answers

Multiple Choice Questions

Answers to Multiple Choice Questions

Index

Preparing Effectively for Essay Examinations[1]

To achieve superior scores on essay exams, a student must (i) learn and understand "blackletter" principles and rules of law for each subject, and (ii) analyze how those principles of law arise within a test fact pattern. One of the most common misconceptions about law school is that you must memorize each word on every page of your casebooks or outlines to do well on exams. The reality is that you can commit an entire casebook to memory and still do poorly on an exam. Reviewing hundreds of student answers has shown us that most students can recite the rules. The ones who do **best** on exams understand how problems (issues) stem from the rules which they have memorized and how to communicate their analysis of these issues to the grader. The following pages cover what you need to know to achieve superior scores on your law school essay exams.

The "ERC" Process

To study effectively for law school exams you must be able to *"ERC"* (*E*lementize, *R*ecognize, and *C*onceptualize) each legal principle listed in the table of contents of your casebooks and course outlines. *Elementizing* means reducing the legal theories and rules you learn, down to a concise, straightforward statement of their essential elements. Without a knowledge of these precise elements, it is not possible to anticipate all of the potential issues which can arise under them.

For example, if you are asked, "what is self-defense?', it is **not** sufficient to say, "self-defense is permitted when, if someone is about to hit you, you can prevent him from doing it." This layperson description would leave a grader wondering if you had actually attended law school. An accurate elementization of the self-defense principle would be something like this: "Where one reasonably believes she is in imminent danger of an offensive touching, she may assert whatever force she reasonably believes necessary under the circumstances to prevent the offensive touching from occurring." This formulation correctly shows that there are four separate, distinct elements which must be satisfied for this defense to be successfully asserted: (i) the actor must have a *reasonable belief* that (ii) the touching which he seeks to prevent is *offensive*, (iii) the offensive touching is *imminent*, and (iv) the actor must use no greater force than she *reasonably believes is necessary under the circumstances* to prevent the offensive touching from occurring.

---

1. To illustrate the principles of effective exam preparation, we have used examples from Torts and Constitutional Law. However, these principles apply to all subjects. One of the most difficult tasks faced by law students is learning how to apply principles from one area of the law to another. We leave it to you, the reader, to think of comparable examples for the subject-matter of this book.

Recognizing means perceiving or anticipating which words within a legal principle are likely to be the source of issues, and how those issues are likely to arise within a hypothetical fact pattern. With respect to the self-defense concept, there are four *potential* issues. Did the actor reasonably believe that the person against whom the defense is being asserted was about to make an offensive contact upon her? Was the contact imminent? Would the contact have been offensive? Did the actor use only such force as she reasonably believed was necessary to prevent the imminent, offensive touching?

Conceptualizing means imagining situations in which each of the elements of a rule of law have given rise to factual issues. *Unless a student can illustrate to herself an application of each element of a rule of law, she does not truly understand the legal principles behind the rule!* In our opinion, the inability to conjure up hypothetical problems involving particular rules of law foretells a likelihood that issues involving those rules will be missed on an exam. It is therefore *crucial* to (i) *recognize* that issues result from the interaction of facts with the appropriate words defining a rule of law; and ii) develop the ability to *conceptualize* fact patterns involving each of the words contained in the rule

For example, an illustration of the "reasonable belief" portion of the self-defense principle in tort law might be the following:

> One evening, A and B had an argument at a bar. A screamed at B, "I'm going to get a knife and stab you!" A then ran out of the bar. B, who was armed with a concealed pistol, left the bar about 15 minutes later. As B was walking home, he suddenly heard running footsteps coming up from behind him. B drew his pistol, turned and shot the person advancing toward him (who was only about ten feet away when the shooting occurred). When B walked over to his victim, he recognized that the person he had killed was not A (but was instead another individual who had simply decided to take an evening jog). There would certainly be an issue whether B had a reasonable belief that the person who was running behind him was A. In the subsequent wrongful-death action, the victim's estate would certainly contend that the earlier threat by A was not enough to give B a reasonable belief that the person running behind him was A. B could certainly contend in rebuttal that given the prior altercation at the bar, A's threat, the darkness, and the fact that the incident occurred within a time frame soon after A's threat, his belief that A was about to attack him was "reasonable."

An illustration of how use of the word "imminent" might generate an issue is the following:

> X and Y had been feuding for some time. One afternoon, X suddenly attacked Y with a hunting knife. However, Y was able to wrest the knife away From X. At that point X retreated about four feet away from Y and screamed: "You were lucky this time, but next time I'll have a gun and you'll be finished."Y, having good reason to believe that X would subsequently carry out his threats (after all,

> X had just attempted to kill Y), immediately thrust the knife into X's chest, killing him. While Y certainly had a reasonable belief that X would attempt to kill him the **next time** the two met, Y would probably **not** be able to successfully assert the self-defense privilege since the "imminency" element was absent.

A fact pattern illustrating the actor's right to use only that force which is reasonably necessary under the circumstances might be following:

> D rolled up a newspaper and was about to strike E on the shoulder with it. As D pulled back his arm for the purpose of delivering the blow, E drew a knife and plunged it into D's chest. While E had every reason to believe that D was about to deliver an offensive impact on him, E probably could not successfully assert the self-defense privilege because the force he utilized in response was greater than reasonably necessary under the circumstances to prevent the impact. E could simply have deflected D's prospective blow or punched D away. The use of a knife constituted a degree of force by E which was **not** reasonable, given the minor injury which he would have suffered from the newspaper's impact.

"Mental gymnastics" such as these must be played with every element of every rule you learn.

Issue-Spotting

One of the keys to doing well on an essay examination is issue-spotting. In fact, issue spotting is **the** most important skill you will learn in law school. If you recognize all of the legal issues, you can always find an applicable rule of law (if there is any) by researching the issues. However, if you fail to perceive an issue, you may very well misadvise your client about the likelihood of success or failure. It is important to remember that (1) an issue is a question to be decided by the judge or jury; and (2) a question is "in issue" when it can be disputed or argued about at trial. The bottom line is that if **you don't spot an issue, you can't discuss it**.

The key to issue-spotting is to approach a problem in the same way as an attorney would. Let's assume you're a lawyer and someone enters your office with a legal problem. He will recite the facts to you and give you any documents that may be pertinent. He will then want to know if he can sue (or be sued, if your client seeks to avoid liability). To answer your client's question intelligently, you will have to decide the following: (1) what theories can possibly be asserted by your client; (2) what defense or defenses can possibly be raised to these theories; (3) what issues may arise if these theories and defenses are asserted; (4) what arguments can each side make to persuade the factfinder to resolve the issue in his favor; and (5) finally, what will the **likely** outcome of each issue be. **All the issues which can possibly arise at trial should be discussed in your answer.**

How to Discuss an Issue

Keep in mind that *rules of law are the guides to issues* (i.e., an issue arises where there is a question whether the facts do, or do not, satisfy an element of a rule); a rule of law *cannot dispose of an issue* unless the rule can reasonably be *applied to the facts.*

A good way to learn how to discuss an issue is to start with the following mini-hypothetical and the two student responses which follow it.

Mini-Hypothetical

A and B were involved in making a movie which was being filmed at a bar. The script called for A to appear to throw a bottle (which was actually a rubber prop) at B. The fluorescent lighting at the bar had been altered, the subdued blue lights being replaced with rather bright white lights. The cameraperson had stationed herself just to the left of the swinging doors which served as the main entrance to the bar. As the scene was unfolding, C, a regular patron of the bar, unwittingly walked into it. The guard who was stationed immediately out-side the bar, had momentarily left his post to visit the restroom. As C pushed the barroom doors inward, the left door panel knocked the camera to the ground with a resounding crash. The first (and only) thing which C saw, how-ever, was A (who was about 5 feet from C) getting ready to throw the bottle at B, who was at the other end of the bar (about 15 feet from A). Without hesita-tion, C pushed A to the ground and punched him in the face. Plastic surgery was required to restore A's profile to its Hollywood-handsome pre-altercation form.

Discuss A's right against C.

Pertinent Principles of Law:

1. Under the rule defining the prevention-of-crime privilege, if one sees that someone is about to commit what she reasonably believes to be a felony or misdemeanor involving a breach of the peace, she may exercise whatever degree of force is reasonably necessary under the circumstances to prevent that person from committing the crime.

2. Under the defense-of-others privilege, where one reasonably believes that someone is about to cause an offensive contact upon a third party, she may use whatever force is reasonably necessary under the circumstances to prevent the contact. Some jurisdictions, however, limit this privilege to situations in which the actor and the third party are related.

First Student Answer

"Did C commit an assault and battery upon A?

"An assault occurs where the defendant intentionally causes the plaintiff to be reasonably in apprehension of an imminent, offensive touching. The facts state that C punched A to the ground. Thus, a battery would have occurred at this point. We are also told that C punched A in the face. It is reasonable to assume that A saw the punch being thrown at him, and therefore A felt in imminent danger of an offensive touching. Based upon the facts, C is liable for an assault and battery upon A.

"Were C's actions justifiable under the defense-of-others privilege?

"C could successfully assert the defense of others and prevention of crime privileges. When C opened the bar doors, A appeared to be throwing the bottle at B. Although the "bottle" was actually a prop, C had no way of knowing this fact. Also, it was necessary for C to punch A in the face to assure that A could not get back up, retrieve the bottle, and again throw it at B. While the plastic surgery required by A is unfortunate, C could not be successfully charged with assault and battery."

Second Student Answer

"Assault and Battery:

"C committed an assault (causing A to be reasonably in apprehension of an imminent, offensive contact) when A saw C's punch about to hit him, and battery (causing an offensive contact upon A) when he (i) C knocked A to the ground, and (ii) C punched A.

"Defense-of-Others/Prevention-of-Crime Defenses:

"C would undoubtedly assert the privileges of defense-of-others (where defendant reasonably believed the plaintiff was about to make an offensive contact upon a third party, he was entitled to use whatever force was reasonably necessary to prevent the contact); and prevention-of-crime defense (where one reasonably believes another is about to commit a felony or misdemeanor involving a breach of the peace, he may exercise whatever force is reasonably necessary to prevent that person from committing a crime).

"A could contend that C was not reasonable in believing that A was about to cause harm to B because the enhanced lighting at the bar and camera crash should have indicated to C, a regular customer, that a movie was being filmed. However, C could probably successfully contend in rebuttal that his belief was reasonable in light of the facts that (i) he had not seen the camera when he attacked A, and (ii) instantaneous action was required (he did not have time to notice the enhanced lighting around the bar).

"A might also contend that the justification was forfeited because the degree of force used by C was not reasonable, since C did not have to punch A in the face after A had already been pushed to the ground (i.e., the danger to B was no longer present). However, C could argue in rebuttal that it was necessary to knockout A (an individual with apparently violent propensities) while the opportunity existed, rather than risk a drawn-out scuffle in which A might prevail. The facts do not indicate how big A and C were; but assuming C was not significantly larger than A, C's contention will probably be successful. If, however, C was significantly larger than A, the punch may have been excessive (since C could presumably have simply held A down)."

Critique

Let's examine the First Student Answer first. It mistakenly phrases as an "issue" the assault and battery committed by C upon A. While the actions creating these torts must be mentioned in the facts to provide a foundation for a discussion of the applicable privileges, there was no need to discuss them further because they were not the issue the examiners were testing for.

The structure of the initial paragraph of First Student Answer is also incorrect. After an assault is defined in the first sentence, the second sentence abruptly describes the facts necessary to constitute the commission of a battery. The third sentence then sets forth the elements of a battery. The fourth sentence completes the discussion of assault by describing the facts pertaining to that tort. The two-sentence break between the original mention of assault and the facts which constitute this tort is confusing; the facts which call for the application of a rule should be mentioned *immediately* after the rule is stated.

A more serious error, however, occurs in the second paragraph of the First Student Answer. While there is an allusion to the correct principle of law (prevention of crime), the **rule is not defined**. As a consequence, the grader can only guess why the student thinks the facts set forth in the subsequent sentences are significant. A grader reading this answer could not be certain that the student recognized that the issues revolved around the **reasonable belief** and **necessary force** elements of the prevention-of-crime privilege. Superior exam-writing requires that the pertinent facts be **tied** directly and clearly to the operative rule.

The Second Student Answer is very much better than the First Answer. It disposes of C's assault and battery upon A in a few words (yet tells the grader that the writer knows these torts are present). More importantly, the grader can easily see the issues which would arise if the prevention-of crime-privilege were asserted (i.e., "whether C's belief that A was about to commit a crime against B was reasonable" and "whether C used unnecessary force in punching A after A had been knocked to the ground"). Finally, it also utilizes all the facts by indicating how each attorney would assert those facts which are most advantageous to her client.

Structuring Your Answer

Graders will give high marks to a clearly-written, well-structured answer. Each issue you discuss should follow a specific and consistent structure which a grader can easily follow.

The Second Student Answer above basically utilizes the *I-R-A-A-O format* with respect to each issue. In this format, the *I* stands for the word *Issue*, the *R* for *Rule of law*, the initial *A* for the words *one side's Argument*, the second *A* for *the other party's rebuttal Argument*, and the *O* for your *Opinion as to how the issue would be resolved.* The *I-R-A-A-O* format emphasizes the importance of (1) discussing *both* sides of an issue, and (2) communicating to the grader that where an issue arises, an attorney can only advise her client as to the *probable* decision on that issue.

A somewhat different format for analyzing each issue is the *I-R-A-C format.* The *"I"* stands for *"Issue;"* the *"R"* for *"Rule of law;"* the *"A"* for *"Application of the facts to the rule of law;"* and the *"C"* for *"Conclusion." I-R-A-C* is a legitimate approach to the discussion of a particular issue, within the time constraints imposed by the question. The *I-R-A-C format* must be applied to each issue; it is not the solution to an entire exam answer. If there are six issues in a question, for example, you should offer six separate, independent *I-R-A-C* analyses.

We believe that the *I-R-A-C* approach is preferable to the *I-R-A-A-O* formula. However, either can be used to analyze and organize essay exam answers. Whatever format you choose, however, you should be consistent throughout the exam and remember the following rules:

First, *analyze all of the relevant facts.* Facts have significance in a particular case *only as they come under the applicable rules of law.* The facts presented must be analyzed and examined to see if they do or do not satisfy one element or another of the applicable rules, and the essential facts and rules must be stated and argued in your analysis.

Second, you must communicate to the grader the *precise rule of law* controlling the facts. In their eagerness to commence their arguments, students sometimes fail to state the applicable rule of law first. Remember, the *"R"* in either format stands for "Rule of Law." Defining the rule of law *before* an analysis of the facts is essential in order to allow the grader to follow your reasoning.

Third, it is important to treat *each side of an issue with equal detail.* If a hypothetical describes how an elderly man was killed when he ventured upon the land of a huge power company to obtain a better view of a nuclear reactor, your sympathies might understandably fall on the side of the old man. The grader will nevertheless expect you to see and make every possible argument for the other side. Don't permit your personal viewpoint to affect your answer! A good lawyer never does! When discussing an issue, always state the arguments for each side.

Finally, don't forget to *state your opinion or conclusion* on each issue. Keep in mind, however, that your opinion or conclusion is probably the *least* important part of an exam answer. Why? Because your professor knows that no attorney can tell her client exactly how a judge or jury will decide a particular issue. By definition, an issue is a legal dispute which can go either way. An attorney, therefore, can offer her client only her best opinion about the likelihood of victory or defeat on an issue. Since the decision on any issue lies with the judge or jury, no attorney can ever be absolutely certain of the resolution.

Discuss All Possible Issues

As we've noted, a student should draw *some* type of conclusion or opinion for each issue raised. Whatever your conclusion on a particular issue, it is essential to anticipate and discuss *all of the issues* which would arise if the question were actually tried in court.

Let's assume that a negligence hypothetical involves issues pertaining to duty, breach of duty, proximate causation and contributory negligence. If the defendant prevails on any one of these issues, he will avoid liability. Nevertheless, even if you feel strongly that the defendant owed no duty to the plaintiff, you *must* go on to discuss all of the other potential issues as well (breach of duty, proximate causation and contributory negligence). If you were to terminate your answer after a discussion of the duty problem only, you'd receive an inferior grade.

Why should you have to discuss every possible potential issue if you are relatively certain that the outcome of a particular issue would be dispositive of the entire case? Because at the commencement of litigation, neither party can be *absolutely positive* about which issues he will win at trial. We can state with confidence that every attorney with some degree of experience has won issues he thought he would lose, and has lost issues on which he thought victory was assured. Since one can never be absolutely certain how a factual issue will be resolved by the factfinder, a good attorney (and exam-writer) will consider *all* possible issues.

To understand the importance of discussing all of the potential issues, you should reflect on what you will do during the actual practice of law. If you represent the defendant, for example, it is your job to raise every possible defense. If there are five potential defenses, and your pleadings only rely on three of them (because you're sure you will win on all three), and the plaintiff is somehow successful on all three issues, your client may well sue you for malpractice. Your client's contention would be that you should be liable because if you had only raised the two additional issues, you might have prevailed on at least one of them, and therefore liability would have been avoided. It is an attorney's duty to raise *all* legitimate issues. A similar philosophy should be followed when taking essay exams.

What exactly do you say when you've resolved the initial issue in favor of the defendant, and discussion of any additional issues would seem to be moot? The answer is simple. You simply begin the discussion of the next potential issue with something like, "Assuming, however, the plaintiff prevailed on the foregoing issue, the next issue would be…" The grader will understand and appreciate what you have done.

The corollary to the importance of raising all potential issues is that you should avoid discussion of obvious non-issues. Raising non-issues is detrimental in three ways: first, you waste a lot of precious time; second, you usually receive absolutely no points for discussing a point which the grader deems extraneous; third, it suggests to the grader that you lack the ability to distinguish the significant from the irrelevant. The best guideline for avoiding the discussion of a non-issue is to ask yourself, "would I, as an attorney, feel comfortable about raising that particular issue or objection in front of a judge"?

Delineate the Transition From One Issue to the Next

It's a good idea to make it easy for the grader to see the issues which you've found. One way to accomplish this is to cover no more than one issue per paragraph. Another way is to underline each issue statement. Provided time permits, both techniques are recommended. The essay answers in this book contain numerous illustrations of these suggestions.

One frequent student error is to write a two-paragraph answer in which all of the arguments for one side are made in the initial paragraph, and all of the rebuttal arguments by the other side are made in the next paragraph. This is *a bad idea*. It obliges the grader to reconstruct the exam answer in his mind several times to determine whether all possible issues have been discussed by both sides. It will also cause you to state the same rule of law more than once. A better-organized answer presents a given argument by one side and follows that immediately in the same paragraph with the other side's rebuttal to that argument.

Understanding the "Call" of a Question

The statements **at the end of** an essay question or of the fact pattern in a multiple-choice question is sometimes referred to as the "call" of the question. It usually asks you to do something specific like "discuss," "discuss the rights of the parties," "what are X's rights?" "advise X," "the best grounds on which to find the statute unconstitutional are:," "D can be convicted of:," "how should the estate be distributed," etc. The call of the question should be read carefully because it tells you exactly what you're expected to do. If a question asks, "what are X's rights against Y?" or "X is liable to Y for:..." you don't have to spend a lot time on Y's rights against Z. You will usually receive absolutely no credit for discussing facts that are not required by the question. On the other hand, if the call of an essay question is simply "discuss" or "discuss the rights of the parties" then **all** foreseeable issues must be covered by your answer.

Students are often led astray by an essay question's call. For example, if you are asked for "X's rights against Y" or to "advise X", you may think you may limit yourself to X's viewpoint with respect to the issues. This is **not correct**! You cannot resolve one party's rights against another party without considering the issues which might arise (and the arguments which the other side would assert) if litigation occurred. In short, although the call of the question may appear to focus on one of the parties to the litigation, a superior answer will cover all the issues and arguments which that person might **encounter** (not just the arguments she would **make**) in attempting to pursue her rights against the other side.

The Importance of Analyzing the Question Carefully Before Writing

The overriding **time pressure** of an essay exam is probably a major reason why many students fail to analyze a question carefully before writing. Five minutes into the allocated time for a particular question, you may notice that the person next to you is writing furiously. This thought then flashes through your mind, "Oh, my goodness, he's putting down more words on the paper than I am, and therefore he's bound to get a better grade." It can be stated **unequivocally** that there is no necessary correlation between the number of words on your exam paper and the grade you'll receive. Students who begin their answer after only five minutes of analysis have probably seen only the most obvious issues, and missed many, if not most, of the subtle ones. They are also likely to be less well organized.

Opinions differ as to how much time you should spend analyzing and outlining a question before you actually write the answer. We believe that you should spend at least 12-18 minutes analyzing, organizing, and outlining a one-hour question before writing your answer. This will usually provide sufficient time to analyze and organize the question thoroughly *and* enough time to write a relatively complete answer. Remember that each word of the question must be scrutinized to determine if it (i) suggests an issue under the operative rules of law, or (ii) can be used in making an argument for the resolution of an issue. Since you can't receive points for an issue you don't spot, it is usually wise to read a question *twice* before starting your outline.

When to Make an Assumption

The instructions on an exam may tell you to *"assume"* facts which are necessary to the answer. Even where these instructions are *not* specifically given, you may be obliged to make certain assumptions with respect to missing facts in order to write a thorough answer. Assumptions should be made when you, as the attorney for one of the parties described in the question, would be obliged to solicit additional information from your client. On the other hand, assumptions should *never be used to change or alter the question.* Don't ever write something like "if the facts in the question were ..., instead of ..., then ... would result." If you do this, you are wasting time on facts which are extraneous to the problem before you. Professors want you to deal with *their* fact patterns, not your own.

Students sometimes try to "write around" information they think is missing. They assume that their professor has failed to include every piece of data necessary for a thorough answer. This is generally *wrong.* The professor may have omitted some facts deliberately to see if the student *can figure out what to do* under the circumstances. In some instances, the professor may have omitted them inadvertently (even law professors are sometimes human).

The way to deal with the omission of essential information is to describe (i) what fact (or facts) are missing, and (ii) why that information is important. As an example, go back to the "movie shoot" hypothetical we discussed above. In that fact pattern, there was no mention of the relative strength of A and C. This fact could be extremely important. If C weighed 240 pounds and was built like a professional football linebacker, while A tipped the scales at a mere 160 pounds, punching A in the face after he had been pushed to the ground would probably constitute unnecessary force (thereby causing C to forfeit the prevention-of-crime privilege). If the physiques of the parties were reversed, however, C's punch to A's face would probably constitute reasonable behavior. Under the facts, C had to deal the *"knockout"* blow while the opportunity presented itself. The last sentences of the Second Student Answer above show that the student understood these subtleties and correctly stated the essential missing facts and assumptions.

Assumptions should be made in a manner which keeps the other issues open (i.e., necessitates discussion of all other possible issues). Don't assume facts which would virtually dispose of the entire hypothetical in a few sentences. For example, suppose that A called B a "convicted felon" (a statement which is inherently defamatory, *i.e.,* a defamatory statement is one which tends to subject the plaintiff to hatred, contempt or ridicule). If A's statement is true, he has a complete defense to B's action for defamation. If the facts don't tell whether A's statement was true or not, it would *not* be wise to write something like, "We'll assume that A's statement about B is accurate, and therefore B cannot successfully sue A for defamation." So facile an approach would rarely be appreciated by the grader. The proper way to handle this situation would be to state, "if we assume that A's statement about B is not correct, A can not raise the defense of truth." You've communicated to the grader that you recognize the need to assume an essential fact and that you've assumed it in such a way as to enable you to proceed to discuss all other potential issues.

Case Names

A law student is ordinarily *not* expected to recall case names on an exam. The professor knows that you have read several hundred cases for each course, and that you would have to be a memory expert to have all of the names at your fingertips. If you confront a fact pattern which seems similar to a case which you have reviewed (but you cannot recall the name of it), just write something like, "One case held that ..." or "It has been held that ..." In this manner, you have informed the grader that you are relying on a case which contained a fact pattern similar to the question at issue.

The only exception to this rule is in the case of a landmark decision. Landmark opinions are usually those which change or alter established law.[2] These cases are usually easy to identify, because you will probably have spent an entire class period discussing each of them. *Palsgraf v. Long Island Rail Road* is a prime example of a landmark case in Torts. In these special cases, you may be expected to remember the case by name, as well the proposition of law which it stands for. However, this represents a very limited exception to the general rule which counsels against wasting precious time trying to memorize case names.

---

2. The only subject to which this does not apply is Constitutional Law, since here virtually every case you study satisfies this definition. Students studying Constitutional Law should try to associate case names with holdings and reproduce them in their exam answers.

How To Handle Time Pressures

What do you do when there are five minutes left in the exam and you have only written down two-thirds of your answer? One thing *not* to do is write something like, "No time left!" or "Not enough time!" This gets you nothing but the satisfaction of knowing you have communicated your personal frustrations to the grader. Another thing *not* to do is insert the outline you may have made on scrap paper into the exam booklet. Professors rarely will look at these items.

First of all, it is not necessarily a bad thing to be pressed for time. The person who finishes five minutes early has very possibly missed some important issues. The more proficient you become in knowing what is expected of you on an exam, the greater the difficulty you may experience in staying within the time limits. Second, remember that (at least to some extent) you're graded against your classmates' answers and they're under exactly the same time pressure as you. In short, don't panic if you can't write the "perfect" answer in the allotted time. Nobody does!

The best hedge against misuse of time is to *review as many old exams as possible*. These exercises will give you a familiarity with the process of organizing and writing an exam answer, which, in turn, should result in an enhanced ability to stay within the time boundaries. If you nevertheless find that you have about 15 minutes of writing to do and five minutes to do it in, write a paragraph which summarizes the remaining issues or arguments you would discuss if time permitted. As long as you've indicated that you're aware of the remaining legal issues, you'll probably receive some credit for them. Your analytical and argumentative skills will already be apparent to the grader by virtue of the issues that you have previously discussed.

Write Legibly

Make sure your answer is legible. Students should *not* assume that their professors will be willing to take their papers to the local pharmacist to have them deciphered. Remember, your professor may have 75-150 separate exam answers to grade. If your answer is difficult to read, you will rarely be given the benefit of the doubt. On the other hand, a legible, well-organized paper creates a very positive mental impact upon the grader.

Many schools allow students to type their exams. If you're an adequate typist, you may want to seriously consider typing. Typing has two major advantages. First, it should help assure that your words will be readable (unless, of course, there are numerous typos). Second, it should enable you to put a lot more words onto the paper than if your answer had been handwritten. Most professors prefer a typed answer to a written one.

There are, however, a few disadvantages to typing. For one thing, all the typists are usually in a single room. If the clatter of other typewriters will make it difficult for you to concentrate, typing is probably **not** wise. To offset this problem, some students wear earplugs during the exam. Secondly, typing sometimes makes it difficult to change or add to an earlier portion of your answer. You may have to withdraw your paper from the carriage and insert another. Try typing out a few practice exams before you decide to type your exam. If you do type, be sure to leave at least one blank line between typewritten lines, so that handwritten changes and insertions in your answers can be made easily.

If you decide against typing, your answer will probably be written in a "bluebook" (a booklet of plain, lined, white paper which has a light blue cover and back). It is usually a good idea to write only on the odd numbered pages (i.e., 1, 3, 5, etc.). You may also want to leave a blank line between each written line. Doing these things will usually make the answer easier to read. If you discover that you have left out a word or phrase, you can insert it into the proper place by means of a caret sign ("∧"). If you feel that you've omitted an entire issue, you can write it on the facing blank page. A symbol reference can be used to indicate where the additional portion of the answer should be inserted. While it's not ideal to have your answer take on the appearance of a road map, a symbol reference to an adjoining page is much better than trying to squeeze six lines into one, and will help the grader to discover where the same symbol appears in another part of your answer.

The Importance of Reviewing Prior Exams

As we've mentioned, it is ***extremely important to review old exams.*** The transition from blackletter law to essay exam can be a difficult experience if the process has not been practiced. Although this book provides a large number of essay and multiple-choice questions, ***don't stop here***! Most law schools have recent tests on file in the library, by course. We strongly suggest that you make a copy of every old exam you can obtain (especially those given by your professors) at the beginning of each semester. The demand for these documents usually increases dramatically as "finals time" draws closer.

The exams for each course should be scrutinized ***throughout the semester.*** They should be reviewed as you complete each chapter in your casebook. Generally, the order of exam questions follows the sequence of the materials in your casebook. Thus, the first question on a law school test may involve the initial three chapters of the casebook; the second question may pertain to the fourth and fifth chapters, etc. In any event, ***don't wait*** until the semester is nearly over to begin reviewing old exams.

Keep in mind that no one is born with the ability to analyze questions and write superior answers to law school exams. Like any skill, it is developed and perfected only through application. If you don't take the time to analyze numerous examinations from prior years, this evolutionary process just won't occur. Don't just **think about** the answers to past exam questions; take the time to **write the answers down**. It's also wise to look back at an answer a day or two after you've written it. You will invariably see (i) ways in which the organization could have been improved, and (ii) arguments you missed.

As you practice spotting issues on past exams, you will see how rules of law become the sources of issues on finals. As we've already noted, if you don't **understand** how rules of law translate into issues, you won't be able to achieve superior grades on your exams. Reviewing exams from prior years should also reveal that certain issues tend to be lumped together in the same question. For instance, where a fact pattern involves a false statement made by one person about another, three potential theories of liability are often present — defamation, invasion of privacy (false, public light) and intentional infliction of severe emotional distress. You will need to see if any or all of these apply to the facts.

Finally, one of the best means of evaluating if you understand a course (or a particular area within a subject) is to attempt to create a hypothetical exam for that topic. Your exam should contain as many issues as possible. If you can write an issue-packed exam, you probably know that particular area of law. If you can't, then you probably haven't yet acquired an adequate understanding of how the principles of law in that subject can spawn issues.

As Always, a Caveat

The suggestions and advice offered in this book represent the product of many years of experience in the field of legal education. We are confident that the techniques and concepts described in these pages will help you prepare for, and succeed, at your exams. Nevertheless, particular professors sometimes have a preference for exam-writing techniques which are not stressed in this work. Some instructors expect at least a nominal reference to the **prima facie** elements of all pertinent legal theories (even though one or more of those principles is **not** placed into issue). Other professors want their students to emphasize public policy considerations in the arguments they make on a particular issue. Because this book is intended for nationwide consumption, these individualized preferences have **not** been stressed. The best way to find out whether your professor has a penchant for a particular writing approach is to ask her to provide you with a model answer to a previous exam. If an item is not available, speak to upperclass students who received a superior grade in that professor's class.

One final point. While the rules of law stated in the answers to the questions in this book have been drawn from commonly used sources (i.e., casebooks, hornbooks, etc.), it is still conceivable that they may be slightly at odds with those taught by your professor. In instances where a conflict exists between our formulation of a legal principle and the one which is taught by your professor, *follow the latter!* Since your grades are determined by your professors, their views should always supersede the views contained in this book.

Essay Exam Questions

Question 1

A and B met on the street one afternoon. A called B a "sissy." B said, "I'll show you who's a sissy, let's see what you're made out of?" They squared off and began a combination fist-fight and wrestling match. A appeared to be winning when C, B's brother, came upon the scene. C pulled a knife and thrusted it unsuccessfully at A. A's brother, D, then came up, saw A being attacked with a knife, and pulled a pistol and shot at C. D missed, but hit and wounded E, an innocent passerby who had just stepped out of a barbershop. D did not have a license to carry a firearm. B and C fled after D's shot.

D picked up C's knife, which C had dropped while fleeing. D took it home. It had a value of $25. When C later found out that D had his knife, he went to D's house. C walked up to D's door and knocked. D answered the door and told C to "get off his land." When C refused, D let his dog, Homer, loose. Homer chased C off D's property, but never bit C.

Discuss the various tort liabilities of the parties.

Question 2

Defendant bought a car for $50,000. The car had interior gold fixtures, genuine leopard fur on the seats, a slide-out bar, a TV set, and other like accessories. In order to protect the car from vandalism and theft, Defendant equipped it himself with a system, which, if a door was opened, caused an alarm to sound and induced a severe electric shock to a person touching the handle of the door as it opened.

Baker, a commercial photographer, seeing the car parked at a downtown curb, induced his friend, Art Archer, to get into the car as a gag for the purpose of taking a picture of Art at the wheel. Art was reluctant but finally agreed. Art took hold of the handle of the door on the sidewalk side. The door was unlocked. As he started to open the door, he received a shock. Such a shock ordinarily would not seriously injure a healthy person, but because of his pre-existing heart condition, the shock caused Art to stagger back, collapse on the sidewalk and die shortly thereafter.

As he fell, his wife Sue Archer, who witnessed the incident, ran to help him but was knocked down when he fell against her. As a result of this experience, she was unable to sleep, and frequently experienced headaches, nausea and vomiting.

Neither Art nor Baker knew that the car was wired to induce electrical shocks. Neither had seen a sign on the front windshield which could be read from the sidewalk and which stated, "Beware, this car is equipped with a protective device — DO NOT TOUCH!" Suit is brought against Defendant for damages for the death of Art and the injury to Sue Archer.

What result? Discuss.

Question 3

Peter, a movie producer, leased the Calumet Saloon in a small western community in order to film an indoor barroom scene for a picture. According to the script, Dan was to enter the barroom and take a shot at Jim. This was to be followed almost immediately by a second shot by Dan which would appear to hit Jim. Shortly before the scene was made, a prop man accidentally inserted live ammunition into Dan's gun, instead of the blanks that were intended. When Dan shot at Jim, a bullet pierced Jim's cowboy hat. Jim realized that when the second shot came he probably would be killed. Since the script called for a crowd in the saloon to be yelling loudly, there was no opportunity to advise Dan of his error within the few seconds available between shots. Jim was holding a bottle in his hand. He raised his arm to throw the bottle at Dan. Since this gesture was not in the script, Dan was quite frightened by Jim's conduct.

At this moment, Fred entered the saloon. Fred was a regular customer of the Calumet Saloon. He had failed to notice a prominent sign by the door stating that the Calumet Saloon would be closed all day. When Fred pushed open the swinging door, it knocked over one of Peter's extremely expensive movie cameras (it cost $25,000) which had been set up immediately to the left of the door. The camera was broken. Fred saw Jim about to throw the bottle at Dan. Fred, to prevent Jim from throwing the bottle, knocked Jim to the floor and punched him in the face.

(1) What are Jim's rights, if any, against Dan and Fred? Discuss.

(2) What are Dan's rights, if any, against Jim? Discuss.

(3) What are Peter's rights, if any, against Fred? Discuss.

Question 4

A storage shed on the suburban yard of Construction Co. (Conco) caught fire on a Sunday morning. Dennis, Conco's draftsman at its downtown office, happened to be bicycling by on a personal errand. He broke into the yard office through a closed window and notified the local volunteer fire department. He next located ignition keys and moved eight pieces of heavy equipment onto an adjacent field. The heavy equipment consisted of trucks and bulldozers, which were threatened with imminent destruction, but were not damaged.

Unknown to Dennis, the adjacent field belonged to a wholesale florist, Frank. Although the field appeared to be vacant and unused, Frank had planted it with valuable tulip bulbs. Bulbs valued at $9,000 were destroyed under the weight of the heavy equipment.

After firefighters extinguished the fire, Frank asked Dennis to come to his office to discuss the damage. Dennis agreed. As soon as Dennis entered the office, Frank told Dennis, in the presence of four of Frank's employees, that Dennis would have to remain at the office until he summoned the president of Conco and the president had arrived at the office. When the president arrived an hour later, Frank told Dennis he could leave, and Dennis left.

(1) What are Frank's rights against Dennis and against Conco? Discuss.

(2) What are Dennis' rights against Frank? Discuss.

Question 5

Abel was a fireman who responded to a call that the Babel Hotel was on fire. When he arrived, he was notified that a Miss Cool, an invalid, was alone in a third floor apartment. Abel reached Cool's apartment but the door was locked. Mrs. Jones, who occasionally took care of Cool, had forgotten to leave Cool's wheelchair close to her bed; with the consequence that Cool could not reach the door. Abel finally used his fire axe to break down the apartment door. He picked Cool up, but by this time, the flames of the fire had engulfed the entire hallway outside of Cool's apartment.

A city ordinance required hotels to have four fire exits on each floor, but there were only two on each floor of the Babel Hotel. Unable to get out of the apartment, Abel (with Cool on his shoulder) finally jumped out of Cool's bedroom window. He attempted to land upon the roof of the adjoining building; but when he did, the roof collapsed. Abel and Cool found themselves on the floor of a restaurant. Pierre, the owner of the restaurant, fearing a slowdown in business, quickly ordered three of his employees to move Abel and Cool into the street. This moving aggravated the back injury Abel had sustained in the jump.

Discuss Abel's rights.

Question 6

Henry and his pregnant wife, Wendy, went to Blodger Stadium to watch a baseball game. The parking lot and stadium are owned by the Blodgers, Inc. After Henry paid the parking fee and parked, Wendy, opening her door, hit a Cadillac parked alongside, causing some paint to chip off. Kelly, the owner of the car, jumped out and screamed at Wendy, "You dumb broad, why don't you look what you're doing? I ought to kick your little butt," at which point Wendy fainted at the shock of Kelly's words. Henry then punched Kelly in the mouth, knocking out two teeth. Kelly and Henry then began to scuffle.

John, an onlooker, tried to break up the fight, but was knocked to the ground with a broken nose. John doesn't know who actually hit him. The local police and two security guards employed by the Blodgers, Inc. arrived after about five minutes. The local police took both Henry and Kelly to jail. The two security guards employed by the Blodgers carried Wendy to the stadium infirmary to rest until she recovered consciousness. About 20 minutes later, however, she began to moan heavily. She was immediately taken to a nearby hospital by the local police because no emergency ambulance would have been able to get through to the stadium because of heavy game time traffic. At the hospital it was discovered that Wendy had suffered a miscarriage. Henry and Wendy have now consulted you for advice with respect to their potential rights and liabilities based upon the foregoing.

Discuss.

Question 7

Farmer (F) was burning weeds on his land adjacent to a highway as was customary in the area. The wind was erratic, and from time to time smoke was blown across the highway.

Husband (H) and wife (W) were traveling along this highway in a car owned by W. H was driving the car at about 50 m.p.h. As they approached the area of the smoke, they saw that it was drifting away from the highway although moments earlier they had seen it crossing the highway. As they proceeded, the wind changed, and heavy smoke from the burning brush enveloped the car. H was unable to see, and he immediately applied the brakes. Before he could stop, he ran into T, a driver going in the opposite direction whose car was over the center line. The impact was substantial. H and W were injured and the car damaged. A few moments later a bus, owned by Coach Co. (C) and driven by one of its drivers, crashed into the car and caused further damage and injury to H and W.

The driver of the bus claimed he had not seen the car ahead of him, but admitted he had seen the smoke across the highway when he approached. He said he started through after reducing his speed to about 35 m.p.h. and claimed that when he saw the car, he tried to stop, but it was too late to avoid hitting it. The legal rate of speed on this road was 45 m.p.h.

What are H and W's rights against F, C, the driver of the bus and T?

Question 8

Mr. and Mrs. Parenti are the parents of Alice, age 6, and Sandy, age 7. One evening they left the two children with a 14-year-old babysitter, Barbara. This was the first time that Barbara had taken care of the children. The Parentis had never met Barbara before. Because she arrived at the house about twenty minutes late, they only had time to instruct her of the bedtime hour of the children and assumed she could manage otherwise.

After they left, Barbara was joined by her boyfriend. The two became so interested in each other, that the absence of Alice and Sandy was not noted. The children, meanwhile, went over to the adjacent property to play in Farmer's barn. Farmer had told them many times that he did not mind their playing on his own children's swing in the yard, but that they were not to go in his barn. Twice before he had made them get out of the barn. On this evening, the children saw, just inside the door of the barn, a charcoal grill in which were some live coals. They decided to play "make believe cook" and piled some loose hay on the grill. A fire resulted during which the barn was completely destroyed and Alice and Sandy were badly burned. What are the rights of:

(1) Farmer against the Parentis and Barbara? Discuss.

(2) Alice and Sandy against Farmer? Discuss.

Question 9

An automobile, owned by Ace Auto Rentals (Ace) and rented to and driven by Bruce, collided with an automobile owned and driven by Chuck when Chuck entered a main highway without looking to see if it was safe. Bruce would have been able to avoid the collision except that he was driving at a recklessly high speed. Unknown to Ace, Bruce had no driver's license.

Chuck's car caught fire. Dave, a passenger who had met Chuck through a want ad and was sharing expenses and driving responsibilities while on a cross country trip, escaped without injury. Chuck was trapped in the burning car. Peter, a bystander, tried to pull Chuck out of the car. Peter was severely burned. Chuck died of his burns.

What are Peter's rights, if any, against Ace, Dave, and Chucks' estate? Discuss.

Question 10

Abel and Baker were working on a scaffold lawfully erected over a public sidewalk. Abel, contrary to an express rule of his employer, was not wearing a hard hat.

While trying to park her automobile near one of the supports of the scaffold, Diana maneuvered it into such a position that she knew there was a risk of knocking the scaffold down if she backed up without someone to guide her. She appealed for help to Sam, a stranger who was passing by. Sam just laughed. Angered, Diana proceeded to back her automobile without assistance and knocked a support out from under the scaffold, causing Abel and Baker to fall.

Abel severely fractured his skull and was taken unconscious to a hospital. If he had been wearing his hard hat, he would have suffered only a slight concussion with minimal disability.

Baker sustained a fracture of a vertebra, but he was able to walk and felt only slight pain. The fracture could have been easily diagnosed by x-ray, and a medical doctor of average competence could have successfully treated it by immobilization. Instead of visiting a physician, Baker worked the rest of the day. While driving his car home later that day, Baker stopped at an intersection and his car was struck from the rear by a car driven by Ed. The collision caused only slight damage to Baker's car, but it was sufficiently severe to aggravate the fracture in Baker's back, resulting in paralysis.

Diana and Sam settled Baker's claim against them and received general releases from him. Abel sued Diana and Sam. Baker sued Ed. Assume that Diana, Sam and Ed raise all appropriate defenses.

(1) What rights, if any, does Abel have against Diana? Sam? Discuss.

(2) What rights, if any, does Baker have against Ed? Discuss.

Question 11

Dan, the operator of a large moving van, was approaching an intersection on a four lane street at noon when his engine died and the vehicle came to a complete halt for which Dan was not responsible. Being unable to move the vehicle he left it standing unattended while he went to secure help. The van had stalled on the left-hand side of the double lane in the direction in which it was proceeding just immediately before the intersection (but not within it), leaving ample room for passage in the same direction to the right.

After Dan had gone, Vick, driving a Volkswagen, approached from the same direction and came to a halt to the right of and parallel to the van preparatory to entering the intersection. The large van entirely obscured his vision to the left, but Vick decided to proceed across the intersection. As he did so, he struck a motorcycle approaching from the left on the intersecting street. The cyclist, Peter, saw Vick's car emerging from behind the van and he could have brought his cycle to a halt in time to avoid being struck had it not been for the fact that his brakes were bad. By the time Vick saw Peter it was too late to stop. It is conceded that both Vick and Peter could have seen each other in abundant time to avoid the accident if Dan's van had not obstructed their views. Discuss Peter's rights against Dan and Vick:

(1) assuming there is a provision of the Motor Vehicle Code making it unlawful to leave a vehicle on a public highway unattended;

(2) assuming there is no such statutory provision.

Question 12

Acme Construction Co. had contracted to add two additional lanes to a heavily-used highway in a rural area. To establish the proper grade, Acme had occasion to engage in blasting, since there was much solid rock on or close to the surface.

Signs at the side of the road, at the approaches to the blasting area, warned motorists as follows: "Blasting in progress. Stop all radio transmissions." Baker, a motorist using his two-way radio, failed to observe the sign; there was a premature detonation which was caused, it may be assumed, by the transmission from his radio; and in the ensuing explosion Baker was injured when a boulder hit his car.

Charles, a motorist who stopped at the scene of the accident and then hurried off to summon medical assistance (Baker's radio had been rendered inoperative), was killed when his car swerved from the road and hit a tree. Charles was not wearing his seat belt at the time. The car was so mangled that it was impossible to tell whether Charles would have been killed even if he had been wearing his seat belt, or whether the failure to wear the seat belt was a substantial contributing factor towards his death in that, if suitably restrained by the seat belt, Charles would have escaped fatal secondary impact after his car hit the tree. A statute makes it unlawful to manufacture or sell an automobile unless equipped with seat belts for occupants of the front seat. (Charles' car was not one of those, produced in recent years, that "refuse" to start if the seat belts are not engaged.)

Discuss:

(1) the rights of Baker; and

(2) the rights of those with standing to sue for Charles' death under the pertinent wrongful death statute.

Question 13

ABC Department Store retained Joe to paint the front of its building. When Joe arrived, he asked for a ladder so that he could inspect the facade to determine if any sandblasting was necessary. Malcolm, the store manager, gave Joe a ladder which ABC had purchased from Bloomingdiles a little more than four years ago. At the time of the purchase, the ladder was delivered in a box which had the following statement in large block letters:

CAUTION: THE NORMAL OPERATIONAL LIFE OF A SPELDING LADDER IS THREE YEARS.

The ladder had been manufactured by the Spelding Company which found that the hinges frequently wore out after three years. Malcolm had not seen this warning since the prior manager (who had retired) took the ladder out of the box (which was discarded at that time). Sure enough, while Joe was making his inspection, one of the legs of the ladder collapsed. Joe fell and landed on Mr. Jones. Joe broke his own collarbone and Mr. Jones suffered a broken shoulder and right arm. Mrs. Jones (who was walking beside Mr. Jones when this occurred) began running up and down the sidewalk screaming, "Get a doctor, get a doctor!" In her frenzy, she slipped and broke her left ankle.

Discuss the possible tort claims of the parties, except for Malcolm and the prior manager.

Question 14

Mary White, owner of White's Diner, watched a television advertisement about the "new and improved" Glutton Microwave Oven. The announcer also stated that the Glutton "could be used with your own cookware and was the best and safest microwave on the market."

To test its economic desirability and efficiency, White leased the Glutton from Black's Appliances. Black negligently omitted a manual from the manufacturer which contained on the cover page the following warning:

WARNING! DO NOT USE METAL DISHES OR METAL COOKWARE.

No such warning appeared on the oven itself.

Mary White used a tin plate to cook some food in the Glutton during a busy lunch hour. As a result of the microwaves bouncing off the tin dish, a hole burned through the oven's outer surface and caused exposure of microwaves. Both Mary, and one of her patrons, John Green, eating near the oven suffered blindness. In addition, White's Diner had to be shut down until a new oven could be installed.

What are the rights of White and Green? Discuss.

Question 15

Nerv was an extremely nervous person. He discussed his problems with his friend Phil, a licensed pharmacist who owned and operated a drug store. Phil recommended "Dreamy", a new tranquilizer which was manufactured by Drugco, and did not require a prescription. Dreamy had been extensively tested by Drugco and four months previously had been approved for sale to the public without prescription by the Federal Drug Administration (FDA). Nerv purchased a bottle of Dreamy and began taking it in accordance with the instructions. The label on the bottle stated: "Normal dosage two pills every twelve hours — safe for adult use — not habit forming."

The day after the purchase, Nerv took two Dreamy pills upon arising, had breakfast and then got in his car and headed for the golf course. While driving on a public street, Nerv suddenly became dizzy and lost control of his car. The car swerved onto the sidewalk, hit Ima, seriously injuring her, and then ran into a pole, seriously injuring Nerv.

Subsequent analysis revealed that Nerv's dizziness was caused by an allergic reaction to Dreamy, but that only five persons out of ten thousand would have such a reaction. None of this had been discovered during the extensive pre-marketing tests which led to approval by the FDA. It was also learned that during the four months since Dreamy was first marketed, two other persons had reactions similar to those of Nerv, and Drugco had conducted further tests and had ordered new labels which would contain the following: "CAUTION — Dizziness may result from normal dosage."

What are the rights of Ima against Nerv and Drugco? Discuss.

What are the rights of Nerv against Phil and Drugco? Discuss.

Question 16

Mag, Inc. publishes a magazine and operates a laboratory for testing merchandise of its advertisers. Mag authorizes the use of a symbol that says "Mag Seal of Approval" when Mag's tests indicate the product is safe and wholesome.

Mag examined samples of Tint hair coloring produced by Tintco, Inc. Mag's tests indicate that Tint was effective and satisfactory. Mag authorized Tintco to use Mag's Seal of Approval in advertising Tint and on Tintco's labels placed on containers of Tint. Neither Tintco or Mag was aware that when Tint is brought into direct contact with Balm, an infrequently used prescription scalp medicine, Tint causes hair to turn purple.

Gloria, a contestant in a beauty contest, used Tint on her hair while it was still wet with Balm. As a result, Gloria's hair turned purple and she had to withdraw from the contest. She had been regarded as the favorite. To Gloria's embarrassment, the purple discoloration persisted until her hair grew out.

What are Gloria's rights against:

(1) Tintco? Discuss.

(2) Mag? Discuss.

Question 17

Alan, a high school student, while in a variety store owned by Black, noticed a sign on the wall reading "FREE — PLEASE TAKE ONE" below which was a box of transistor radios. He put one of the radios in his pocket and walked out of the store. Black rushed out of the store after Alan shouting, "Come back here with that radio, you thief!" The street was crowded, and Alan, humiliated by the accusation, eluded Black and ran home.

Later that day, Carl, a customer who resembled Alan, went into the restroom of Black's store. Black, thinking Carl was Alan, locked the restroom door and called the police. There was an open window in the restroom. Carl mounted a chair planning to climb out the window. Carl probably should have realized that it was too far to reach, but he tried anyway. As he put his weight on the back of the chair, the chair tipped. Carl fell to the floor and broke his leg.

Several days later, Alan learned that the "FREE — PLEASE TAKE ONE" sign referred to advertising bulletins which were usually beneath the sign and not to the transistor radios. He immediately offered to return the radio, but Black refused to accept it.

Discuss the rights of Alan and Black against each other and the rights of Carl against Black.

Question 18

Peter carelessly left his wallet containing $100 lying on the cashier's counter in Jim's restaurant and walked away. Jim observed the wallet but neglected to call it to Peter's attention. Immediately thereafter, David, another restaurant patron, paid his bill and picked up Peter's wallet by mistake, thinking it was his own.

As David was leaving the restaurant, Peter saw the wallet in David's hand and recognized it as his own. Before Peter could call out, David boarded a bus owned by Busco. Peter followed and managed to board the bus just as it started to move. He skinned his knee in so doing. He yelled, "Stop, thief!" and worked his way around other passengers to where David stood.

The loud accusation angered David, who, even after he noted that the wallet was not his own, retorted, "Don't you call me a thief! Take your wallet and get out of here." He hurled the wallet at Peter. It struck Peter's face, glanced off and flew out the bus window. Peter attempted to get off the bus, but the bus was so arranged that passengers were required to pay fares as they left. Peter had no money with him and argued with the operator of the bus while the bus travelled several blocks. When the bus was stopped by traffic, Peter jumped out and ran back. He was unable to locate his wallet.

A. What are Peter's rights against:

    (1) Jim? Discuss.

    (2) David? Discuss.

    (3) Busco? Discuss.

B. Does David have any right against Peter? Discuss.

Question 19

Twenty years ago, Resco erected a building in what was then an unsettled area. Resco conducts experimental work in connection with cattle virus diseases in that building. The area surrounding the Resco property has now become a thriving cattle and dairy district.

Cattle ranches in the area tried to induce Zoe, a cattle auctioneer, to establish a local market. Zoe was reluctant to do so because of his fear that the virus might escape from Resco's property and infect cattle.

Some of the ranchers called on Prex, the president of Resco. They told Prex of their desire to establish a market in the area and asked him to make a statement which would dispel Zoe's fears.

Prex called a conference and, without having made any investigation and without naming Zoe, stated that there was "no danger at all" of any virus escaping from the Resco premises, and that only a "driveling idiot" could conclude otherwise. This statement was printed in "News," a local newspaper, and received wide attention. As a result, Zoe was frequently referred to in the community as a "driveling idiot." This caused him considerable embarrassment.

In the belief that Prex's statement concerning the safety of the Resco operation was correct and in order to escape further embarrassment, Zoe established a market in the area for the auction of cattle. Shortly thereafter, without negligence on the part of Resco, the virus escaped from Resco's premises and infected cattle in the area.

To stop the spread of the infection, public authorities ordered the slaughter of all infected or exposed cattle and Zoe had to abandon his market with consequent financial loss to him.

What are Zoe's rights against

(1) Resco? Discuss.

(2) Prex? Discuss.

(3) News? Discuss.

Question 20

Norm is a well-known author who gave a lecture at a private college. During the question period following the lecture, one of the answers about the leaders of the "Women's Lib" movements was as follows: "Some of the top leaders are obviously lesbians. In fact, one of the top leaders at this college is a high school dropout who was once arrested for peddling dope." After this diatribe, pandemonium broke loose in the lecture hall. Polly, the secretary of the relatively small and obscure Women's Lib club at the college, rushed the platform and would have struck Norm, had she not been forcibly restrained. The daily student newspaper, "The Spector," reported the episode, but inaccurately stated that Polly had hit Norm, that "blood gushed from his temple" and that Norm had accused Polly of having been convicted of peddling dope.

This information was obtained by the newspaper from several persons who attended the lecture. Polly read the article and claims that as a result she has not been able to sleep, that she has had to revisit a psychiatrist who had discharged her before the episode as cured from a nervous ailment, that she could not take her examinations at the end of her senior year, and that her graduation had been delayed one year.

What are Polly's rights against Norm and "The Spector?" Discuss.

Question 21

White, a Marine Corps officer, was convicted of murder 38 years ago in a highly publicized trial. The only evidence against him at the trial was the testimony of two former Marines that Japanese prisoners of war had been killed while in the custody of troops commanded by White during the battle for control of Guadalcanal. Eight years later, one of these witnesses who was then dying of cancer confessed that he and the second witness had lied at the trial of White in order to avoid punishment for their own misconduct. When investigation confirmed the truth of the confession, White received a pardon, was released from prison, and entered a religious order where he lived in seclusion under vows of silence and poverty.

Early this year, White developed a serious illness. He reluctantly left the order and entered a hospital for treatment.

News, a daily newspaper in the city in which the hospital is located, has prepared a feature article that fully and truthfully recounts the trial, imprisonment, and the events leading to the pardon of White. The author and editors have relied solely on information available in public records. News has notified White that it intends to publish the article. White objects to the prospect of unwelcome publicity. White and News have been warned by White's doctors that the emotional stress White may suffer if the story is published will impede his recovery.

(1) If the story is published, on what theory or theories might White base an action for damages against News? Discuss.

(2) If White seeks an injunction to prohibit publication of the proposed story, what defenses should News offer, and how should the court rule on them? Discuss.

Question 22

Upon retirement, Bill and Jane Mason purchased a mobile home trailer from Dealer for $65,000. They made a down payment of $10,000 and financed the balance of the purchase price with Finance Company. The Masons moved their mobile home into a space rented from Dream Park, where they paid monthly rental.

Several months later the trailer was removed from Dream Park by Repo, Co., an entity specializing in repossessions. Bill protested the removal and suffered a broken leg when he refused to step down and fell from the step of the trailer as it was being pulled away. He has since been hospitalized. When Bill had advised the Repo Co. employees that they were making a mistake, they curtly responded, "That's what they all say buddy."

Because of mental distress suffered when she learned of these events two hours later, Jane has been hospitalized and under the care of a physician.

Repo Co. had erroneously repossessed the Masons' trailer, believing it was the property of Stranger. Stranger had defaulted on a debt due Finance that was secured by a mortgage on a trailer similar to the Masons' trailer. The Masons were, however, current on their payments to Finance Company.

The fair rental value of the Masons' trailer is $1,000 a month. A small section of the trailer was dented while it was in Finance's possession. It would cost $500 to repair the dent, but the damage is neither serious nor noticeable. The Masons' clothes and other personal possessions are missing from the trailer. The Masons replaced such personal property at the cost of $5,000.

What are the rights of Bill and Jane against Finance Company? Discuss.

Question 23

Disco, a discount retailer, opened a new store. To publicize the event Disco placed the following advertisement in local newspapers:

"Announcing the Grand Opening of Disco's New Store — January 10 — Bargains Galor —Win the Door prize — A week in Paris for Two — Drawing Time 4 P.M. — You Must Be Present to Win."

Ellen, age 15, read the advertisement and came to the opening. When she entered the store she received a numbered slip of paper on which she was directed to write her name and to deposit the slip in a box inside the store. She complied with those directions. At 4 P.M. she was announced as the winner of the doorprize and asked to come to a platform at the front of the store. Ellen did so.

"Ellen, lucky winner of Disco's doorprize."

During the next few days, many of Ellen's schoolmates asked what she had won and Ellen told them it was a trip for two to Paris.

A week after the drawing, when Ellen returned for the tickets and expense money, Mana explained that Disco had never intended to give the winner of the doorprize anything, and that the advertisement and drawing were merely promotional stunts. Ellen felt humiliated when, in response to her schoolmates' continuing inquiries, she had to explain that she would receive nothing as a doorprize.

What are Ellen's rights against Disco? Discuss.

Question 24

One day Ben, a beneficiary of a trust administered by Bank, went to Bank and said to the bank manager in a loud voice: "Although I do not believe it to be true, I have heard that one of the men in the trust department has used trust funds to take trips to Hawaii." About fourteen customers overheard Ben's remarks.

Four men work in the trust department, including Arthur. None of the trust department employees had ever been to Hawaii or misused trust funds. Arthur became extremely upset at Ben's remark.

While Ben was talking to the bank manager, his friend Ed, who had accompanied him to the bank, spoke with Jane, a secretary in the trust department, about how to prepare a will.

Jane told him that it was easy; just type it, sign it and have it notarized. Jane had obtained these instructions from an attorney, Larry, several weeks ago at a cocktail party. Ed died three weeks after making his will, in accordance with these instructions, leaving all of his property to his brother, Bill. However, his will was held to be invalid because it was not property witnessed and his property passed instead to his children.

Discuss the tort liability of the various parties.

Question 25

Able is in the real estate investment business. He is trying to have the zoning ordinance of City amended to permit his company to erect a high rise apartment. Opposition to the amendment is headed by Mrs. Bird, a well known socialite, and Cross, the owner of several small apartment houses and office buildings.

Able hired detectives, who, in accordance with Able's instructions, followed Mrs. Bird on public streets, tape-recorded her statements whenever she appeared in public to discuss the amendment, and looked with binoculars into the windows of her home from adjacent premises. These activities ceased after one month, but they had embarrassed and humiliated Mrs. Bird so that she required psychotherapy.

Cross was interviewed on station XYTV on a live television broadcast concerning the proposed zoning amendment. During the interview, Cross stated: "I can't believe the City Council will approve Able's idiotic and stupid proposal. The guy had to be flying on something to propose that one." Able has been greatly disturbed by the broadcast, but is unable to establish any actual monetary loss as a result thereof.

Following the broadcast, Able advised various suppliers with whom he did business that he would not do business with anyone who had anything to do with Cross. Some of these suppliers, who were tenants at will of Cross, terminated their tenancies. Others, whose leases will expire shortly, have notified Cross that they will vacate at the end of their respective terms.

What are:

(1) Mrs. Bird's rights against Able;

(2) Able's rights against Cross and XYTV; and

(3) Cross's rights against Able?

Discuss.

Essay Exam Answers

Answer to Question 1

A v. B *(Assault and Battery):*

A could sue B for assault and battery. An assault occurs where one person intentionally causes another person to be in apprehension of harmful or offensive contact. (*See* ELO Ch.2-III(A).) A battery occurs where one person intentionally inflicts such harmful or contact bodily contact on another. (*See* ELO Ch.2-II(A).) Here, the assault arguably occurred when B initially cocked his fist to hit A and the battery when B actually struck A. To these actions B would assert the defenses of (1) *consent* (that A "squared off" with him), and (2) if A had thrown the initial punch, *self-defense* (where one reasonably believes that another is about to cause an imminent, offensive contact upon him/her, he/she can exercise whatever force is reasonably necessary under the circumstances to prevent such contact). In most jurisdictions, one cannot validly consent to conduct which constitutes a criminal act, especially if it involves breach of the peace. If this is such a state, B's consent defense would fail. (*See* ELO Ch.4-II(H)(1).) Whether B could prevail on the self-defense claim would depend on whether A was the initial aggressor. Here, the facts are not clear as to who threw the first punch. It seems somewhat more likely that B was the initial aggressor because A merely called B a sissy, while B's statement "I'll show you who's a sissy; let's see what you're made of" is considerably more aggressive and may well have been accompanied by a raised fist. If all A did initially was to insult B, B cannot claim self-defense, as words alone do not constitute an assault. If A was in fact the initial aggressor, B's self-defense claim would probably prevail, since it is probably not excessive force to defend oneself with fists against another's fists. (*See* ELO Ch.4-III.)

Conclusion: More facts are needed to determine who was the initial aggressor. If B was the initial aggressor, A can recover against B for nominal, compensatory (for mental suffering and physical injury), and possibly *punitive damages* (if B's conduct was outrageous or malicious). If A was the initial aggressor, B can claim self-defense and avoid tort liability. If A and B *consented* to fight, it is irrelevant who struck the first blow and they are both liable to each other for their torts.

B v. A *(Assault and Battery):*

The discussion above under *A v. B* would again be applicable, except that the parties would be reversed. Additionally, if A utilized more force than was necessary to protect himself against B (the facts indicated that A was "winning"), the *self-defense* privilege would *not* be available to him, even if B had been the initial aggressor, although the mere fact that A was "winning" does not necessarily mean the A's use of force was excessive. (*See* ELO Ch.4-III(F).)

A v. C *(Assault):*

A would probably assert an action for assault against C based on C's unsuccessful knife attack upon him. The elements of an assault are present: C intentionally caused A to be in apprehension of a harmful contact when he thrust the knife at A. C's possible defenses are (1) that he was acting in defense of B, and (2) that he was effecting a citizen's arrest. Under the *defense of others privilege*, a person may use reasonable force to protect another person, even a complete stranger, against attack. However, as in self-defense, the force used must be reasonable; deadly force may not be used to defend against a non-deadly attack. Here, A was using his fists against B, which probably does not rise to the level of deadly force, while the knife C used clearly is deadly force. Thus C would probably lose the defense of others privilege and would be liable to C. Furthermore, if A did not consent to fight B and B was the initial aggressor, C would lose the defense of others privilege because most courts would hold that C had stepped into B's shoes. If B were not entitled to use force in self-defense, C would not be entitled to use force on B's behalf and would lose the privilege. (*See* ELO Ch.4-IV.)

Under the *citizen's arrest claim*, C would be privileged to use force to effect a warrantless arrest because a felony (assault and battery) had been committed, and C would not lose the privilege even if he arrested the wrong person. So, even if B were the aggressor, C would have a defense against tort liability to A. However, because C used deadly force, he will probably lose the privilege regardless of who the initial aggressor was, since even a police officer may use deadly force to apprehend a suspect after the commission of a crime only where it is necessary to prevent escape and where the suspect poses a significant threat of death or serious physical injury to others. Here, even if A were beating B severely, there is no indication that A was about to escape. Furthermore, as a matter of public policy, it is unlikely that courts would afford private citizens the privilege to use deadly force to effect an arrest.

Conclusion: C will lose his defense of others privilege if B was the initial aggressor. C will lose the defense of others privilege if A was the initial aggressor but A's use of force was non-deadly. C will probably not prevail on his citizen's arrest claim because he used deadly force. If C loses his privileges, he will be liable to A for nominal, compensatory (here, for mental suffering), and possibly punitive damages.

B v. D (Assault):

B would probably assert an action for assault against D if he (1) saw D aiming the pistol in his direction, or (2) reasonably believed that D would fire at him after having shot at C. As discussed above, D would assert the defense of others and citizen's arrest privileges. D would prevail on the *defense of others claim* only if B were the initial aggressor and D's use of deadly force was not excessive. Here, D's use of deadly force was probably not excessive, since C was attacking A with a knife, which clearly is deadly force. D is more likely to prevail on the citizen's arrest defense than in the above example (if the courts will ever allow citizens to use deadly force to effect an arrest), since he can convincingly argue that C posed a significant risk of death. He will still have to show that he acted to prevent C's escape. The fact that D did not have a license to carry the firearm would be of no relevance to the assertion of these privileges. (*See* ELO Ch.4-III(G).)

C v. D (Assault, Conversion):

C could assert an action for assault against D based upon (1) D's shooting at him during the altercation, and (2) letting Homer loose (one is liable for instrumentalities which he/she set into motion). (It is assumed that Homer was of sufficiently large size to make C apprehensive of offensive touching, such as a dog bite). C could also sue D for conversion (intentionally causing a substantial interference with plaintiff's ownership interest in a chattel) because D took C's knife back to his home. If, however, the interference were characterized as being minor in nature, D would then be liable only for trespass to chattels. (*See* ELO Ch.3-III.)

With respect to the shooting, D would assert the defense of others and citizen's arrest privileges (discussed above). With respect to setting the dog loose, D would argue that he was privileged to use reasonable force in expelling C from his land since the latter was trespassing. This defense is probably available to D, since he warned C to get off his land before he released the dog. He might lose this defense, however, if C can convince a court that he was in hot pursuit of a chattel (the knife) wrongfully taken from him by D, and thus privileged to enter D's land. Whether C prevails on this point will depend on how much time elapsed between D's wrongful possession of the knife and C's attempt to reclaim it. C might try to argue that use of a dog to defend one's property is excessive force and thus vitiates D's defense of property claim, but given that dogs are very frequently used to guard property and in light of the fact that Homer didn't actually harm or even catch C, this argument is unlikely to win. (*See* ELO Ch.4-V.)

D's wrongful possession of C's knife is probably a conversion, ***not a trespass to chattels***, because (1) he has exercised total control over it by taking it and removing it to his home (assuming he had no intention to return it), and (2) he acted in bad faith by knowingly taking C's property. D would thus be liable to C for the full value ($25) of the knife, since in a conversion, title is deemed to have passed to the wrongdoer. D might try to assert a ***defense of necessity***, *i.e.*, that he took the knife to prevent C from committing harm either to the community at large (***a defense of public necessity***) or to himself or to A in retaliation for the fight (***a defense of private necessity***). His claim of public necessity will probably not prevail, because in such cases the danger to the community must be severe and must threaten a substantial number of people, such as a fire. He might prevail on the private necessity defense, where the threatened danger can be less severe, in which case he would either have to compensate C for the value of the knife or return the knife and compensate C for the temporary loss of its use. (*See* ELO Ch.4-VIII.)

Conclusion: C will probably not prevail on the assault claim based on the shooting. C will probably not prevail on the assault claim based on the dog attack because of D's defense of property privilege, although more facts are necessary to determine whether C can defeat that privilege with a reclamation of property claim. C will probably prevail on the conversion claim and recover the full value of the knife. If D convinces a court that he acted out of necessity, he will have to compensate C for his actual loss.

D v. C (Trespass):

As discussed above, D might sue C for trespass (intentionally encroaching upon the land of another). However, D can probably recover only ***nominal damages*** for this tort, since C did not damage his property. (*See* ELO Ch.3-I(D).)

E v. D (Assault and Battery):

E would sue D for battery and possibly assault. Although D was aiming at C instead of E, the intent element would probably be satisfied under the transferred intent doctrine (where the defendant intended to do an act with respect to a particular individual, and as a consequence thereof a different person was harmed, the defendant's intention will be transferred to the latter). (*See* ELO Ch.2-I(D).) The assault action may fail, however, because the facts indicate that E had "just" stepped out of the barber shop, and therefore he presumably did not have an opportunity to be in apprehension of the contact prior to the moment when it occurred. (*See* ELO Ch.2-V(E).)

D would assert the defense of others and citizen's arrest crime privileges to the foregoing torts, as discussed above. Thus, D would appear to have no liability to E.

E v. A or C or B (Assault and Battery):

An intentional tortfeasor is liable for all of the consequences of his/her actions, whether foreseeable or not. If A was the initial aggressor or consented to the fight and A appeared to be likely to cause B serious injury and C's only possibility of avoiding this harm was through use of the knife (*i.e.*, A was substantially larger and stronger than C), C's attempt to stab A would have been privileged. Therefore, A would be liable for the injury which D caused to E: However, if use of a knife was unnecessary (*i.e.*, C could have simply pulled A off of his brother), then use of the knife constituted excessive force; and C would be liable to E for the damages sustained from D's shot. Furthermore, if B were the initial aggressor, C would lose his privilege even if his use of force was not excessive, and would be liable to E. B is also liable to E if he was the initial aggressor, or if he consented to the fight. (*See* ELO Ch.2-III.)

Answer to Question 2

Estate of Art ("EA") v. Defendant ("D"):

The type of action EA will bring will depend on the state statutes governing such suits. In general, survival statutes allow the decedent's estate to sue for personal injuries to the decedent. Survival statutes are often accompanied by wrongful death statutes, which give the decedent's family a cause of action for the injured party's death. In such states, where the death is instantaneous, there is no survival action at all, since all damages are sustained after death; *e.g.*, the decedent did not experience pain and suffering before death and lost no wages prior to death. Here, assuming that both a survival statute and a wrongful death statute are in force, EA will not have a cause of action for Art's death, since he died instantaneously. Art's family (Sue Archer) will have to bring a wrongful death action to recover for his death. (*See* ELO Ch.10-IV.)

Sue Archer ("SA") v. D for injury to A (Battery, Negligence)

Battery: SA will assert a wrongful death action against D predicated upon battery (intentional infliction of an offensive touching upon the plaintiff). D arguably committed this tort when he knowingly equipped the vehicle to cause an electric shock to any person touching it. While D obviously did not desire to seriously injure anyone (the facts state that a healthy person would *not* be seriously harmed by a shock), the fact is immaterial since D did intend to cause an offensive touching upon anyone tampering with the car. (*See* ELO Ch.2-IV(B).)

D would initially assert the defense of ***property privilege***. One may ordinarily utilize the degree of force which he/she reasonably believes is necessary under the circumstances to prevent another from taking or tampering with his/her property. However, force capable of causing death or serious injury is *not* permissible, unless non-deadly force is not sufficient and the owner reasonably believes that without deadly force, death or serious bodily harm will occur. Here, it is clear that D could not have reasonably believed that death or serious bodily harm would occur; he only wanted to protect his car. However, D would contend that the degree of force was reasonable because it was not deadly force; a normal, healthy person would not have suffered any permanent injury. He would also argue that a brief electric shock was reasonable in light of the fact that D was seeking to protect a $50,000 car. SA would contend in rebuttal that an electric jolt is not reasonable force because (given the surprise which could occur) even a healthy person could go into shock and subsequently die. (*See* ELO Ch.4-V(A)(1).)

Whether the use of electric shock device constituted unreasonable force may depend on additional facts. In many states, for example, it is illegal to carry for self-defense purposes "stun guns" that administer a comparable jolt. A court could also conclude that the risk of innocent passersby being shocked if they tried, for example, to turn off headlights D had inadvertently left on was so great as to make the use of such a device an unreasonable use of force. (See negligence discussion below).

If SA prevailed on the battery issue, D would be liable to SA for A's death. It is well established that an intentional tortfeasor is responsible for all injuries which his/her victim suffered, whether foreseeable or not (Rest. 2d Sections 16 and 435).

Negligence: SA will also assert a wrongful death action against D based on a negligence theory. The tort of negligence occurs when one person's conduct imposes an unreasonable risk on another person who is injured as a result. Here, SA would argue that in designing an anti-theft device, D acted unreasonably by including a mechanism capable of administering a severe shock. In determining whether D's conduct was reasonable under the circumstances, a court might consider whether such shock devices were legal. A court might also consider custom as evidence of reasonableness; *i.e.*, was it common for shock devices to be included in anti-theft systems. A court might determine that such devices are inherently unreasonable because of the risk that persons who, as discussed above, tried to do a good deed by turning off D's headlights, or persons who were fleeing an attacker and sought refuge in D's car, would be severely injured. (*See* ELO Ch.5-III.)

SA would also argue that D was negligent in leaving his car unlocked. Given the expensive accessories and the consequent strong likelihood that someone would try to enter the vehicle if it appeared easy to do so, D probably failed to act reasonably in neglecting to lock the car door, particularly in light of the fact that he specifically designed the shock device to be triggered when a door was opened. (*See* ELO Ch.5-IV(F)(2).)

SA will have to show that D's negligence was the ***proximate cause*** of A's injury. D's conduct did in fact cause the loss, and SA would argue that the injury that resulted was reasonably foreseeable at the time that D acted negligently (*i.e.*, it was reasonably foreseeable that someone would try to enter D's car). However, D will contend that A's conduct was a superseding cause: an intervening cause that is sufficient to prevent D from being liable. D will probably lose on this point, since both the intervening cause and the kind of harm that results usually must be unforeseeable for a court to relieve the defendant of liability. (*See* ELO Ch.6-IV.) Although courts will usually find an unforeseeable intervening cause that is a crime or intentional tort to be a superseding cause, A's intentional tort was foreseeable. A court might be reluctant to relieve D of liability in these circumstances, for fear of encouraging people to take unreasonably dangerous measures in anticipation of foreseeable torts. With respect to A's heart condition, if D's conduct is found to have been negligent and the basic injury (*i.e.*, the shock) to A foreseeable, D will be liable for A's death, even if A's death was unforeseeable. The negligent defendant takes his plaintiff as he finds him. (*See* ELO Ch.6-III(D)(1)(a).)

SA will have to show actual damages as a result of D's negligence. Here, the actual damages are A's death. Under most wrongful death statutes, SA could sue for lost economic support, lost companionship (including sexual relations), and sometimes grief.

SA v. D for injuries to SA (Battery, Negligence):

Apparently, SA was *not* injured when knocked to the ground by her husband. She appears to be primarily concerned with the right to recover for her mental distress.

If SA is successful in her contention that D had committed a battery against A, D will be liable to her for her injuries as well since, as discussed above, an intentional tortfeasor is responsible for virtually all consequences that flow from his tort, whether foreseeable or not.

Since SA might *not* be successful in contending that D was an intentional tortfeasor, she would also contend that D was negligent. She would argue, as above, that D acted unreasonably in installing the shock device and in leaving his door unlocked.

D could contend in rebuttal that (1) SA was not a foreseeable plaintiff (*i.e.*, he could not reasonably foresee the harm to SA as a consequence of his allegedly negligent conduct), and (2) he was *not the proximate cause* of SA's harm (A's intentionally tortious conduct in committing a trespass to D's chattel was an unforeseeable, intervening consequence). However, SA could probably successfully contend in rebuttal that (1) she was a foreseeable plaintiff, since she was among the class of persons who might be harmed by D's negligent conduct (either on the theory that a person stunned by an electric shock would be likely to stumble backwards into a would-be rescuer or that someone who witnessed a family member's death as a result of D's conduct would be severely traumatized), and (2) A was foreseeable intervening factor (it was foreseeable that someone would attempt to enter D's car). (*See* ELO Ch.6-III(D)(5).) SA should prevail on these issues, and therefore, she should be able to successfully sue D for negligence.

There are three views as to when someone who suffers mental distress can recover from a negligent tortfeasor.

The traditional view is that an impact must be made upon the plaintiff for that person to sue for *mental distress*. If this is such a jurisdiction, D will contend that there was no impact upon SA as a direct consequence of his action in the sense of a physical injury, distinct from the physical symptoms of mental distress. While A fell upon SA, the facts suggest that SA was not physically injured by this contact. Given that the policy behind requiring physical injury is to have assurance that the claim of suffering is not feigned, it is unlikely that the physical impact here would be sufficient.

Most courts, in addition to allowing recovery when an impact occurs, permit a plaintiff to recover for mental distress so long as he/she was in the zone of danger. The facts are silent as to how far SA stood from A at the time of the incident. However, assuming she was *not* within a very few feet of D's car, it is unlikely that SA will be deemed to have been in the zone of danger.

Finally, a few jurisdictions permit ***damages for emotional distress*** if, upon weighing the following factors, recovery would be appropriate: (1) the relationship of the plaintiff and the victim, (2) whether the plaintiff contemporaneously observed the incident which resulted in the victim being injured, and (3) the extent to which the actual physical harm to the plaintiff is manifest. Since SA was A's wife, she personally observed the incident, and her mental distress was manifested in physical symptoms (vomiting, nausea, etc.), all of the possible elements necessary to satisfy this theory appear to be met. (*See* ELO Ch.8-IV(B).)

D's defenses: D would argue in response to the battery claim that A ***consented*** to the harm which occurred because the sign in D's front window warned of a protective device. SA would argue in rebuttal, however, that the warning was not adequate because (1) it was only in the front windshield, rather than on the side (where someone would be likely to attempt to enter the vehicle), and (2) the warning did not describe the particular type of danger which a trespasser would encounter (the term "protective device" is too vague; the sign should have specifically indicated that an intruder would receive an electric jolt). Furthermore, Baker ("B") could probably testify that A did not see the sign and thus did not consent to the harm. SA should succeed on this issue.

D would argue in response to the negligence claim that A assumed the risk of harm based on the same facts. Here, SA will prevail because A clearly did not expressly assume the risk, and a court will not find implied ***assumption of risk*** unless the defendant can show that the injured party (here, A) (1) actually knew of the risk in question, and (2) voluntarily consented to bear the risk. Again, B will testify that A did not see the sign and did not voluntarily consent. (*See* ELO Ch.11-III.)

D may also try to defend against the negligence claim on the grounds that A was contributorily negligent in entering his car. At common law, a plaintiff whose own negligence contributes proximately to his injury is barred from recovery. Here, a court could find that it was not reasonable under the circumstances for A to enter D's car. However, a court could also find that it was so unforeseeable that A would be shocked by opening the door that his negligence did not proximately cause his injuries. Furthermore, if a court finds D's conduct to be willful, wanton, or reckless, he will not be able to use the contributory negligence defense. (*See* ELO Ch.11-I.)

SA v. Baker ("B") (Negligence):

SA might contend that B failed to act reasonably in persuading A to attempt to enter D's car and that, since A died as a consequence of B's suggestion, he should be liable to SA. However, words alone ordinarily do not constitute unreasonable conduct when spoken to an adult (who is presumably in full control of his/her faculties and actions).

Conclusion:

SA will probably win the wrongful death action based on battery. She will be able to recover nominal, compensatory, and possibly punitive *damages* for this intentional tort. If she loses on the battery claim, she might prevail on negligence grounds, but proximate cause issues make this less sure than the battery claim. If SA wins on negligence, she will get damages for loss of economic support, lost companionship, and possibly grief.

D will be liable to SA for her mental distress if SA wins the battery claim. Whether D will be liable for SA's mental distress on a negligence theory will depend on how the court finds on proximate cause and on what rule the jurisdiction follows on liability for mental distress suffered as a result of witnessing injury to another.

Answer to Question 3

Jim v. Dan (Assault, Battery and Negligence)

Assault and Battery:

Did Dan assault or commit a battery upon Jim? An assault occurs where the defendant intentionally causes the plaintiff to be reasonably in apprehension of an imminent, offensive touching. A battery is an intentional harmful or offensive touching. The intent required for both assault and battery is not intent to harm another; instead, it is intent to do the act itself. Here, although Dan shot at Jim, Dan never intended to make Jim fearful of his life; he thought he was merely playing a role in a scene with a fellow actor. Therefore, no assault occurred. Dan also did not intend to inflict harmful physical contact on Jim, because he believed he was only firing blanks. Thus, there was no battery. (*See* ELO Ch.2-IV(A)(1), V(B).)

Negligence:

Did Dan act reasonably under the circumstances? The tort of negligence occurs when one person's conduct imposes an unreasonable risk on another person who is injured as a result. Here, Jim would have to argue that Dan failed to act reasonably under the circumstances. Jim could contend that Dan failed to act with due care in not checking the gun prior to firing it. However, a reasonable actor probably relies upon the prop person to tend to this detail. Thus, Dan should prevail on this issue. (*See* ELO Ch.5-II.)

Did Jim suffer actual injury? Dan would argue that Jim had suffered no actual injury and thus could not recover. Generally, the plaintiff may not recover for mental harm alone without physical injury, and nominal damages will not be awarded in a negligence action (unlike intentional tort suits). Jim could try to recover for damage to the hat (if it belongs to him and not the studio). However, since Dan probably did not breach his duty of care to Jim, the negligence action will probably **not** be successful. (*See* ELO Ch.II(A)(4).)

In summary, Jim probably has no right of recovery against Dan.

Jim v. Fred (Assault and Battery):

Assuming Jim saw Fred coming toward him, the elements of an assault appear to be satisfied. A battery occurred when Fred intentionally inflicted harmful physical contact on Jim by (1) knocking him to the ground, and (2) punching him in the face.

Is the "defense of others" privilege available to Fred? One can ordinarily defend others to the same extent that the protectee could have utilized force. Although at common law this privilege was limited to defense of one's family members, courts today allow bystanders to use reasonable force to defend complete strangers against attack. Since Dan had the right to protect himself from Jim's bottle-throwing, Fred would argue that he had the right to subdue Jim. Jim could contend in rebuttal, however, that the force utilized by Fred was excessive (*i.e.*, Fred didn't have to punch him in the face; he could have simply held Jim down) and therefore the privilege was forfeited. Fred could respond that punching Jim was a reasonable way of assuring that he would be restrained. The facts are silent as to the relative sizes of Jim and Fred. Assuming they were of approximately equal stature, Fred's assertion that he did *not* use excessive force since Jim was obviously a very violent individual (one who appeared to be about to throw a bottle at another) would probably be successful. However, if Fred were substantially larger than Jim (to the extent that he could have restrained Jim somewhat easily), Fred's punch probably would have constituted excessive force. (*See* ELO Ch.4-IV(A)(1).)

Jim could argue that Fred was mistaken in his assumption that Jim was the aggressor who needed to be subdued, because Jim was in fact defending himself against Dan. Jim would contend that this mistake vitiated Fred's *"defense of others" privilege*. Most courts would hold that Fred has stepped into Dan's shoes, and that if Dan would not have been entitled to use force because he was the initial aggressor, Fred would also lose the privilege. Here, however, Dan had no knowledge that he was firing real bullets, and thus, believing that Jim was attacking him without provocation, he probably would have been privileged to defend himself against Jim. Therefore, Fred would probably not lose the privilege on grounds of mistake. (*See* ELO Ch.4-IV(A)(2).)

Is the "prevention of crime" privilege available to Fred? A private citizen can ordinarily use reasonable force to prevent a felony that seems about to be committed in his/her presence (a few states require that a felony must actually have been committed; but we will assume that is not the case in this instance). Since throwing a bottle at another person is probably a felony, the discussion above with respect to the defense of others privilege would be equally applicable here too.

Dan v. Jim (Assault):

Did Jim assault Dan? Jim clearly assaulted Dan by raising a bottle to throw at him. Because this gesture was not in the script, it was reasonable for Dan to fear that Jim meant to strike him. Jim had the intent necessary for assault because he meant to cause Dan to fear such contact. (*See* ELO Ch.2-V(A).)

Dan will probably not be able to recover against Jim, however, because Jim has the *"self defense" privilege*. Jim will be entitled to this privilege as long as (1) he reasonably believed that Dan was about to harm him, and (2) the degree of force he used to defend himself was not excessive. Here, it was reasonable for Jim to believe Dan was about to harm or even kill him, because Dan had just shot a real bullet into Jim's hat and because the script called for Dan to fire another shot at Jim. Jim did not use excessive force because the room was too noisy for Dan to hear any warnings of his error. Furthermore, he is privileged to use the degree of force necessary to prevent the harm, and where the threatened harm is death, he is privileged to use deadly force. A thrown bottle probably does not rise to the level of deadly force and seems clearly within the range of force necessary to prevent an imminent shooting. (*See* ELO Ch.4-III(G).)

In summary, Dan probably has no right of recovery against Jim.

Peter v. Fred (Trespass and Negligence):

Did Fred Commit a trespass? A trespass occurs where one intrudes upon the land of another, even if the trespasser mistakenly thinks he is entitled to enter. Since Peter was renting the saloon, and the sign was clearly posted (and therefore no implied consent argument could be made), Fred's action probably constituted a trespass. In many jurisdictions a trespasser is liable for all injuries or losses occasioned by his/her trespass, regardless of whether those losses were accidental or not. Thus, Fred would probably be liable for the value of the camera. (*See* ELO Ch.3-I(C)(1).)

Negligence:

Did Fred act reasonably under the circumstances? If the incident involving the injury did not occur in a jurisdiction which holds a trespasser liable for all damages occasioned by the trespass, Peter would also sue Fred in negligence (*i.e.*, arguing that he acted unreasonably under the circumstances in failing to see the prominently displayed "Closed For Day" sign).

In a negligence action, however, Fred would argue that he did not **breach a duty of care** by acting unreasonably under the circumstances. Fred would argue that a reasonable person in that small western town would not look for a warning sign on the door of a saloon which he regularly frequented, particularly where the saloon was routinely open for business during the relevant time and had not, to his knowledge, previously been used as a film set or for any other unusual purpose. Whether this argument would prevail might depend on to what extent the filming of the movie was common knowledge in the town. Thus, to determine whether Fred acted reasonably under the circumstances might depend on additional facts. (*See* ELO Ch.5-IV(C)(2).)

Was Fred's conduct the proximate cause of Peter's loss? If Fred did act unreasonably, then Peter would have to show that Fred's negligent conduct was the proximate cause of his loss. While Fred's conduct clearly did in fact cause the loss, an issue in this action would be whether the extent of the loss ($25,000) was so unforeseeable in light of the allegedly negligent conduct (*i.e.*, pushing open the door without seeing the sign), that proximate causation should be deemed to be lacking. Peter would contend, however, that $25,000 in damages was not unforeseeable; since the pushed door could have hit someone in the face, causing harm in that amount. (*See* ELO Ch.6-III(C).)

Fred would respond that $25,000 in *damages* was not foreseeable, because (1) under normal circumstances, people do not stand behind swinging doors because of the risk of injury, and (2) the remoteness of the town made it highly unusual for a film to be produced in its local saloon (and thus for expensive camera equipment to be situated behind the door). Whether Fred would prevail of this argument might depend on whether he pushed the door with unusual force and, as above, whether the film production was common knowledge in the town.

Was Peter contributorily negligent? If Fred is found to have been negligent and the $25,000 in damages foreseeable, Fred might raise the affirmative defense that Peter was ***contributorily negligent***. Fred would argue that Peter should have taken greater measures to protect the film site, such as hiring guards to prevent people from entering the saloon, placing more signs in front of the site, or locking or barricading the entry. The success of this defense would depend on what a reasonable person in Peter's circumstances would have done. Thus, additional facts, such as what standard precautions are used in the film industry, are needed. If Peter is held contributorily negligent, he will be totally barred from recovery against Fred. If this is a ***comparative negligence*** jurisdiction, then the damages would be apportioned between Fred and Peter. (*See* ELO Ch.11-I(D), II(B).)

In summary, Peter can recover the value of the camera and any other ***damages*** occasioned by Fred's conduct on a trespass theory. On a negligence theory, whether and how much Peter can recover will depend on additional facts.

Answer to Question 4

Frank ("F") v. Dennis ("D") and Conco ("C") (Trespass):

Is D liable to F for trespass? A trespass occurs when a person intentionally enters someone else's land without permission, or when a person places an object on someone else's land without permission. The fact that such encroachment is the result of a good faith mistake is irrelevant. Since D intentionally moved the vehicles upon F's land, he would be liable for all damage resulting from such action, whether foreseeable or not (there is no proximate causation requirement with respect to intentional torts). Thus, D would be liable to F for $9,000, the value of the destroyed bulbs. (*See* ELO Ch.3-I(C).)

Can D escape liability with a claim of necessity? D might attempt to defend by claiming his trespass was privileged as a *public necessity* (*i.e.*, that the injury or inconvenience to the property owner was outweighed by the potential public loss of life and property). There would be no point in arguing that a *private necessity* was present, since the actor is still liable for the actual harm caused by his conduct in that instance. Where public necessity is applicable, however, the actor is relieved of all liability. D could argue that a public necessity existed because the vehicles at C's plant could have caught fire, exploded, and injured the persons responding to the fire alarm. While F could contend in rebuttal that since the yard was located in a suburban area, little or no threat was posed to the public at large, and D was acting only to protect the private interest of his employer. Whether D will be found to have acted out of public necessity will depend on additional facts, such as the likelihood of explosion, the size of the fire, the presence of flammable materials near the fire, the density of population in the area, etc. However, fires generally pose a risk to the public at large because they spread quickly and are very dangerous to life and property, so D (and thus C) will probably prevail. (*See* ELO Ch.4-VIII(C),(D).)

F v. D and C (Negligence):

F would probably also sue D for negligence. The tort of negligence occurs when one person's conduct imposes an unreasonable risk on another person who is injured as a result.

Did D **breach his duty of due care** toward F by acting unreasonably? Since there was very little harm apparent to F's land and the potential of great damage of personal injury if the vehicles were not removed from C's premises, D probably did not act unreasonably. (*See* ELO Ch.8-I(A).)

Even if D did act unreasonably under the circumstances, it is not clear that D's actions were the *proximate cause* of F's losses (*i.e.*, was the manner and/or extent of the loss reasonably foreseeable in light of the allegedly negligent conduct?). Assuming the ground appeared to be barren (*i.e.*, there was no visible evidence that something had been planted under it), D could probably successfully argue that he couldn't foresee a $9,000 loss from destroyed tulip bulbs; although F will contend that there is always the possibility that damage could result when heavy items are moved onto someone's land (*e.g.*, underground pipes could be broken). (*See* ELO Ch.6-III(D).)

In summary, D (and therefore C, also) should prevail in the event F brought a negligence action against them.

Is Conco liable for the intentional acts or negligence of Dennis? Under the doctrine of *respondeat superior*, if an employee commits a tort while in the scope of his employment, the **employer** will be jointly liable with the **employee**. Here, although D committed the tort(s) on a Sunday, while on a personal errand, and at a facility at which he usually did not work, D probably did act within the scope of his employment because he probably acted with an intent to further his employer's business purpose (*i.e.*, to preserve the equipment necessary for the employer's operations). Even if part of his motivation was to prevent harm to the public, his employer will still probably be liable, because an employee acts within the scope of his employment even if his intent to serve his employer is coupled with a separate personal purpose. *Respondeat superior* covers both intentional torts (*i.e.*, trespass) and torts of omission (*i.e.*, negligence). (*See* ELO Ch.12-II(C).) As a matter of law, C will probably be liable, and as a practical matter, none of the parties is likely to challenge this, since F wants a deep pocket defendant, D probably can't pay the **damages** himself, and C is probably glad to pay the $9,000 (and is probably insured anyway) instead of the much greater loss it would have had if D had not moved the equipment.

D v. F (False Imprisonment and Intentional Infliction of Severe Emotional Distress):

A false imprisonment ("F.I.") occurs where the defendant has intentionally confined the plaintiff within definite physical boundaries. Here, although D was clearly confined within definite physical boundaries (the office space), it does not appear from the facts that the confinement was enforced in any way. D might contend that when he was told, in the presence of four of F's employees, he would "have to" remain in the office, his will was overcome, and therefore an F.I. had occurred. However, where a plaintiff voluntarily submits to purely verbal commands unaccompanied by force or threats, there is no F.I. F will argue that D was simply told to remain there and apparently no threats were made. Merely telling D that he would have to wait for the president is not in itself a threat; perhaps F meant only that the president was the only person with the authority to settle the matter. Furthermore, there is no F.I. where the plaintiff's confinement results solely from his desire to clear himself from suspicion in a criminal setting; here, D's confinement may well have resulted simply from his desire to clear up the matter of the damage to F's property, as would seem apparent from his agreement to meet with F in the first place. (*See* ELO Ch.2-VI(F)(1).) If nonetheless an F.I.

were held to have occurred, F might contend that D **consented** to the alleged F.I. since he voluntarily went to F's premises; but this defense would fail since D presumably did so with the belief that he would be free to leave whenever he chose to go. If an F.I. occurred, it appears that D can recover only nominal damages since he suffered no real loss. (*See* ELO Ch.4-II(A).)

D might also sue F for the **intentional infliction of severe emotional distress.** This tort arises where the defendant intentionally, through outrageous conduct, causes the plaintiff to suffer severe emotional distress. However, since F's employees apparently did not actually threaten D with any type of physical harm, it is unlikely that F's conduct would be considered "outrageous" in this instance. (*See* ELO Ch.2-VII(C).)

Conclusion:

D will be liable to F for the damages resulting from his trespass. Additional facts are needed to determine whether D can avoid paying damages with a public necessity defense. If D is liable and must pay damages, C will be liable under *respondeat superior.* Neither D nor C will be liable on a negligence theory. Any false imprisonment or intentional infliction of emotional distress claims by D against F will fail.

Answer to Question 5

Abel ("A") could assert negligence actions against Babel ("B") and Jones ("J"). He could also assert intentional torts against Pierre ("P") and his employees.

We'll assume that there is no applicable statute which prevents Abel from suing for injuries sustained in the course of his employment as a result of another's negligence.

A v. B (Negligence):

A would argue that by only having two fire exits on Cool's ("C's") floor, B acted unreasonably under the circumstances and that A was injured as a result of B's unreasonable conduct.

Did B fail to act reasonably under the circumstances? A would have to show that B was under a ***legal duty*** to conduct itself according to a certain standard of care in order to avoid unreasonable risk to others, and that B breached that standard of care. The duty that B, as owner of the premises, owed to A will depend on whether this is a jurisdiction that distinguishes among categories of people when they are on another's property. If this jurisdiction does distinguish among, *e.g.*, trespassers, invitees, and licensees, then B probably did not owe A a duty to make the premises safe for him, because firefighters are generally deemed to be licensees, not invitees. Property owners are not usually held to have an affirmative duty to make their premises safe for licensees, presumably because such persons enter their property in emergencies, so it would be unreasonable to require owners to make advance preparations for their safety. (*See* ELO Ch.9-V(B)(3).) It is nonetheless possible that a court might find that in light of the particular negligent conduct involved here (failure to have required fire exits), it was sufficiently foreseeable that this would endanger a firefighter since a firefighter would probably only be on the premises in the event of a fire, and that B should therefore be liable even though the firefighter was a licensee.

Many jurisdictions have rejected the above categories and instead use a single "reasonable person" standard of liability. (*See* ELO Ch.9-VII.) If this is such a jurisdiction, B will probably be deemed to have a duty to provide escape routes in the event of fire for those who are inside the building, whether they are guests, invitees, or public employees attempting to be of aid to those inside. Furthermore, B will probably be deemed to have had a duty to A since peril invites rescue, and therefore B should have foreseen that firemen would respond to a fire at the hotel. The city ordinance will probably be considered as evidence of what is at least the minimum standard of care.

Violation of a ***statute*** establishes a lack of due care where the (1) legislation (a) clearly defines a standard of conduct to which the defendant did not conform, and (b) was intended to prevent the type of harm which occurred and (2) plaintiff was within the class which the statute sought to protect, which would be either the

public at large or anyone in the hotel. Although the violation here involves only a city ordinance and not a statute and thus does not establish negligence *per se*, it would clearly be very strong evidence of negligence. Since B would appear to have no excuse for failing to have four fire exits on C's floor, B would ***not*** be deemed to have acted with due care. (*See* ELO Ch.5-VIII(B)(1).)

Was B's negligence a "but for" cause of A's injuries? A defendant's failure to have acted reasonably must be a "but for" cause of the plaintiff's harm. B could argue that his failure to have two additional fire exits was not the actual cause of A's injuries since (1)A's path onto the hallway (where additional exits would have been located) was entirely blocked by the fire, and (2) J's failure to leave the wheelchair at Cool's ("C") bedside was the direct cause of A's injuries. While the latter contention would probably fail (*i.e.*, J's conduct would probably be deemed to be a contributing, but not superseding, cause of A's injuries), B's first contention appears to be well taken. Additional facts might be necessary to determine whether A or B should prevail on this point. It would be helpful to know, for example, where the additional exits should have been placed, or what additional city regulations might exist on the placement of emergency exits. If an exit were supposed to be accessible from the rooms of all long-term residents, or if the hotel were required to house invalids only in rooms with fire exits directly accessible to them, then B's negligence would clearly be a "but for" cause of A's injuries. If, however, the exits would have been off the hallway, then B's negligence clearly would not be a "but for" cause of A's injuries. (*See* ELO Ch.6-I.)

Was B's negligence the proximate cause of A's injuries? A must show that there is a sufficiently close causal link between B's negligence andA's injuries that B should be held liable.

B would contend that its conduct was not the proximate cause of A's injuries since the unforeseeable intervening acts of (1) J in forgetting to leave the wheelchair by C's bed, and (2) P in deliberately moving A after he had fallen to the ground, extinguished the chain of causation. However, A could probably successfully contend in rebuttal that (1) it was foreseeable that an invalid staying at the hotel might be unable to vacate the premises regardless of whether someone negligently parked the former's wheelchair, because invalids generally require more time to move from one place to another, and (2) P's conduct did not cause A's injury (but rather, merely aggravated the injury after it had been sustained). Given the nature of the injury, assuming that B's negligence was a "but for" cause, it would probably be very difficult to divide the harm and determine what harm was caused by B and what by P. This is not an instance where the subsequent intervening factor is so remote in time or in logic that it should relieve B of liability. (*See* ELO Ch.6-IV(A)(1).) Indeed, if additional facts showed that B should have placed an exit from C's room (and thus B's conduct created the danger), then it would clearly be foreseeable that someone attempting to escape a burning building without the benefit of a fire exit would be likely to be injured in the attempt, and that those injuries could be aggravated even by well-intentioned efforts to remove that person to safety. (See also proximate cause discussion under *A v. J* below.)

B might also try to argue that A was an unforeseeable plaintiff and that therefore its negligence was not the proximate cause of A's injuries. However, A would probably be deemed to be a member of the general class of persons as to which there was a foreseeability of harm, because it is foreseeable that a firefighter would be in a burning building. (*See* ELO Ch.III(D)(5).)

Conclusion: Whether A will prevail in a negligence action will hinge on whether B's negligence was a "but for" cause of A's injuries. This determination requires additional facts.

A v. J (Negligence):

A would contend that J failed to act reasonably by not leaving the wheelchair at C's bedside.

Did J fail to act reasonably under the circumstances? J probably failed to act reasonably under the circumstances in neglecting to leave the wheelchair close to C's bed. She should have recognized the possibility of an emergency occurring which would require C to unlock the door. By making C reliant on others for mobility, J also put those who would come to C's aid at risk of harm from whatever danger C needed to flee. (*See* ELO Ch.5-III.)

Was J's negligence a "but for" cause of A's injuries? J's negligence was probably a "but for" cause of A's injuries, because if she had placed the wheelchair next to C's bed, C might have been able to escape on her own, and A would not have had to enter the building to rescue her. Even if she could not have escaped without help, she might have been able to unlock the door, saving valuable time and enabling A to escape with her through the fire exit before the fire engulfed the hallway. (*See* ELO Ch.6-I(A)(1).)

Was J's negligence the proximate cause of A's injuries? J's negligence will probably be found to have proximately caused A's injuries, because (1) it is foreseeable that an invalid who is rendered immobile by someone else's negligent act will require assistance in an emergency; and (2) her negligence created the danger in a "but for" sense, as discussed above, and thus neither an attempted escape nor an attempted rescue from that danger will be a superseding cause. P's conduct will also not be a superseding cause, as discussed above under proximate cause, *A v. B.* (*See* ELO Ch.6-IV(B).)

Conclusion: In summary, it appears that A could successfully sustain a negligence action against J.

A v. P and his employees (Assault and Battery):

While P did not actually participate in moving A, he would still be liable since the employees were acting pursuant to his direction. A should be able to successfully sue P and his employees for assault (intentionally causing the plaintiff to be in apprehension of an imminent, offensive touching) and battery (intentionally causing an offensive contact upon the plaintiff) since they accosted and then moved him. While the defendants could argue that A was a trespasser and therefore they had the right to use reasonable force to eject him, A could probably successfully contend in rebuttal that where the situation is one in which the property owner is not entitled to use deadly force, the owner cannot eject an intruder if this is likely to cause injury. (*See* ELO Ch.4-V(A)(1).) Here, deadly force would clearly be inappropriate and excessive, as it must have been obvious from A's uniform that he was a firefighter and from the condition of A and C that they had just been in a fire. Thus, they were clearly not intruding in a malicious manner. In addition, a reasonable person would conclude that individuals who had just fallen through a roof were injured and in need of medical attention and thus should not be moved. A would also argue that he was privileged to be in P's restaurant under the private necessity doctrine (the interest in saving his life outweighed any business interruption to P). Where someone is privileged by private necessity to enter someone else's property, the owner cannot interfere with the exercise of that privilege and is liable for any damages resulting from such interference. (*See* ELO Ch.4-VIII(D).)

Damages: Assuming A were successful in his lawsuit against B, J, P, and the latter's employees, or any of them, he would be able to recover for any past and prospective lost income, medical bills, and pain and suffering attributable to the incident. A might be able to get punitive damages from B if a jury found that its conduct was "reckless" or "willful and wanton." (*See* ELO Ch.10-II(A)(1).) A might get punitive damages from P (and his employees) if a jury found their conduct was outrageous or malicious. (*See* ELO Ch.2-V(M).) If A's injury is found to be an indivisible harm, then the defendants are jointly and severally liable; each defendant is liable for A's total harm. However, A can only recover the amount of his actual damages, so A will be able to collect the amount from only one defendant. Depending on the jurisdiction, that defendant may be able to seek contribution from the other defendants, either on an equal share basis or on a ***comparative negligence*** basis (except that P and his employees, as intentional tortfeasors, have no right of contribution from their fellow wrongdoers). Even if A were insured against hospitalization or loss of income, he would ***not*** be obliged to offset any reimbursement against this judgment as a consequence of the collateral source rule. (*See* ELO Ch.10-I(E)(1).)

Answer to Question 6

Wendy ("W") v. Blodgers, Inc. ("B") (Negligence):

W could sue B in negligence for her miscarriage, and the pain and suffering that resulted from it.

Duty: The duty that B owed W as the owner of the property where the injury was inflicted will depend on whether this jurisdiction distinguishes among categories of persons on another's land. In some jurisdictions, the owner's duty varies according to the status of the person on her land. If this is such a jurisdiction, then B owed W a duty to make the premises safe and assist her in the event of an emergency because, as a customer who had paid for a ticket to the game and for parking in the lot, W was a business invitee. The owner's duty to invitees to use reasonable care may require that the owner exercise control over third persons on the premises; thus, W will argue that B had a duty to take reasonable security measures to protect her from K's assault. (*See* ELO Ch.9-VI(C)(3)(d).)

If this jurisdiction has rejected the categories of invitee, etc., and instead uses a single "reasonable person" standard of liability, then B owed W a duty to exercise reasonable care under the circumstances.

Here, the fact pattern is such that whether B had a particular duty to an invitee or simply that of a reasonable person will probably not affect the outcome of the case in a significant way.

Breach of Duty: Depending on the jurisdiction, W will argue that B either failed to make the premises safe for invitees or did not act reasonably under the circumstances in failing to (1) prevent Kelly's ("K's") conduct, and (2) provide her with an immediate examination and the proper medical aid.

B would probably contend in rebuttal that it did not act unreasonably in failing to prevent K's conduct since it occurred spontaneously (B would have to have a security guard at every single parking place in order to prevent the type of incident about which W is complaining), and furthermore, because K's conduct consisted primarily of speech, it was not possible for B's guards to anticipate it or to know while it occurred that it was dangerous. From where they were standing, they may not have been able to discern that his words were threatening. A court would probably conclude that B met its duty (regardless or what duty was required by the jurisdiction) by having security guards in the parking lot, unless additional facts showed that the security guards were somehow delinquent in performing their job. (*See* ELO Ch.9-VI(C).)

B would also argue that it was not B's responsibility to have a doctor and an extensive medical facility at the stadium (they're a baseball organization, not a hospital); and so the infirmary where first aid care could be administered was sufficient. B probably did not fail to act reasonably in not having a complete medical facility.

Whether B did not act with due care in providing W with an immediate medical examination (or at least sending her to a hospital promptly) would depend upon the obviousness of W's pregnancy. If it were obvious, B probably should have recognized that immediate medical attention might be necessary to avert a miscarriage. However, if W was in the early stages of her pregnancy and it was not noticeable, then B probably would have acted reasonably in simply having W rest in its infirmary until she regained consciousness and could drive home. Thus, additional facts would be required to advise W with respect to this issue.

Actual Causation: If B were found to have breached its duty of care by not preventing K's conduct, then its actions would be an actual (or "but for") cause of W's harm.

If B failed to act reasonably in not obtaining immediate medical attention for W, B would not be the actual cause of W's harm unless it could be shown that the miscarriage could have been prevented had such aid been promptly administered. Thus, if B can show that the miscarriage occurred when W struck the ground, actual causation would be absent (assuming B had not failed to act reasonably in not averting K's conduct). Again, more facts would have to be obtained to advise W as to the likelihood of success with respect to this issue. (*See* ELO Ch.6-I(A)(1).)

Proximate Cause: If W can establish that B breached its duty of care and that its breach actually caused her injuries, she must still show that B's conduct proximately caused her injuries; *i.e.*, that there is a sufficiently close causal link between B's negligence and her injuries that B should be liable. Here, a court would probably find that it was reasonably foreseeable that failure to prevent an assault on a customer would result in injuries to the customer, and that failure to provide adequate medical attention would either cause injuries or aggravate existing ones. (*See* ELO Ch.6-III(C).)

Conclusion: B is probably not liable to W because B does not seem to have breached its duty of care to W.

W v. Police (Negligence):

W might sue the police for negligence on the grounds that they acted unreasonably under the circumstances by taking her to the hospital in a police car rather than an ambulance. She would argue that this negligence caused the miscarriage because she could not receive proper medical care en route to the hospital.

Even if she could prove that this conduct caused the miscarriage, W would probably lose this suit because a court would probably find that the police would have acted unreasonably under the circumstances (*i.e.*, heavy traffic that precluded use of an ambulance) had they *not* taken her to the hospital in their police car. (*See* ELO Ch.5-IV(A).)

W v. K (Assault, Intentional Infliction of Mental Distress):

W would probably sue K for assault and intentional infliction of mental distress. An assault occurs where the defendant has intentionally caused the plaintiff to be in reasonable apprehension of an imminent, offensive touching. Although words alone are usually not sufficient to constitute an assault even a slight overt act accompanying those words can be sufficient for an assault. Here, K "jumped out" of his car. A court could find that this was an overt act that made it reasonable for W to be apprehensive that he was about to carry out the action threatened by his words. Indeed, for K to have committed an assault, he need not have intended to actually touch her; the required intent is merely that he intended to put her in **apprehension** of such contact. (*See* ELO Ch.2-V(C).)

The tort of **intentional infliction of mental distress** requires intent, a showing that the defendant's conduct was extreme and outrageous, and actual severe distress on the part of the plaintiff. Here, even if W could show intent (that K (1) desired to cause her emotional distress, (2) knew with substantial certainty that she would suffer emotional distress, or (3) recklessly disregarded the high probability that she would suffer emotional distress), she would probably not be able to establish that K's conduct was extreme and outrageous. In general, a defendant's conduct does not rise to this level when he has merely insulted the plaintiff or hurt her feelings. A court could possibly find that K's conduct was outrageous because a threat of physical violence against a pregnant woman would foreseeably cause her intense anxiety and fear for the welfare of her unborn child. Again, resolution of this issue might depend upon how pregnant W appeared to be. (*See* ELO Ch.2-VII(C).)

Defenses: K might argue that he should not be liable because he was acting in **defense of his property.** In general, a person may use reasonable force to defend his property. Here, although K arguably used words and not force, a court might find that he acted unreasonably in the face of what was merely a negligent act by W, particularly if she was in late pregnancy and thus less able to maneuver among parked cars and more likely to suffer severe mental distress from a threat of violence. Additional facts, such as which car was parked first and thus who was responsible for the cars being too close to each other, might also affect the viability of such a defense. (*See* ELO Ch.4-V(A)(1).)

Conclusion: W can probably recover from K for assault. Whether she can recover for intentional infliction of emotional distress will depend on additional facts. If W were successful upon either theory, she would be able to recover for the miscarriage as well as mental suffering, since an intentional tortfeasor is normally liable for all of the consequences of his/her act. She might be able to recover punitive damages if K's conduct is found to be particularly outrageous or malicious. Even if B or the police were found to have been negligent after K's initial conduct, K would still be liable for all of her injuries.

K v. H; H v. K (Assault and Battery):

Between H and K, the party who will be able to recover from the other for assault and battery (the intentional infliction of harmful or offensive bodily contact) will depend on who was the initial aggressor. H will argue that he was privileged in punching K in the mouth first because *he was acting in defense of W.* The success of this defense would depend upon whether H reasonably believed that W was in imminent danger of serious injury (*i.e.,* whether K was about to kick W) and on whether H used reasonable force in acting to protect W. Whether H will prevail on this point will depend on additional facts, such as what actions K took after W fainted. If he moved towards her aggressively, then H probably acted reasonably. If he merely stood still or recoiled in surprise, then H probably acted unreasonably. (*See* ELO Ch.4-IV(A)(1).)

If H acted unreasonably and thus was not privileged in punching K, he'd probably prevail on a *self-defense claim*, arguing that he used the force that was reasonably necessary to prevent further offensive contact from H. (*See* ELO Ch.4-III(E).)

If H acted reasonably and his first punch was privileged, then liability for the rest of the altercation would depend on who threw the next punch and thus became the aggressor (*i.e.,* did H charge K after the latter had been knocked to the ground, or did K jump back up and attack H?).

J v. H or K (Assault and Battery):

J would argue that he was attempting to effect a warrantless arrest for a breach of the peace committed in his presence, and that therefore *his action was privileged.* He should be able to recover from the party who was the aggressor (either H, if H was not privileged, or whoever threw the second punch).

K v. W (Trespass to Chattels, Negligence):

K will try to recover from W for the damage to his car, either on a trespass to chattels theory or on a negligence theory. Trespass to chattels is intentional interference with another person's use or possession of property. Here, W probably did not have the required intent; at most, she acted negligently if she did not act with reasonable care in opening her car door. (*See* ELO Ch.3-II(C).) Thus, K's claim will be an ordinary negligence action. Whether W acted reasonably under the circumstances may depend on additional facts. Was she in advanced pregnancy? If so, she may have had difficulty getting into her car and so scraped K's car in spite of exercising as much care as she could. Furthermore, W may be able to assert that K was contributorily negligent if K parked his car after H and W parked their car and if K parked unreasonably close to their parking space. If W was negligent and K was not contributorily negligent, K can recover for the actual damage to the car. If W was negligent but K was contributorily negligent, K cannot recover. (*See* ELO Ch.11-I(A).)

Answer to Question 7

HW v. F (Public Nuisance, Negligence):

Public Nuisance: H and W ("Plaintiffs") might try to sue F for their injuries on a public nuisance claim, asserting that F's conduct interfered with their ability to use the public highway, a right common to the general public. The factors a court might consider in determining whether F's conduct amounted to a public nuisance are the type of neighborhood, the nature of the act complained of, the proximity of the act to those injured, the frequency, continuity, and duration of the act, and the damage that results from it. Here, the neighborhood is a rural area with a sparse population, which would appear to give the farmer more leeway in his conduct. However, because of the deliberate nature of the act (burning weeds) and its creation of a visual obstruction in close proximity to a public road, a court might find F's conduct unreasonable in spite of the sparse population of the surrounding area. The frequency of the act is not clear from the facts, although it does not appear to have been a constant activity (unlike a public utility, for example, that constantly emits pollutants), which would weigh in F's favor. The damage that resulted in this instance appears to have been substantial. A court might also look at whether burning weeds was reasonably necessary to F's farming enterprise, which it probably was; however, even if it was reasonably necessary as a general matter, a court might conclude that F could have waited until the wind had changed. While a court could probably find either way on whether F's conduct was a public nuisance, it seems most likely that a court would not find that it was. (*See* ELO Ch.5-II(A)(2).)

Even if a court did not hold that F's conduct was a public nuisance, Plaintiffs would have to show that the injury to them was different in kind from the actual injury or possibility of injury to the public at large in order to recover. Here, Plaintiffs would have to argue that the injury to the public at large was the interference with its ability to use the highway, while the particular injury to Plaintiffs was the damage they suffered in the accident caused by F's burning of weeds. Whether a court would find this injury sufficiently different in kind is not clear. Plaintiffs probably have a better chance to recover from F on a negligence theory. (*See* ELO Ch.15-II(B).)

Negligence: Plaintiff would contend that F was negligent in burning weeds on land adjacent to a highway when the wind was blowing in the direction of that highway.

Duty: Landowners generally have a duty to prevent unreasonable risk of harm to persons off their land where artificially created, hazardous conditions on their land pose such a risk. Here, Plaintiffs would argue that burning weeds next to a highway under the wind conditions described in the fact pattern constituted such hazardous, artificially created conditions, and that F had a duty to prevent the risk of an accident arising from obstructed visibility to persons driving on the highway adjacent to his land . (*See* ELO Ch.9-II(A)(2).)

Breach of Duty: Plaintiffs would contend that F failed to act with due care (*i.e.*, reasonably under the circumstances) by permitting smoke to drift over a highway and thereby obscure the vision of potential drivers. Although F could contend that it was "customary" to burn weeds in that manner, that fact alone would not preclude a finding that F's conduct was negligent. Furthermore, regardless of whether F's act was customary or served a purpose, he presumably could have waited until the wind pattern changed before burning his weeds. Plaintiffs would contend that his failure to do so was unreasonable. Plaintiffs should prevail on this point. (*See* ELO Ch.5-IV(D)(1).)

Actual Causation: F might contend that the actual cause of the Plaintiff's harm was T's misconduct in being over the center line of the highway. However, unless additional facts show otherwise, a jury could infer that T crossed the center line as a consequence of being unable to see the divider by reason of the smoke generated from F's fire. Plaintiffs should prevail on this issue also. (*See* ELO Ch.6-I(A)(1).)

Proximate Causation: Where there is a subsequent, unforeseeable intervening factor between the defendant's allegedly negligent conduct and the Plaintiff's harm, some courts hold that the defendant's liability is extinguished. F might contend that since there were several intervening factors between his allegedly negligent conduct and Plaintiffs' harm (the wind shifting, T being over the center line and the bus driver hitting plaintiffs from the rear), proximate causation is absent. However, Plaintiffs could probably successfully contend in rebuttal that (1) wind shifts are not "unforeseeable", and in any case F should have observed the wind shifts as they occurred, (2) T was probably over the dividing line as a consequence of the smoke (rather than T's own negligence), and (3) the possible negligence of the bus driver would merely be a contributing (rather than a superseding) cause of their harm. (*See* ELO Ch.6-IV.)

Contributory Negligence ("CN"): F might argue that he should not be liable because Plaintiffs were contributorily negligent in continuing down the highway with knowledge that the wind could shift, and thereby blow the smoke across it. Plaintiffs could contend in rebuttal, however, that they acted reasonably since they waited until smoke was no longer over the highway before proceeding. Furthermore, if there was no emergency lane, they could not be expected to stop their car on the highway and wait an indefinite period of time until F had finished burning the weeds. The purpose of Plaintiff's travel and whether they reduced their speed before proceeding into the affected area would also be relevant to whether they were contributorily negligent. (*See* ELO Ch.11-I(A).)

In a few states, if F were successful with respect to the assertion immediately above, he would also contend that H's CN was imputable to W. However, most jurisdictions no longer impute the negligence (or CN) of one spouse to the other. (*See* ELO Ch.12-VI.)

In a ***comparative negligence*** jurisdiction, if Plaintiffs were found to have been negligent, the court would reduce Plaintiffs recovery in proportion to Plaintiffs' share of the fault. In a "pure" comparative negligence system, Plaintiffs would recover damages (reduced according to their fault) even if their fault were found to be greater than F's. In a "50%" system (the more common type), plaintiffs would recover only if their negligence were less than F's. (*See* ELO Ch.11-II(D).)

More facts are necessary to determine whether Plaintiffs were negligent.

Assumption of Risk: F might also contend that Plaintiffs voluntarily assumed the risk that the wind might shift, and as a consequence an accident could result. For Plaintiffs to have assumed the risk, they must have known of the risk and voluntarily consented to bear that risk. Here, Plaintiffs did know of the risk (they had seen the smoke over the highway previously and observed the shift of the wind) and voluntarily chose to drive over that section of highway in spite of the risk of the wind shifting again. Whether this assumption of risk will constitute contributory negligence depends on whether the assumption of risk was reasonable under the circumstances. Here, whether it was reasonable will depend on additional facts, such as the availability of alternate routes, emergency lanes, or the purpose of Plaintiffs' travel (*i.e.*, were they en route to the hospital for urgent medical treatment). If the assumption of risk was reasonable, then it will not constitute contributory negligence, but F will still be entitled to an assumption of risk defense and Plaintiffs will be barred from recovery. (*See* ELO Ch.11-III.)

Conclusion: Plaintiffs could probably successfully sue F in a negligence action and recover for their past and prospective pain and suffering, medical bills, lost income and loss of consortium. Whether their recovery would be barred or reduced by contributory negligence, assumption of risk, or comparative negligence will depend on the jurisdiction and on additional facts.

H and W against bus driver and C (Negligence):

Plaintiffs would sue the driver of the bus and C under a negligence theory (*i.e.*, that the former acted unreasonably in knowingly driving into an area in which there was poor visibility). C would be liable for the driver's errors or omissions under a ***vicarious liability*** theory (an ***employer*** is liable for the acts or omissions of his/her ***employees*** within the scope of the employment arrangement). (*See* ELO Ch.12-II.)

Breach of Duty: C and the bus driver could contend that the latter acted reasonably under the circumstances since he slowed to 35 m.p.h. (10 m.p.h. below the legal rate of speed). However, Plaintiffs could probably successfully contend that the bus driver acted unreasonably in proceeding down a highway which was clearly engulfed in smoke. In such circumstances, the bus driver should have stopped altogether since there was always the possibility that vehicles might be present within the obscured area. Also, by stopping the bus, the bus driver could have reduced the seriousness of injury in the event that another driver, unable to see in the smoke, collided with the bus. (*See* ELO Ch.8-I.)

CN/Last Clear Chance ("LCC"): C and the bus driver would contend that Plaintiffs were CN (discussed above under *H/W v. F*). If they were held to be CN, Plaintiffs would invoke the LCC doctrine (where the defendant had the LCC to avoid the accident and failed to exercise this opportunity, the plaintiff's CN is negated). Since the bus driver proceeded into the obscured area well after the Plaintiffs' allegedly negligent conduct occurred, Plaintiffs' assertion of the LCC doctrine against bus driver and C should be successful. (*See* ELO Ch.11-I(I).)

If this is a comparative negligence jurisdiction, Plaintiffs may or may not be able to assert the LCC doctrine, depending on the state.

Conclusion: Plaintiffs can probably recover from C and the bus driver on a negligence theory. If Plaintiffs are shown by additional facts to have been negligent, their ability to recover will depend on whether this is a contributory negligence jurisdiction or a comparative negligence jurisdiction. If the former, Plaintiffs will still recover under the last clear chance doctrine. If the latter, Plaintiffs may or may not be able to recover on that basis.

H/W v. T (Negligence):

Did T fail to act with due care? Additional facts are needed to determine whether T failed to act reasonably under the circumstances. If T was surprised by the sudden wind shift, and attempted to stop his vehicle as soon as his vision became completely obscured, T probably would not be deemed to have acted negligently. However, if T consciously proceeded into an area obscured with smoke, then he would probably be deemed to have acted unreasonably under the circumstances.

Damages: Assuming (1) Plaintiffs successfully sued F, C, T and the bus driver as joint and several tortfeasors, and (2) it was not possible to distinguish between the injuries caused by the secondary impact and those suffered when the Plaintiffs collided with T's car, Plaintiffs would be entitled to recover the full amount of their judgment, or any portion thereof, from each of the defendants. Plaintiffs, however, may only recover the amount of their actual damages. In addition, depending on the jurisdiction, the defendant(s) against whom damages are awarded may be able to seek contribution from the other defendants, either on an equal share basis or on a comparative negligence basis. If P's injury is found to be a divisible harm, then liability will be apportioned according to the injury each defendant caused. (*See* ELO Ch.7-I(B).) Finally, C would probably have a right of indemnity from the bus driver. (*See* ELO Ch.7-V(B)(1).)

Answer to Question 8

Farmer ("F") v. Parentis ("Ps") and Babysitter ("B") (Negligence):

F will contend that the Ps and B ("Defendants") were jointly and severally liable to him in negligence as a result of Ps' hiring of an incompetent babysitter and B's not preventing the children ("Kids") from leaving the house and not properly supervising them outside of the house. Alternatively, F will sue for B's negligence and will try to hold Ps liable under *respondeat superior*.

Duty: The defendants had a duty to act with the care that a "reasonable person" would exercise under the circumstances.

Breach of Duty: F will argue that the Ps failed to act reasonably under the circumstances by entrusting Kids to a 14-year-old teenager whom they had not met before and who had already demonstrated her irresponsibility by arriving 20 minutes late. However, assuming B was of sufficient physical stature and not obviously unintelligent, the Ps would argue that 14-year-olds are commonly used as babysitters and older babysitters would be more likely to have, and thereby be distracted by, boyfriends. The Ps will probably prevail on this issue. (*See* ELO Ch.5-IV(A).)

F would also argue that B acted negligently failing to notice the children's absence and thus failing to properly supervise them once they were out of the house.

Since she is only fourteen, B will probably be held to a standard of care that is that of a reasonable child of similar age, intelligence, and experience. Here, although the facts do not indicate how the Kids evaded B (*i.e.*, did they climb out a rear window?), they do indicate that she was distracted by her boyfriend. A court could find that judged by such a standard, B acted unreasonably by failing to discover and prevent the Kids' departure, or at the very least by failing to notice their absence and investigate. (*See* ELO Ch.5-IV(B)(6).)

Causation: Assuming Ps are not found negligent and B is found negligent, F must still show that B's conduct both actually and proximately caused his loss.

F can probably show that B's conduct was the **actual ("but for") cause** of his loss. If B had not acted unreasonably, the children would not have entered the barn, piled the hay on the grill, and started the fire that caused the loss.

F will argue that B's conduct **proximately caused** his loss because it was reasonably foreseeable that B's negligence would cause F harm. F would argue that children are frequent trespassers, that these particular children had trespassed before, and that since he was the immediate neighbor, his was the property the Kids would be most likely to enter. He would also argue that it was foreseeable that the Kids would cause property damage if they were unattended, given their young age (these arguments will work against F on the issue of contributory negligence; see **Kids v. F** below). Defendants will try to argue that F's placement of a charcoal grill inside the barn was a superseding intervention that should relieve them of liability, and that it was *not* foreseeable that F would suffer losses in such an unusual manner (*i.e.*, the Kids pretending to play "cook"). Nevertheless, it probably is foreseeable that children of ages 6 and 7 could accidentally start a fire when unsupervised. Thus, F should prevail on this issue. (*See* ELO Ch.6-IV(B).)

Are Ps liable for B's negligence? If Ps were not negligent in hiring Barbara, F will nonetheless try to recover from them under the *respondeat superior* doctrine. Under *respondeat superior*, if an employee commits a tort while in the scope of his employment, the employer will be jointly liable with the employee. A threshold issue here is whether B was Ps' employee or an **independent contractor**, which would depend on whether B would be deemed to be under the Ps' control (if she were not, B would be an independent contractor and the Ps would not be liable for her omissions). The Ps could contend that (1) since no instructions were (apparently) given to B, and (2) babysitting is never supervised by the principal, *respondeat superior* is *not* applicable. However, since minimal skill was required for B's job and it was to be carried out exclusively at the Ps home, the Ps probably would be vicariously liable for B's conduct (if negligent) because B clearly committed the tort while in the scope of Ps' employment. (*See* ELO Ch.12-II(B), III.)

Was F contributorily negligent ("CN")? F was probably not contributorily negligent under the analysis set forth below (**Kids v. F**). If he were, he would be barred from recovery. If he were but this jurisdiction used a comparative negligence approach, his recovery would be reduced in proportion to his fault. (*See* ELO Ch.11-I.)

Conclusion: F will be able to recover damages for the loss of his barn from B and from Ps for B's negligence. Ps will probably have a right of indemnity from B.

The Kids v. F (Negligence):

While a landowner normally has no duty to trespassers, F would have an obligation to make his premises safe if the following factors are satisfied: (1) the landowner must have known that the children would be likely to trespass, (2) the owner had reason to know of the condition and that the condition in question posed an unreasonable risk of serious bodily harm, (3) it must be unlikely that children would perceive or appreciate the risk involved, (4) the utility in maintaining the condition must be outweighed by its danger to children, and (5) the owner failed to use reasonable care to eliminate the danger or protect the children. Here, F was aware of the Kids' propensity to enter his land (he had explicitly instructed them to stay away from his barn). F also knew of the condition (a grill with hot coals in it placed by the open door of the barn) because he created it, and he presumably should have known that it posed an unreasonable risk of serious injury to the children, since hot coals easily ignite dry materials (such as the nearby hay) and children are often tempted to play with fire. (*See* ELO Ch.9-IV(B)(3)(b).)

Although the Kids' young age would tend to indicate that they did not realize the danger posed by the hot coals, F could argue that even very young children are able to appreciate the risk of burning substances, since one of the first lessons most parents teach their children is "don't play with matches." F would also argue that the children were aware generally that the barn was a dangerous place for them, since he had specifically warned them twice before not to enter it. F would also argue that the utility of being able to use his grill in the barn outweighed the risk that the children would be hurt by it, especially since he did not expect them to be outside and trespassing at night and he had already told them not to enter the barn. Although Kids would argue that F did not exercise reasonable care in eliminating the danger (*i.e.*, he could have doused the coals with water or he could have made the barn more secure against the Kids' entry), F would counter that he does not have an obligation to make his premises child-proof, but simply to use reasonable measures to make it safe, and that his repeated warning to them to stay out was sufficient. Although F did have a duty to the children, he probably did not breach it.

Were Kids CN or did they assume the risk ("AOR")? Assuming F was negligent, F could argue that the Kids were CN. As discussed above under ***F v. Ps and B***, the standard of care children are held to is usually that of a reasonable child of similar age, intelligence, and experience. Where a child engages in a potentially dangerous activity that is normally pursued only by adults (such as driving a car), however, the child will be held to the standard of care that a reasonable adult would exercise. Here, F would argue that grilling is a potentially dangerous activity that is usually pursued only by adults and that therefore the Kids should be held to an adult standard. Kids would argue that they did not engage in such an activity because they did not mean to actually grill; they were playing "make believe grill" and did not know there were live coals in the grill. Resolution of this issue might hinge on additional facts; *i.e.*, whether the Kids in fact observed any live coals, etc. If the Kids are held to an adult standard, they will probably be CN. If they are held to a reasonable child standard, whether they are CN will depend on whether the reasonable child of that age, etc., would be aware of the risks involved with grills, charcoal, and burning materials. In addition, if the Kids have any particular knowledge of the risks involved (they had been specifically instructed on the dangers of barbecues, or had previously witnessed materials set on fire by charcoal), they would be barred from recovery. (*See* ELO Ch.5-IV(B)(6)(d).)

As above, if the Kids were CN, they will not recover, and in a comparative negligence jurisdiction, their recovery would be reduced by their share of the fault. F will also argue that they assumed the risk of burning themselves when they began playing with the coals or that they ***assumed the risk*** of any harm that would befall them in the barn by entering it.

An implied assumption of risk occurs where the plaintiff voluntarily assumed a known risk. The Kids will contend that children of their ages would normally not recognize the risks involved in "playing" with coals. F will, of course, argue in rebuttal the Kids should have realized that fire was very dangerous. If charcoal grills were common in the neighborhood, the risk probably should have been apparent to a child of six or seven years. F will also argue that the Kids assumed the risk of any harms that would occur to them in the barn because he warned them not to enter, thereby giving them knowledge of the risk. The Kids would respond that F's warnings were not sufficient to give them knowledge of the risk, and that they thought that he simply didn't want them there. A court could probably go either way on the AOR issue, although it is somewhat more likely that the Kids would prevail because courts tend to be sympathetic to injured children. (*See* ELO Ch.11-III(C).)

Conclusion:

Kids probably cannot recover from F because he did use reasonable care in protecting the children from the harm by warning them repeatedly to stay out of his barn and because he could not foresee that they would be trespassing at night, when children of their age are usually not outside. However, because courts tend to be sympathetic to injured children, and given the Kids' young age and F's knowledge of their tendency to trespass, a court could conceivably find against F.

Answer to Question 9

Peter ("P") v. Ace ("A") (Negligence, Vicarious Liability):

P would contend that A was negligent in leasing a car to Bruce ("B"), because he did not have a license. P will also assert that A is vicariously liable for B's negligence.

Did A act reasonably under the circumstances? A will be found liable to P for negligence if its conduct imposed an unreasonable risk of harm on P. Here, a court could find that A did not act reasonably under the circumstances because it did not verify that B had a driver's license. This oversight probably does not conform to the company's policy for the procedure to be used in making rentals, and such conduct is almost certainly against the law as well. Common sense also indicates that A's conduct was unreasonable, since lack of possession of a valid driver's license suggests that someone is either an incompetent or inexperienced driver. (*See* ELO Ch.5-IV(A).)

A might argue that its conduct did not impose an unreasonable risk on P on the rationale that, under the *Cardozo view of duty*, a defendant had a duty to the plaintiff if harm to the latter was reasonably foreseeable in light of the defendant's alleged failure to act with due care. A might conceivably contend that since the harm to P (the accident) occurred (presumably) miles away from its alleged negligence (where it rented the car to Bruce), it had no duty to P. However, P could probably successfully argue in rebuttal that cars are inherently mobile, and that therefore anyone who is within an area within which that person might drive is a foreseeable plaintiff. (*See* ELO Ch.6-III(D).)

Was A's conduct the actual cause of P's harm? P will have to show that A's negligence was the *"but for" cause* of P's injuries. It seems clear that "but for" A's negligent conduct, the accident would not have occurred, because B would not have been driving on the road in the rental car when C's car entered the highway. (*See* ELO Ch.6-I(A)(1).)

Was A's conduct the proximate cause of P's harm? Where the plaintiff's harm is the consequence of an unforeseeable, intervening factor, some jurisdictions hold that the defendant's conduct is not the proximate cause of the plaintiff's injuries. A might contend that the subsequent negligent conduct of B and C were intervening factors which precluded A from being the proximate cause of P's injuries. However, P could probably successfully contend in rebuttal that negligent driving of persons on a highway is a foreseeable, intervening factor and thus does not relieve A of liability. (*See* ELO Ch.6-IV(C)(3).)

A might also argue that P's intervention was not foreseeable (because there are not usually bystanders next to major highways) and that his intervention should therefore be superseding (the "unforeseeable plaintiff" problem). However, courts often use a less strict foreseeability rule where rescuers are concerned, on the grounds that "danger invites rescue", and that where the defendant's negligent conduct created the danger that harmed the rescuer, the defendant should be liable. Thus, A will probably be liable to P for its own negligence. (*See* ELO Ch.6-III(D)(2).)

Is A liable for B's negligence? If this jurisdiction has a relevant bailment or auto consent statute, the owner of a car (the bailor) will be vicariously liable for any negligence committed by someone using the car with the owner's permission (the bailee). As a threshold matter, P will have to show B was negligent. B seems to have been clearly negligent here by driving at a recklessly high speed (thus not acting reasonably under the circumstances), thus putting other drivers and passersby at risk of harm. B's negligence seems to have been a ***"but for" cause*** of P's injuries (had he not driven so fast, he either would not have collided with C or the impact might not have been so severe as to cause a fire). As above, B's negligence was the ***proximate cause*** of P's injuries because (1) merging traffic was foreseeable on a highway, (2) negligence by other drivers was foreseeable, and (3) P was a rescuer injured by a danger created by B's negligence. Here, A would be liable for B's negligence under a bailment statute as long as B's use of the car did not exceed the scope of A's consent to B's use of the car (which it presumably did not). (*See* ELO Ch.12-V(B)(1).)

If there is no bailment statute in effect in this jurisdiction, the mere existence of the bailment will not make A vicariously liable for B's negligence.

P v. Dave ("D") (Vicarious Liability):

Is D vicariously liable for the acts of C? P might contend that since B and C were sharing expenses and driving, they were engaged in a ***joint enterprise***, and so D is liable for the negligent conduct of C (discussed below). Persons who engage in a joint enterprise are vicariously liable for the negligent conduct of the other members of the enterprise. There are usually four requirements for a joint enterprise: (1) an express or implied agreement between the members, (2) a common purpose to be carried out by the members, (3) a common pecuniary interest in that purpose, and (4) an equal right of control in the enterprise. (*See* ELO Ch.12-IV(B).) Here, there was an express agreement between C and D to pursue a common purpose, that they would drive across country in C's car and share expenses. However, they do not seem to have had a common pecuniary purpose, in the sense of a shared business objective. They met through a want ad and presumably had different reasons for travelling across country, reasons which may have been purely social. Furthermore, sharing expenses is not usually enough to constitute the common pecuniary interest required for a joint enterprise. Finally, where a trip is merely social or does not have a common business purpose, courts are reluctant to find that a passenger had common right of control with the driver. Thus, D will probably not be vicariously liable for C's negligence.

P v. C's Estate (Negligence):

There appears to be little question but that C failed to act reasonably under the circumstances by entering the highway without looking. Causation also seems satisfied; if C had not entered the highway without looking, he would not have hit B. The proximate cause discussion above (*P v. A*) is equally applicable here.

Was P contributorily negligent or did he assume the risk? Each of the defendants might contend that P was contributorily negligent (*i.e.*, failed to act reasonably under the circumstances) by attempting to pull D from the burning car and that P should be barred from recovery. It is common knowledge that vehicles have gas tanks, and that burning cars might explode. However, P should be able to successfully argue in rebuttal that it is not unreasonable to attempt to save someone from what is almost certain death (in fact, it is laudable conduct). (*See* ELO Ch.11-I(D).)

The defendants might additionally contend that P assumed the risk, since the ordinary person is aware that a burning car might burst into flames. However, P could probably successfully contend in rebuttal that his action was really not voluntary, in the sense that seeing another human being in danger places one under a certain compulsion to save that person. (*See* ELO Ch.5-IV(E).)

Conclusion:

A will be liable to P for its negligence and possibly for B's negligence (if there is a bailment statute in effect). C's estate will be liable to P for C's negligence. D will not be liable because there was not a joint enterprise between C and D. P was not contributorily negligent and did not assume the risk. P will be able to recover any past and prospective lost income, medical expenses, pain, suffering and embarrassment (*i.e.*, scars) resulting from the incident. (*See* ELO Ch.10-I(A)(2).)

P's injuries will probably be found to be an indivisible harm, so that defendants will be jointly and severally liable; each defendant will be liable for P's total harm, although P can only recover the amount of the actual damages. If P recovers that amount from a single defendant, that defendant may be able to seek contribution from the others (depending on the jurisdiction), either on an equal share basis or on a comparative negligence basis. (*See* ELO Ch.7-II(A).)

Answer to Question 10

Abel v. Sam (Negligence):

One is ordinarily under no obligation to gratuitously aid or assist another, unless there is some special relationship between the defendant and plaintiff, which there is not here. Thus, Sam ("S") had no duty to assist Diana, even though the likelihood that an accident might occur increased as a consequence of his refusal to help. Consequently, S would have no liability to Abel ("A"). (*See* ELO Ch.8-II(A)(2).)

A v. Diana ("D") (Assault, Battery and Negligence):

A would probably attempt to sue D for assault (intentionally causing another to be in apprehension of an imminent, offensive touching) and battery (intentional infliction of an offensive or harmful bodily contact). The intent required is not intent to harm, but intent to do the act; furthermore, the defendant must have known with substantial certainty that a particular effect (*i.e.*, plaintiff's apprehension or the offensive contact) would occur as a result of that act. It is not clear from the facts whether D had the requisite intent for the torts of assault and battery. The facts indicate that D knew she would collide with the scaffolding if she did not have parking assistance, but they do not indicate whether she knew there were people on the scaffolding. Whether she had the necessary intent will depend on whether she knew with substantial certainty that they were there. (*See* ELO Ch.2-V(B).)

If D knew that people were on the scaffolding, a battery would have occurred when the scaffolding (which was physically associated with A and Baker) was struck and (again) when A struck the ground at the conclusion of his fall. (*See* ELO Ch.2-IV(D).) The assault would have occurred either immediately before D hit the scaffolding (if A saw her coming) or while A was falling (knowing that he would strike the ground shortly).

If additional facts show that D had the necessary intent, then D would be liable for all of A's injuries, even though he may have been negligent in not wearing a hard hat. Intentional tortfeasors are liable for virtually all consequences of their torts, regardless of how unforeseeable they may be. (*See* ELO Ch.2-IV(F).)

Negligence: Alternatively, A would sue D in negligence.

There appears to be little doubt that D failed to act with due care (*i.e.*, did not act reasonably under the circumstances) by attempting to park with knowledge that she might strike the scaffolding without someone to guide her. D's negligence clearly was the ***"but for" cause*** of A's injuries; if she had not parked recklessly, A would not have been knocked to the ground and injured. There would also seem to be no proximate causation problem, since there was no intervening factor between D's conduct and A's injuries. (*See* ELO Ch.6-I(A)(1), III.)

Defenses: It probably could not be successfully argued that A *assumed the risk* by failing to wear his hard hat, since A had no awareness of the particular danger involved (D's unsafe driving).

D would contend that A was *contributorily negligent* in having failed to wear the hard hat and that A should be barred from recovery. A would probably be found to have acted unreasonably under the circumstances by not wearing a hard hat while working on a scaffolding in violation of company policy. For this negligence to constitute contributory negligence, it must have been either a "but for" cause of A's harm or a substantial factor in it. Here, the facts are explicit that A would have suffered only a slight concussion if he had been wearing a hard hat. Thus, A's negligence was a substantial factor in causing his harm. Proximate cause in the contributory negligence context requires that the harm that the plaintiff suffered be the same sort of harm that the plaintiff should have acted to protect himself from. Here, A was negligent because he failed to wear a hard hat, which would have protected him from head injuries in the event of a fall. Since that is precisely the harm A suffered, A's negligence as to his own safety will be a proximate cause of his harm. Thus, A would be barred from recovery in negligence. (*See* ELO Ch.11-I(E)(3).)

In a *comparative negligence* jurisdiction, A's recovery would be reduced in proportion to his fault. In a "pure" comparative negligence system, he could still recover reduced damages even if his fault was greater than D's. In a "50%" system, he could recover reduced damages only if his fault was not greater than D's. (*See* ELO Ch.11-II(C)(2)(a)(i).)

In some states, D could assert that A had a *duty* to mitigate his damages. Although in most states this "duty" applies only to actions a plaintiff could have taken after the harm (*e.g.*, seeking medical attention), a few states apply it also to safety precautions a plaintiff should have taken before the harm, such as wearing a seat belt or a motorcycle helmet. If this is such a jurisdiction, A could not recover for the damages that could have been avoided had he worn his hard hat (injury in excess of a slight concussion). (*See* ELO Ch.11-II(K).)

Conclusion: D is probably liable to A for assault and battery. A will be able to recover *compensatory damages* (for mental suffering and physical injury) and, if a court finds D's conduct was sufficiently outrageous, punitive damages. D is probably liable to A for negligence also, but A's recovery will probably be either barred or reduced as a result of A's own negligence. To the extent A is able to recover damages, A can recover medical expenses, lost earnings, physical pain, mental distress, and hedonistic damages.

Baker ("B") v. Ed (Negligence):

The facts are silent as to why Ed struck B. Assuming Ed was merely inattentive, there would seem to be little doubt that Ed acted unreasonably under the circumstances (and was therefore negligent). It is possible, however, that Ed was not negligent and that he hit B's car simply because B was driving erratically as a result of his previous injuries. Additional facts are needed to determine whether B has a cause of action against Ed. (*See* ELO Ch.5-IV(A).)

If additional facts show that Ed acted negligently, his negligence was clearly a *"but for" cause* of the injuries B suffered; if he had not hit B's car, the facts suggest B's fracture would not have resulted in paralysis. There is also *no proximate causation* problem because a defendant ordinarily takes the plaintiff as he/she finds the latter, and there was no intervening factor between Ed's conduct and the enhancement of B's injury. (*See* ELO Ch.6-II(D)(1).) Ed's liability would, however, be reduced to the extent the injury which B incurred as a consequence of D's conduct could be distinguished from the fracture and paralysis which Ed caused. (*See* ELO Ch.7-I(B)(2).)

Defenses: If Ed was negligent, he might assert that B was contributorily negligent. If B's erratic driving as a result of his previous injuries contributed to the accident, Ed would argue that B was (a) negligent in not seeking medical attention earlier, and (b) negligent in getting behind the wheel in his condition. However, it is not clear that B had acted unreasonably in *not* obtaining immediate medical attention, since he had felt only a slight pain. Similarly, he may have felt perfectly capable of driving and had no indication that his condition would worsen. More facts are needed to determine whether B was contributorily negligent. (*See* ELO Ch.11-I(D).)

Conclusion: More facts are needed to determine whether Ed was negligent and whether B was contributorily negligent.

Answer to Question 11

Peter ("P") v. Dan ("D") (Negligence, assuming the statute is applicable):

P will sue D for negligence, claiming that D's violation of the Motor Vehicle Code was negligence *per se* by D. Under this doctrine, if the plaintiff can establish that the statute was addressed to a class of persons including herself, that the statute was designed to guard against the kind of harm she suffered, and that the violative act was the actual cause of her harm, then the defendant is negligent *per se* (*i.e.*, did not act reasonably under the circumstances) and cannot argue that the statutory standard of care is too high. (*See* ELO Ch.5-VIII(A)(1).)

Class of persons: Here, P could probably convince a court that the statute sought to protect users of public highways and that he belonged to this class of persons (this answer assumes that "public highway" as defined in the statute would include a four lane street). (*See* ELO Ch.5-VIII(D)(1).)

Particular harm: P will argue that the statute was designed to protect against the particular harm Peter suffered: injuries from an accident caused by obstructed vision due to an unattended vehicle on the highway. However, D may be able to convince a court that the statute was really designed to protect against individuals voluntarily parking their vehicles on highways, and that it was not aimed at vehicles left stranded by malfunction. Whether P or D will prevail on this point would depend on the wording of the statute. (*See* ELO Ch.5-VIII(D)(2).)

Causal relationship: P will argue that D's violation **actually caused** the harm that P suffered because if the van had not been left unattended in the street (since D couldn't move it, D would have had to remain with it), either Vick ("V") or P would not have proceeded through the intersection, since D would have been there to help other drivers navigate around the van.

P will also argue that D's violation **proximately caused** the harm because the causal link between D's leaving the van unattended and P's injury is not so attenuated that it would be unfair to hold D liable. P will argue that it was foreseeable that other drivers would try to pass by the van even if their view of oncoming traffic was obstructed, and so V's conduct should not be a superseding cause, even if V was negligent. Furthermore, P will argue that his faulty brakes and consequent inability to stop before being hit by V should not be a superseding cause because it was foreseeable that individuals with vehicles in less than perfect condition (and thus less able to respond adequately to the risk D created) would approach the vicinity. (*See* ELO Ch.6-IV(A)(1).)

P will probably prevail on causation.

Was D's violation excusable? In some states, the statute would be viewed as establishing a rebuttable presumption of negligence. In other states, the statutory violation establishes negligence *per se*, but the defendant has the right to show that his violation was excusable. This answer will assume that this is a negligence *per se* jurisdiction, although D would probably use the same arguments to try to rebut a presumption of negligence.

D would offer two excuses for his violation: (1) that he was confronted with an emergency not of his own making (his van's failure to operate), and (2) compliance would have involved a greater risk of harm to himself or to others than his violation. D would argue that if he had remained with the van, he might have been hit by oncoming traffic. He would also argue that he could not remove the van from the thoroughfare on his own, and that he thought that he could get the van removed faster if he sought help than if he remained in the street. (*See* ELO Ch.5-VIII(D)(3)(b)(iii)-(iv).)

P would counter that D's conduct was not excusable, since a police car would undoubtedly arrive sooner or later, at which time an emergency vehicle could be alerted. D should prevail because the statute was probably aimed at situations where a driver had voluntarily left the vehicle on a highway. Otherwise, one whose car has stalled might have to wait at the vehicle for hours (until the police or an emergency vehicle arrived).

Defenses: Even if P establishes D's negligence *per se* and D's violation is not excused, D can still assert the defenses of ***contributory negligence and assumption of risk***.

D would argue that P was contributorily negligent in proceeding into the intersection with knowledge that another vehicle might come from behind the van. However, P could contend that it was reasonable to assume that V would drive safely (*i.e.*, a driver whose view of traffic from a perpendicular direction is obstructed should "inch out", so that oncoming cars from the obscured direction would be able to avoid a collision). The facts are silent as to whether a green light was facing P's direction at the time he entered the intersection. If not, P probably did fail to act reasonably (since V would have assumed that no vehicle would be approaching from P's direction). If P had a "go" or green signal, then he probably was not contributorily negligent by proceeding into the intersection. (*See* ELO Ch.11-I(D).)

D would also argue that P was negligent in operating his motorcycle with faulty brakes. Whether P acted reasonably under the circumstances will hinge on additional facts: did P know prior to the accident that his brakes were faulty? Or did the brakes cease to work suddenly as a result of an instantaneous mechanical problem? If the former, then P was probably contributorily negligent and his recovery should either be barred or reduced in proportion to his negligence. If the latter, P was not contributorily negligent.

Assumption of the risk could not be successfully asserted since P was not aware that V was proceeding into the intersection (until it was too late). However, D might successfully assert an assumption of the risk defense if he formulates the risk that P assumed as the risk of operating his motorcycle on a major road with faulty brakes. As above, additional facts are needed to determine whether this defense will work; for P to have assumed the risk, he must have known in advance that the brakes were faulty. If P is found to have assumed the risk, then P will be barred from recovery. (*See* ELO Ch.11-III(D)(2).)

Conclusion: Based upon the conclusion above that the statute was not intended to cover this situation, D probably is **not** negligent *per se* by reason of his failure to observe the statute. Furthermore, even if D was negligent *per se* by virtue of the statutory violation, his violation will probably be excused in light of the emergency situation.

If D is not negligent *per se*, P will still assert a negligence claim against him but would probably lose (see the following discussion).

P v. D (Negligence, assuming no statute):

Without a statute, the issue of whether D was negligent would again hinge on whether he acted reasonably under the circumstances. Here, the standard of conduct would be what a reasonable person would have done in D's position. P would argue that D failed to act reasonably in leaving his vehicle unattended (*i.e.*, D should have remained by it to alert other drivers as to the hazard). However, D could probably successfully argue in rebuttal that it was reasonable to immediately search for assistance, and thereby remove the road impediment as quickly as possible. Thus, D probably has no liability to P. (*See* ELO Ch.5-IV(A).)

P v. V (Negligence):

P would argue that V did not act reasonably under the circumstances by proceeding into an intersection when his view was obstructed without "inching out." Assuming V did not have a green light, his conduct was probably negligent since he should have entered the intersection slowly, thereby allowing intersecting drivers the opportunity to stop or swerve around him.

Causation is satisfied here, because if V had not proceeded into the intersection, he would not have hit P, and because it was foreseeable that another driver would be approaching the intersection (especially if V did not have a green light). (*See* ELO Ch.6-III(C).)

Defenses: V will argue that P was contributorily negligent or that he assumed the risk. The outcome will be the same here as it was above (see **P v. D**).

Effect of Motor Vehicle Code: The Motor Vehicle Code will not affect P's case against V because V did not violate the Code; thus, it is irrelevant here whether the Code is in effect or not.

Conclusion: V is probably liable to P. If P knew of his faulty brakes in advance, P's recovery will either be barred or, in a ***comparative negligence*** jurisdiction, reduced in proportion to his fault. To the extent that P can recover ***damages*** from V, V will be liable for medical expenses, lost earnings, physical pain, mental distress, and hedonistic damages.

Answer to Question 12

Baker ("B") v. Acme ("A") (Abnormally Dangerous Activity and Negligence):

Abnormally Dangerous Activity ("ADA"): Where a defendant is engaged in an ADA, he/she is strictly liable to all foreseeable plaintiffs who are injured or suffer property damage as a consequence of it. Factors to be considered in determining if an activity should be characterized as an ADA include: (1) the degree of risk of serious harm posed by it, (2) whether the risk can be eliminated by the exercise of due care, (3) whether the activity is a matter of common usage to the community in which it is being undertaken, and (4) whether the value of the activity to the community exceeds the risk of harm posed by it. B will contend that blasting is an ADA, and therefore he should be able to recover for the personal injuries and property damage which he suffered. A will argue in rebuttal that since the activity was carried on in a rural area, it was appropriate to the place where it was being undertaken, and that the utility of adding additional lanes to a heavily-used highway outweighed the risk posed by the blasting necessary to carry out the construction. However, most courts would probably find that A's blasting was not appropriate, because even though it was conducted in a rural (and thus presumably less populated) area, it nonetheless put the many drivers on the heavily-used highway at risk. Furthermore, the degree of risk was high, and the harm threatened severe. Finally, some courts have imposed a *per se* abnormally hazardous rule for the use of explosives, rejecting the above-cited factors. Thus, A's blasting would probably be found to be an ADA. (*See* ELO Ch.13-II(C)(1).)

Defenses: A would assert the defense of **assumption of risk** ("AOR") and therefore since B should have been knowledgeable of the blasting, he assumed the risk of the alleged ADA. However, B will argue in rebuttal that AOR requires a voluntary assumption of a known risk. Since he failed to observe the sign, for whatever reason, B was not aware of the risk and the necessity for ceasing all radio transmission. Additionally, even had he observed the sign an AOR would not have occurred because (1) A's sign does not clearly communicate that a radio transmission could actually activate the blasting, and (2) one would not necessarily understand that a 2-way radio (as opposed to a normal AM-FM type of radio) would detonate the blasting charges. Thus, it is unlikely that A would avoid recovery on an AOR defense. (*See* ELO Ch.11-III(C)(2).)

A might contend that B's **contributory negligence** ("CN") in not observing the sign bars recovery by him. However, CN ordinarily does not bar a plaintiff from strict liability recovery, especially where the type of negligence exhibited by the plaintiff consisted of being merely inattentive and not discovering a risk he should have discovered. In such circumstances, courts usually place responsibility for preventing the harm that results from abnormally hazardous activities upon the person who has subjected others to the abnormal risk. Furthermore, B could argue that his failure to observe the sign should not bar his recovery because even an explosion that was detonated when planned would have posed an abnormal risk to passing drivers; nothing in the facts indicates that an on-schedule explosion would not have occurred in a similar fashion (projecting boulders onto the highway). (*See* ELO Ch.13-III(C).)

Negligence: B would alternatively sue A under a negligence theory, contending that A had failed to act reasonably in creating a situation whereby a passing car on a highly-travelled highway could prematurely activate an explosion. A should have recognized that a passing motorist might fail to observe or understand its sign, and therefore cause an explosion to occur. B would argue that A failed to exercise due care because merely posting a sign is not sufficient to protect others from the dangers of an explosion; rather, A should have had the state close down the highway during the portion of construction that involved blasting. (*See* ELO Ch.5-IV(A).)

B will have to show that A's negligent conduct both actually and proximately caused his injuries. Here, had A either not engaged in blasting or closed the highway before blasting, B clearly would not have been injured. A's conduct also proximately caused the injuries because it is foreseeable that drivers might not see the sign or might not see the sign in time to turn off their radios before entering the zone of danger. (*See* ELO Ch.6-III.)

Defenses: A might contend in rebuttal that B was *CN* by reason of his failure to observe and conform his conduct to the sign. However, B could probably successfully argue in rebuttal that a reasonable person would not have (1) observed the sign (it is unclear as to how conspicuous it was from the highway at the speeds at which cars ordinarily travel), and (2) taken the sign to pertain to two-way radios (rather than AM-FM radios).

The AOR discussion above (under ADA) would also be applicable here.

Conclusion: Thus, B should be able to recover for his personal and property injuries from A under either an ADA or negligence theory.

Charles' ("C") Survivors v. B (Negligence):

C's survivors would bring an action under the state's wrongful death statute, seeking recovery for economic support, companionship, and grief.

C's survivors would contend that B had failed to act reasonably under the circumstances by failing to observe and obey A's sign. As discussed above, however, this assertion would probably *not* be successful. (However, we'll still discuss the additional potential issues, since this conclusion could be incorrect.)

B could also argue that C was not a foreseeable plaintiff (*i.e.*, was not within the zone of danger created by B's allegedly negligent conduct), since C (apparently) came upon the scene subsequent to the explosion and B's injury. However, since calamity invites rescue, rescuers are ordinarily deemed to be foreseeable plaintiffs. (*See* ELO Ch.6-III(D)(2).)

B could also argue that C was *CN* in (1) swerving off the road, and (2) neglecting to wear his seat belt. However, his survivors could probably successfully contend in rebuttal that (1) his loss of control of the car as a result of driving quickly was reasonable in that failing to obtain medical assistance for B as promptly as possible could have resulted in the latter's demise, and (2) the failure to fasten the seat belt did not contribute to the occurrence of the accident (and the CN doctrine is ordinarily not applicable in such instances), and (3) there is no evidence that C's failure to wear a seat belt contributed in any way to his death. The latter two points are significant because the injured party's negligence must have been a "but for" cause of or a substantial factor in that party's harm before it will constitute CN. (*See* ELO Ch.11-I(E)(1).)

Survivors v. A (ADA, Negligence):

C's survivors will bring a wrongful death action against A, asserting that A should be both strictly liable on an ADA theory and liable on a negligence theory. However, the ADA theory will probably be unavailing because the plaintiff must ordinarily show that his/her injuries were sustained as a consequence of the particular type of risk associated with the ADA (*i.e.*, blasting). In this instance, C's death was a consequence of B's injured condition, not the ADA. (*See* ELO Ch.13-III(B).)

C's survivors should be able to successfully recover from A under a negligence theory, as discussed above under *B v. A*, on the grounds that A failed to exercise due care by blasting next to a busy highway. They would argue that A's negligence proximately caused C's death because A's negligence created the danger from which C tried to rescue B; rescue attempts are foreseeable in the face of harm.

Survivors v. the car's manufacturer ("M") (Products Liability: Negligence, Warranty, Strict Liability):

C's survivors might contend that M is liable to them for wrongful death under a products liability theory. Under this doctrine, one who manufactures a product that is defective is liable for any personal injuries proximately caused by the defect. A products liability action can be based on a negligence theory, a warranty theory, or on a strict liability theory. Here, Survivors would base their action on a design defect claim, on the rationale that all of the cars that M manufactured that were the same model as C's car lacked a safety feature (namely, a mechanism that would prevent the car from starting unless the seat belt were attached), and that that safety feature made the design defective and unreasonably dangerous. (*See* ELO Ch.14-IV(E).)

On a negligence theory, Survivors would argue that M acted unreasonably under the circumstances by choosing a design that did not include an automatic seat belt or an ignition block, and that this choice posed an unreasonable danger to C. Here, Survivors would argue that M should have foreseen that many people do not fasten their seat belts, and that therefore M did not exercise due care by failing to design a "mandatory" seat belt. (*See* ELO Ch.14-IV(B).)

On a strict liability theory, Survivors would have to show that M's failure to include such a safety feature in the design made the car *defective* and unreasonably dangerous to the extent that if a reasonable consumer knew of the true characteristics of the car, he or she would not use it. This theory would be hard for Survivors to argue convincingly, since C probably knew that the car did not have the additional safety feature in question, and yet he used the car anyway. (*See* ELO Ch.14-III(B).)

On a warranty theory, Survivors would have to show that M breached an *implied warranty of merchantability* that the car was "fit for the ordinary purposes for which such goods are used" (UCC § 2-314(1)). Most states allow consumers to recover from manufacturers on the grounds that a manufacturer's warranty extends to remote purchasers, not simply to the immediate purchaser (*i.e.*, the distributor or retailer). (*See* ELO Ch.14-II(C)(1).)

Defenses: As a threshold issue, it seems unlikely that a court would find that the car was unreasonably dangerous, because the car was equipped with seat belts for front seat occupants, as required by statute. M would use the statutory standard as evidence that the car was reasonably safe for its intended use. Survivors will try to use evidence of the later safety feature (the mechanism that prevents the car from starting when the seat belts are not fastened) as proof that a higher safety standard was feasible, but a court will look at whether the original design was reasonably safe as of the time of manufacture and of sale to C. (*See* ELO Ch.14-IV(B)(2).)

M might also assert a "state of the art" defense, arguing that the level of technology existing at the time the car was manufactured did not permit a safer design. While courts usually hold such a defense is relevant to the defect issue, it is not usually dispositive. More facts are needed to ascertain whether the technology was available at the time. (*See* ELO Ch.14-IV(B)(4).)

M would also argue that it was unduly expensive to install the additional safety feature. Again, the persuasiveness of this defense will depend on additional facts.

M might argue that its design was as safe as the design used by other car manufacturers at the time. This defense may not work if a court finds that the entire industry was unreasonably behind in installing safety features. (*See* ELO Ch.14-IV(E)(1)(a).)

However, even if additional facts show that M cannot escape liability with the above defenses, M can probably avoid liability by arguing that: (1) the car was not utilized in a reasonably anticipated manner (*i.e.*, vehicle operators would be expected to make use of a seat belt which was inserted into the vehicle), (2) C assumed the risk of enhanced injury when he neglected to utilize the seat belt, and (3) C's heirs (who would have the burden of proof) are unable to show proximate cause: that if the seat belt were utilized, C would not have been killed. Therefore, a products liability action probably would *not* be successful. (*See* ELO Ch.14-IX.)

Survivors v. the car's seller ("S") (Products Liability: Negligence, Warranty, Strict Liability):

Survivors might also try to sue S for wrongful death on a products liability theory. A retailer will have *strict liability* and warranty liability, even if there is nothing the retailer could have done to discover the *defect*, if the product is defective and unreasonably dangerous. A retailer is someone who is in the business of selling goods. Here, Survivors could sue S as long as S is not a private individual who sold the car to C. (*See* ELO Ch.14-III(B).)

As above, whether the design was unreasonably dangerous may hinge on whether the technology for additional safety features existed at the time, what the prevailing standard was in the industry, and how expensive it would have been to install the additional feature even if it was possible to do so. Again, S will point to the seat belt statute as evidence that the car was not unreasonably dangerous, while Survivors will use the subsequently-developed ignition block feature as evidence of a feasible alternative.

Survivors will probably not be able to recover from S on a warranty theory, because, even without the mechanism, C's car (which did contain seat belts) would probably be deemed to have been reasonably fit for the ordinary purposes for which a vehicle is used (*i.e.*, to drive in relative safety from one location to another). (*See* ELO Ch.14-II(C)(1).)

Survivors also probably cannot prevail on a strict liability theory, because, as discussed above under *Survivors v. M*, C did not use the car as anticipated (*i.e.*, he did not wear his seat belt) and by doing so, assumed the risk of not using a safety feature of which he was aware. (*See* ELO Ch.14-IX(B).)

Survivors probably could not recover from S on a negligence theory, unless S knew or should have known that the car was unreasonably dangerous and did not at least warn C. Here, as discussed above (*Survivors v. M*), the car probably was not unreasonably dangerous, and S probably described the extant seat belts and how they functioned when C purchased the car. (*See* ELO Ch.14-I(C)(3)(b).)

Thus, Survivors probably cannot recover from S on a products liability theory.

Answer to Question 13

Mr. and Mrs. Jones (the "Jones'") and Joe ("J") would each sue Spelding ("S"), Bloomingdiles ("B") and ABC (collectively, "Def's"), under a products liability ("PL") theory. If additional facts show that the hinges were not made by S, plaintiffs would also sue the manufacturer of the hinges. Under the PL theory, one who manufactures or sells a product that is defective and thereby unreasonably dangerous is liable for any personal injuries caused by the defect. PL actions can be based on a negligence theory, a warranty theory, or a strict liability theory. Here, none of the plaintiffs was a purchaser of the ladder, so they will not be able to use an implied warranty theory. Instead, plaintiffs will base their claims on negligence and on strict liability.

Who may be a plaintiff: In general, any reasonably foreseeable user or purchaser of a defective product will have standing to sue ***manufacturer or seller*** under a negligence or a strict liability theory. Here, although J was not a purchaser, he was a reasonably foreseeable user, because it was foreseeable that ABC, the purchaser, would provide the ladder for any workmen who came to do repairs on its premises. The Jones' will also probably have standing to sue, because courts have generally been willing to extend products liability protection to reasonably foreseeable bystanders. Here, where the purchaser was a large department store, it was foreseeable that customers might pass in the vicinity of repair work. Thus, all of the plaintiffs have standing. (*See* ELO Ch.14-I(B)(2)(c).)

Who may be a defendant: Permissible defendants here are the seller, the manufacturer, and, if the hinges were not made by S, component manufacturers. Plaintiffs could not sue ABC because a seller must have sold the item in the ordinary course of its business. Since ABC merely loaned the ladder to J, it would ***not*** be a commercial supplier unless the court was willing to extend the PL doctrine to bailors. (*See* ELO Ch.14-I(C).)

Was the product in a defective (i.e., unreasonably dangerous in light of its anticipated use) condition when it left S and B? Plaintiffs would argue that the ladder was unreasonably dangerous because (a) the hinges were not strong enough to withstand ordinary use for more than three years, and (b) because the warning on the box was inadequate. Plaintiffs would argue that S failed to design the product in a reasonably safe way because the ladder has a structural weakness (the hinges) that makes it unreasonably dangerous. (*See* ELO Ch.14-IV(A).)

Whether plaintiffs would prevail on this point would depend on additional facts (*i.e.*, what uses was the ladder designed and marketed for, what sort of hinges are usually used by other manufacturers in that type of ladder, what is the usual life span of a ladder, etc.). Plaintiffs would also argue that S should have affixed some type of metallic warning to the ladder itself as to the 3-year life span and when it would expire, since it should have anticipated that someone would remove the box and neglect to advise subsequent users of its limited period of use. (*See* ELO Ch.14-V.)

S and B could contend that the ladder was *not* in an unreasonably dangerous condition when it left each of them since the box carrying the item conspicuously stated that its operational life was only 3 years. Thus, the ladder became defective only when the prior manager removed and discarded the box in which the item was contained. However, S and B probably should have foreseen that the box would be removed and that the warning would fail to be communicated to subsequent users. Additionally, the term "normal operational life" is arguably too vague to advise a potential user that the hinges might break. Furthermore, if a court found that the ladder was defective by virtue of its flimsy hinges, any warning, even an adequate one, would not make the ladder "un-defective." Plaintiffs should prevail on this issue. (*See* ELO Ch.14-V(B)(2).)

Will plaintiffs recover under either a negligence or a strict liability theory? If the ladder is found defective and unreasonably dangerous, plaintiffs can probably recover from both S and B. For strict liability, plaintiffs have to show that the item was manufactured or placed in the stream of commerce by the defendant. Here, S manufactured the ladder, and both S and B placed it in the stream of commerce. Plaintiffs must also show that the product, by virtue of its defect, actually and proximately caused their injuries. Here, if the hinges had not been too weak and the warning inadequate, none of the plaintiffs would have been hurt. Furthermore, as discussed above, all of the plaintiffs were foreseeable. (*See* ELO Ch.14-III(B)(2).)

S and B might contend that ABC's subsequent intervening conduct in discarding the box and not warning subsequent users of the ladder's 3-year life was an unforeseeable condition which extinguished their liability to the plaintiffs. Furthermore, ABC's conduct was the sort of foreseeable conduct that an adequate warning would have protected against. (*See* ELO Ch.14-IX(C)(2).)

S and B might also contend that while it was foreseeable that a defective ladder should collapse, and possibly that a party using it would fall on another; it was *not* reasonably foreseeable that someone observing the incident would panic, and as a consequence break his/her ankle by slipping. However, people frequently act slightly irrationally when exposed to extreme stress, and so this contention should fail. Witnessing one's spouse in an accident of this sort would be extremely upsetting to most reasonable people. Whether Mrs. Jones can recover for her injuries will be discussed below. (*See* ELO Ch.14-III(H)(3)(b).)

Finally, plaintiff must show that the defect existed when the product left the hands of the defendant. Here, the flimsy hinges and the inadequate warning clearly existed while the ladder was in the possession of both S and B. (*See* ELO Ch.14-III(H)(4).)

If the ladder is found to be defective, plaintiffs can probably recover from S on a negligence theory. Plaintiffs would argue that S failed to act with due care in designing a product with weak hinges and by putting a warning about the life span of the ladder on disposable packaging that most people would not retain. Causation would be satisfied, as discussed above. (*See* ELO Ch.14-I(C)(1).)

Plaintiffs may be able to recover from B on a negligence theory, if they can show that B had reason to know that the product was unreasonably dangerous and failed to warn customers of the danger. B may be able to avoid negligence liability by arguing that it did not have reason to know of the defect because the warning on the box did not give it reason to suspect that the hinges were inadequate, and because retailers usually have no duty to inspect goods. However, a court could find that the warning was sufficient to give B notice that the ladder was defective in some way, even if it did not specify that the hinges were bad. (*See* ELO Ch.14-I(C)(3).)

Can Mrs. Jones recover for her injuries? In general, a plaintiff can recover from a negligent tortfeasor for mental distress experienced out of fear for the safety of others, as long as the plaintiff was also in the zone of danger created by the defendant's conduct and the plaintiff is closely related to the party who was injured. Here, Mrs. Jones was clearly in the zone of danger and was closely related to Mr. Jones, her husband. Thus, at least on a negligence theory, Mrs. Jones could recover for her own injuries. On a strict liability theory, a court would probably also allow Mrs. Jones to recover, since her actions were reasonably foreseeable in response to the event she witnessed, an event caused by the defective ladder. (*See* ELO Ch.14-IV(B)(1)-(2).)

Conclusion: Plaintiffs can probably recover from S and B (and from the hinge manufacturer, if it is not the same as S) in products liability on a strict liability theory. Plaintiffs can probably recover from S (and the hinge manufacturer) on a negligence theory, and possibly from B as well.

The Jones' and J v. ABC (Negligence):

Plaintiffs will argue that ABC acted unreasonably in failing to advise J that the ladder's operational life had been exceeded. (Since he was at ABC's premises for a business purpose, ABC owed J a ***duty to remedy*** any defect of which they should have been aware.) Additionally, the Jones' will argue that ABC was negligent in not roping off the area around J and the ladder so that passersby would not be injured by his activities. (*See* ELO Ch.9-VI(C).)

Was ABC's negligence the proximate cause of the plaintiffs' harm? Plaintiffs will assert that ABC's failure to warn J ***actually and proximately caused*** their injuries. If they had warned him, he would probably not have used the ladder and no one would have been hurt. The Jones' will argue that they were foreseeable plaintiffs because ABC could have foreseen that customers or other passersby would be in the vicinity of the repairs. (*See* ELO Ch.6-III(D)(5).)

ABC will argue that it had no duty to the Jones' because they were not necessarily customers and were not in the store when they were injured; thus, they were not business invitees to whom ABC owed a duty of inspection. This argument will probably fail, however, since ABC had created the danger to the Jones' by having J work on the facade of the building with a defective ladder. Furthermore, even if ABC does not own the sidewalk in front of its building, it is probably required under the applicable city code to keep that area safe for the public. A court could find that ABC failed to exercise due care with respect to the Jones', regardless of whether the ladder was defective, because they could foreseeably have been injured in some other fashion by work performed on the facade. (*See* ELO Ch.9-II(B)(3).)

ABC will also argue that it did not know that the ladder was unsafe because the former manager discarded the warning and did not communicate the information it contained to Malcolm. First, the former manager's knowledge would probably be imputed to ABC. Second, under the doctrine of *respondeat superior*, an employer is liable for the tortious acts of its employees. (*See* ELO Ch.12-II(A).)

ABC will try to argue that Mrs. Jones' behavior was not proximately caused by its negligence. This argument will probably fail, as per above discussion.

Thus, ABC will probably be liable to the Jones' and to J for negligence.

Damages: The successful plaintiffs would be able to recover for their past and prospective lost income, medical bills, as well as for pain and suffering resulting from the incident. The Jones' might also be able to recover for loss of consortium for the period during which they were incapacitated. (*See* ELO Ch.10-I(A)(2).)

Indemnification: Both ABC and B (if B is liable) might be able to seek indemnity from S as the manufacturer of the defective ladder and drafter of the inadequate warning (and from hinge manufacturer, if it is separate from S), because where a defendant is liable only because she had failed to discover another's defect, she is usually entitled to indemnity from that party. They would not be entitled to indemnity if a court found that they had reason to know of the defect by virtue of the warning on the box. ABC might also be entitled to indemnity from the former manager. (*See* ELO Ch.7-V(B).)

Answer to Question 14

White and Green v. Manufacturer and Black (Products Liability):

White ("W") and Green ("G") could contend that the microwave manufacturer ("M") and Black ("B") are liable to them under a products liability ("PL") theory. Under a PL theory, one who manufactures or sells a product that is **defective** and thereby unreasonably dangerous is liable for any personal injuries caused by the defect. PL actions can be based on a strict liability theory, a negligence theory, or an express or implied warranty theory. This answer will analyze the plaintiffs' claim on each of these theories.

W and G v. M and B (Strict Liability):

Plaintiffs have to show that the oven was manufactured or sold by the defendants. Here, while it is clear that G made the oven, B will try to avoid liability on the grounds that it was merely a lessor, not a seller. However, many courts have extended strict liability to lessors of defective products. (*See* ELO Ch.14-VII(B).)

Plaintiffs must also show the existence of the defect. Where a product is properly manufactured and designed but it still contains a non-obvious risk of personal injury, the defendant will still be liable if he does not warn about that risk. Here, plaintiffs will argue that the oven should have been accompanied by a permanently-affixed warning label about the non-obvious dangers of using metal cookware in it. (*See* ELO Ch.14-V(A).)

Plaintiffs also must show causation. Here, if M had used a warning label that was attached to the product itself and could not be removed, W would not have put a tin plate inside it. Although M will try to argue that B's removal of the warning from the manual is a superseding cause that should relieve it of liability, a court could find that B's conduct was reasonably foreseeable, and therefore M should have taken measures to safeguard against it. (*See* ELO Ch.14-III(H)(3).) M and B will try to argue that G was an unforeseeable plaintiff because he is not a user or consumer of the product; however, a court would probably find that it is foreseeable that microwaves would be purchased for restaurant use, and that logically, a customer of the restaurant is a user of the oven.

Plaintiffs must also show that the product was defective when it left the hands of the defendants. (*See* ELO Ch.14-III(H)(4).) This is clearly the case with respect to B, who had removed the warning, but M might contend that the oven was not in a defective (*i.e.*, unreasonably dangerous) condition when it left its hands, since a warning manual accompanied the item. However, given the possibility that a vendor might fail to deliver the manual to a purchaser and the great harm that could occur if this happened, the product probably would be considered to have been in a defective condition when it left M.

Defenses: M and B might try to defend on the grounds that W was *contributorily negligent* in misusing the oven (*i.e.*, by putting a metal plate in it). They will argue that the risk associated with using metal in microwaves is obvious (*i.e.*, many people are aware of it). (*See* ELO Ch.14-V(H).) However, a court would probably find that awareness of such a risk requires a special knowledge, and that it was reasonably foreseeable that consumers or users would not have that special knowledge. Furthermore, where misuse of a product is reasonably foreseeable (as it was here), the defendant will be held responsible for protecting against that misuse. (*See* ELO Ch.14-V(I).) Here, a court could find that M's warning was inadequate because it was not attached to the product and thus easily discarded, as it was here. Thus, the product was defective and unreasonably dangerous, and defendants should be liable.

W and G v. M and B (Negligence):

Plaintiffs would argue that M failed to act reasonably by failing to attach a permanent warning about the dangers associated with using metal cookware in the microwave to the oven itself. (*See* ELO Ch.14-I(C)(1).) Plaintiffs would argue that B did not act reasonably by failing to deliver the manual intact to W. Plaintiffs would have to show that the product was defective and unreasonably dangerous, as above.

M would argue that B's negligence was a superseding cause and thus M's conduct was *not the proximate cause* of plaintiffs' harm; however, as above, B's negligence was foreseeable and so does not break the chain of proximate causation. M and B will both try to argue that G was an unforeseeable plaintiff; but, as above, it is foreseeable that microwaves would be sold to restaurants and used in the vicinity of customers. (*See* ELO Ch.14-VI(B).)

Defendants will invoke the contributory negligence via misuse defense discussed above, with the same result, thus, M and B will probably be liable to plaintiffs on a negligence theory. (*See* ELO Ch.14-IX(C)(2).)

W and G v. M (Express Warranty):

W and G might also sue M under an express warranty theory. Plaintiffs will have to show that M made a statement about the oven that turned out not to be true, that this statement formed part of the basis of the bargain, and that plaintiffs were part of the class to whom the statement was addressed. Here, plaintiffs will base their claim on the statement the oven "could be used with your own cookware" (they will not base their claim on the statement that the oven was the "best and safest", since M could probably successfully argue that such a statement was clearly "puffery" and opinion). Plaintiffs will argue that the statement was clearly not true, since the oven was not able to accommodate W's cookware. Plaintiffs do not have to show reliance or even privity to recover for breach of an express warranty. While W will show that the statement formed part of the basis of the bargain (*i.e.*, was part of her understanding of what she was getting when she purchased the oven), a non-privity plaintiff such as G probably does not even have to show that he was aware of the express warranty. Where express warranties are addressed to the public at large, remote buyers, users, or even passersby are often deemed part of the general class to which the warranty was addressed. Thus, both W and G can recover from M on this theory. (*See* ELO Ch.14-II(B).)

W and G v. B (Implied Warranty of Merchantability):

W and G might also sue B for a breach of the implied warranty of merchantability (under UCC Section 2-314, there is an implied warranty in the sales of goods by a merchant that the items will be fit for the ordinary purposes for which they are used). B will argue that this doctrine has traditionally been limited to lawsuits against vendors (rather than lessors) and most courts have required privity between the plaintiff and defendant. However, many courts have extended the implied warranty to lessors of goods. Whether G, a bystander, can utilize this theory will probably depend on whether he can successfully argue that he should be considered a non-purchaser user and on the version of UCC Section 2-318 adopted in this state. (*See* ELO Ch.14-II(C)(1).)

B will argue that the oven was fit for ordinary use, and that W misused the product by putting metal plates in it. However, to be "merchantable", goods must be adequately labeled, and here, the oven clearly was not, since it did not bear a label warning about the use of metal cookware. (*See* ELO Ch.14-II(C)(1)(a)(i).)

Thus, W can recover from B on a implied warranty theory. It is less clear whether G will be able to recover.

Damages: On a strict liability, negligence, or warranty theory, plaintiffs can recover for personal injuries. W can recover for her property damages on any of the theories. W can probably recover damages for the lost business while the diner is closed (*i.e.*, intangible economic harm) only on a warranty theory, although she might be able to "tack on" her intangible economic harm to her other injuries as an additional element of damages under a negligence theory. (*See* ELO Ch.14-VIII.)

W and G v. M (Misrepresentation):

W and G could sue M in an action based on Section 402B of the Second Restatement. Section 402B provides that a seller of goods who makes any misrepresentation on the label or in public advertising will be strictly liable for any physical injury that results, even if the injured person did not buy the product from the defendant. This cause of action is very similar to the breach of express warranty claim discussed above, but it would be preferable for G to use this cause of action if the jurisdiction is one with stricter than average privity or reliance requirements for express warranty claims. For W, this cause of action would have the disadvantage of not allowing recovery for her property damage or her lost business. (*See* ELO Ch.16-IV(C).)

G v. W (Negligence):

G might try to sue W for negligence, asserting that W did not act reasonably under the circumstances by putting a tin plate into a microwave, and that this conduct imposed an unreasonable risk on nearby customers. G would argue that W had a ***duty*** to him as a business invitee to inspect her premises for hidden dangers, and that W ***breached that duty***. G will argue that but for this negligence, he would not have been hurt, and that proximate causation is satisfied because W's negligence directly caused his injuries. (*See* ELO Ch.5-II.)

G will probably not recover from W, however, because W can probably convince a court that she did not breach her duty to G. She will argue that this was the first time she had occasion to use a microwave, that she read the manual before using it, and that the manual contained nothing above the dangers of using metal. Thus, she acted reasonably under the circumstances.

Answer to Question 15

This answer will discuss Nerv's claims first, and Ima's claims second.

Nerv ("N") v. Drugco ("D") (Products Liability):

N will bring a products liability claim against D, probably using either a strict liability theory or a warranty theory.

Strict Liability: On a strict liability theory, N would essentially be alleging that Dreamy was ***defective and unreasonably dangerous***, and that therefore D should be strictly liable as a result. However, Dreamy probably falls within the category of unavoidably unsafe products that nonetheless have high social utility, like prescription drugs. Here, D conducted extensive testing on Dreamy and obtained FDA approval for it. Dreamy's undesirable effects were not apparent during testing and were discovered only after the drug had been put on the market. In such cases, ***courts almost always deny liability.*** As long as the drug was properly prepared and accompanied by warnings of known or reasonably scientifically knowable dangers, the defendant will ***not*** be liable. Here, D did not know of the danger that resulted, so N can recover from D only if D was somehow negligent in conducting its testing, and nothing in the facts indicates that D was negligent. (*See* ELO Ch.14-III(D).)

If N pursues a strict liability suit, he may try to introduce evidence of D's subsequent remedial measures (the increased warning) as evidence that the product was defective. Most courts, however, will either not allow such evidence at all as a policy matter (so as not to discourage manufacturers from making their products safer) or will allow such evidence only to rebut a claim by the defendant that such warnings would have been unreasonably expensive to furnish.

Express Warranty: N may try to sue D for having ***breached*** an express warranty that Dreamy was "safe for adult use." N would have to show that D's statement about Dreamy was not true, that the statement formed part of the basis of the ***bargain***, and that N was part of the class of persons to whom the statement was addressed. N could easily show that his belief in the statement was part of the reason he purchased the product, and that as a consumer he was part of this class of persons to whom it was addressed. N may, however, have trouble convincing a court that the statement was untrue. D would probably point to the context of the statement (it preceded the words "not habit-forming") to show that it was not warranting that the product was absolutely safe from all possible cross reactions or allergic reactions, but merely that it was safe in the sense of being non-addictive. Nothing in the facts indicates that this is not true. D will probably prevail on this issue. (*See* ELO Ch.14-II(B).)

Implied Warranty: N could also sue D for breach of an implied warranty of merchantability.

A breach of the ***implied warranty of merchantability*** occurs where a good which is sold by a merchant is not reasonably fit for the ordinary purposes for which such item is used; UCC § 2-314. N would contend that the Dreamy pills which N utilized were not reasonably fit since dizziness resulted from their use and because the label did not warn of dizziness. (*See* ELO Ch.14-II(C)(1).) D could contend in rebuttal, however, that Dreamy was "reasonably fit" in light of the small proportion of users who would suffer an allergic reaction to it. D would also argue that Dreamy was "reasonably fit" in spite of the lack of additional warnings because D ***did not know*** of the undesirable effects of the pill and could not have known of such dangers. A court could find that where the product is one that is unavoidably ***unsafe but highly beneficial***, it would not be equitable to hold the manufacturer liable on a warranty of merchantability theory where the manufacturer has not been negligent.

N v. Phil ("P") (Products Liability):

N would bring a products liability suit against P as the vendor of Dreamy. He could base his suit on a strict liability theory or on a warranty theory.

Strict Liability: Same result as above (***N v. D***).

Implied Warranty: N could sue P for both a breach of an implied warranty of merchantability and for breach of an ***implied warranty of fitness for a particular purpose***.

On the warranty of merchantability theory, N would probably lose, as above. Indeed, a court would be even less likely to find P liable, since he was not in as good a position as D to discover the hidden dangers of Dreamy.

The warranty of fitness for a particular purpose arises where the seller of a good has reason to know of a particular purpose for which the good is required by the buyer and that the latter is relying upon the former's skill or judgment in selecting it. Here, N described the purpose for which he desired the drug toP, and selected Dreamy based upon P's recommendation. However, as above, Dreamy probably was fit for the particular purpose; nothing in the facts indicates that it did not calm N as it was supposed to. Furthermore, as above, a court might hesitate to impose liability on P when all the available safety and usage information did not reveal that the drug could cause an allergic reaction. (*See* ELO Ch.14-II(C)(2).)

Conclusion: N probably cannot recover for his injuries from either D or P, unless additional facts indicated that D had negligently conducted its testing.

Ima ("I") v. N (Negligence):

I could assert a negligence action against N, based upon the assertion that N failed to act reasonably by driving after taking a tranquilizer without having previously determined if the drug could have an adverse effect upon him (it is relatively common knowledge that tranquilizers sometimes produce unexpected side effects, such as drowsiness). Whether I will prevail on this issue may hinge on additional facts, such as whether Dreamy also bore the warning typically found on tranquilizers to the effect that people should not operate heavy machinery after taking the drug. If N had already begun to experience drowsiness before getting behind the wheel, a court could find that he *failed to exercise due care*. (*See* ELO Ch.5-IV(A).) There may also be a relevant statute in effect in the jurisdiction prohibiting driving while under the influence of tranquilizers. If so, N's violation of this statute would mean that he was negligent *per se*, and thus liable unless he could somehow show that his violation was excused. (*See* ELO Ch.5-VIII(A)(1).) However, absent such additional facts, N could probably successfully contend in rebuttal that since the label on the bottle stated that it was "safe for adult use", he could reasonably assume that it was safe for him to drive immediately after taking the Dreamy.

Thus, whether I can recover from N may depend on additional facts.

I v. D (Products Liability):

I will probably not be able to recover from D on a strict liability or a warranty theory for the reasons discussed above under *N v. D*. Furthermore, even if D were found liable to N, D could probably convince a court that it should not be liable to I because she was a *bystander* whose injury as a result of the defective product was not reasonably foreseeable. This case is not like one in which the defective product is a car; there, it would be foreseeable that a bystander would be injured as a result of the defect and the risk that it posed, that of automobile malfunction. Here, the risk posed by the alleged defect is dizziness, and D's conduct posed no risk of dizziness to I. (*See* ELO Ch.14-VI(B).) To impose liability on D for I's injuries would be to impose a *direct causation rule*, whereby the defendant would be liable for all consequences of its conduct, no matter how far-reaching. This result runs directly counter to the principles that underlie proximate cause. (*See* ELO Ch.6-III(B).)

Answer to Question 16

G v. T:

G should sue T in products liability for breach of an express warranty, breach of the implied warranty of merchantability, and misrepresentation. She should not sue on a strict liability theory because she would probably not be able to show that the product was unreasonably dangerous when viewed from the standpoint of the reasonable consumer and because the measure of damages is not as favorable to her circumstances (*i.e.*, she could not get damages for intangible economic harm). She should not sue on a negligence theory because the facts do not indicate that T was negligent in testing Tint and because the measure of damages would again not be in her favor.

Breach of Express Warranty: G would sue T for having breached its express warranty that Tint was safe and wholesome, as represented by the Mag Seal of Approval on the Tint labels. G would have to show that this warranty was not true, that the warranty formed part of the basis of the bargain, and that she was part of the class of persons to whom it was addressed. G would argue that Tint was not safe and wholesome because it causes hair to turn purple when it comes in contact with the scalp medicine she used, and that it is sufficiently foreseeable that users of Tint might also use other hair products that the product cannot be considered "safe" unless it can be safely used in conjunction with such other products. She could probably show that the Seal of Approval was part of the reason she purchased Tint, and that as a purchaser, she was clearly among the class of persons whom the label's warranty was intended to reach. (*See* ELO Ch.14-II(B).)

T will argue that by using the Seal of Approval, it was warranting that Tint was safe and wholesome when used by itself and that it was not thereby warranting that Tint was free from all possible cross-reactions. T will argue its warranty was therefore true because Tint does not turn hair purple when used alone. T will also argue that because Balm is only infrequently prescribed by doctors, Tint's negative reaction with Balm does not make it generally unsafe and unwholesome. Additional facts may be necessary to resolve this issue (*i.e.*, what percentage of Tint users experienced hair discoloration, whether Balm is so infrequently prescribed as to make it rare or obsolete, whether other hair color products also interact with Balm and similar medicines, etc.).

Breach of Implied Warranty of Merchantability: Under UCC Section 2-314, where the seller of an item is a merchant, there is an implied warranty of merchantability by him/her that the good will be reasonably fit for the ordinary purposes for which it is used. Furthermore, to be merchantable, a good must be adequately packaged and labeled and must conform to any promises or affirmations of fact that are on the label. Although T is not a "merchant" in the sense of being a retailer, most states have extended the implied warranty of merchantability to manufacturers and hold that the manufacturer's warranty extends to remote purchasers. (*See* ELO Ch.14-II(C)(1).)

Here, G would argue that Tint was not merchantable because (1) it was not adequately labeled to warn of possible cross-reactions with other products, and (2) it did not conform to the label's promise (*i.e.*, the Seal of Approval) that the product was safe and wholesome. Her arguments as to safety and wholesomeness would be the same as above (*Express Warranty*).

T will argue that Tint was fit for its ordinary purpose: coloring hair. T will also argue that Tint was adequately labeled because it did not know of the specific reaction with Balm. Whether T will prevail on this point may depend on whether T's testing was adequate (the facts do not suggest that T was negligent) and on whether the Tint label bore any other more general warnings or disclaimers about possible cross-reactions. T will make the same arguments with respect to safety and wholesomeness as above (*Express Warranty*).

Thus, whether G will prevail on an implied warranty theory will depend on additional facts.

Misrepresentation: G could sue T in an action for misrepresentation based on Section 402B of the Second Restatement. Section 402B provides that a seller of goods who makes any misrepresentation on a product label or in public advertising will be strictly liable for any physical injury that results. This cause of action would be very similar to the express warranty claim discussed above, and has the disadvantage for G of not allowing damages for intangible economic harm (see *Damages* below). It might be preferable, however, if the jurisdiction is one with stricter than average privity requirements for an implied warranty action or stricter reliance requirements for an express warranty claim. (*See* ELO Ch.16-IV(C).)

Damages: If G prevails in an action based on a breach of an express or implied warranty, she will be able to recover damages for her physical injury (the persistent discoloration of her hair), mental distress resulting from the injury (humiliation due to disfigurement), and economic loss. Economic loss could include (1) medical expenses (*i.e.*, if she consults a doctor for advice and treatment), (2) lost income (*i.e.*, if she is unable to work due to the discoloration), (3) the difference between what the product would have been worth if not defective and what it was worth with the defect, and (4) possibly lost profits as a result of G's withdrawal from the beauty contest she was favored to win (*i.e.*, the prize money and possibly the contracts for product endorsements and public appearances that usually go to the winner). Because she is a remote purchaser, G will be more likely to recover such lost profits, which are usually considered intangible economic loss, with an express warranty claim than with an implied warranty claim, especially if a court decided that the discoloration did not constitute physical injury (although such a finding seems unlikely). (*See* ELO Ch.14-VIII.)

G v. Mag ("M"):

G would probably sue M for breach of an express warranty and negligent misrepresentation.

Express Warranty: The essence of G's claim against M on this theory would be the same as above (*G v. T, Express Warranty*). M would try to argue that it was not properly a defendant, since it neither manufactured nor sold Tint. However, some courts have found endorsers liable where the plaintiff can show that the defendant made an actual representation as to the quality of a product and that such representation was incorrect. Here, M's Seal of Approval was clearly a representation as to the quality of Tint. Whether G can recover may depend on whether M tested Tint adequately or not and on whether a Court finds that Tint was not safe and wholesome as warranted. (*See* ELO Ch.14-VII(F).)

If M is liable, G's measure of damages will be as above (*Damages*).

Negligent Misrepresentation: G could try to sue M for negligent misrepresentation. She would have to show that M's statement (its Seal of Approval) was not true and that she justifiably relied on the misrepresentation. G will also have to show that M made the misrepresentation in the course of its business and that it had a pecuniary interest in the transaction. (*See* ELO Ch.16-III.) Here, a substantial part of M's business consists of selling advertising space, and its Seal of Approval is a way to attract advertisers. Even if M did not receive direct pecuniary compensation from T for the use of its Seal on the Tint label, the Seal both encourages (and possibly obligates) T to advertise in M's magazine and functions as advertising for the magazine itself.

G may not be able to recover from M on this theory, however, because liability for negligent misrepresentation is usually limited only to persons whom the maker of the misrepresentation intends to reach or whom he knows the recipient intends to reach. Although a court could find that M was aware that T would use its Seal of Approval to market its product to all purchasers, many courts have interpreted liability to third persons for negligent misrepresentation much more narrowly.

If G does convince a court that M should be liable to her for negligent misrepresentation, she can recover reliance damages, and consequential damages (*i.e.,* her physical injury and lost profits, as described above).

Answer to Question 17

Black ("B") v. Alan ("A") (Conversion):

B would probably sue A for conversion (intentionally exercising substantial dominion and control over a chattel belonging to another). B would contend that a conversion occurred when A removed the radio from his store and then eluded B when return of the item was demanded. Thus, B would contend that A is liable to him for the reasonable (forced sale) value of the radio. (*See* ELO Ch.3-III.)

A would assert the *defense of consent*, arguing that B explicitly consented to his conduct by reason of the wall sign. (*See* ELO Ch.4-II(A).) Assuming it was not clear that B was the owner of the store, A could explain that he evaded B because he assumed that the person shouting at him was either a passerby who mistakenly thought A had stolen the radio or a store employee who did not know that the radios were being given away as a promotional offer. A would argue that B's behavior made him apprehensive and embarrassed, and that he wanted to avoid becoming involved in an altercation with such an individual. However, the radios were not in fact free, and B did not in fact consent to A's conversion. Mistake as to ownership is not a defense to conversion, so it seems unlikely that a court would allow A's mistake as to the meaning of the sign to be such a defense. (*See* ELO Ch.III(B).)

A would next argue that since he offered to return the radio (which was still presumably in good condition) he should only be liable for *trespass to chattels*. Under this tort, the owner of the item is only entitled to recover damages equivalent to the interference with his/her ownership rights (*i.e.*, in this instance, probably the reasonable rental value of the radio). (*See* ELO Ch.3-II(B).) However, by the time the case comes to trial, the radio will probably have been in A's possession for a considerable period of time, and a court could find that title had effectively passed to A and that A should therefore be liable to B for its full value.

A v. B (Assault, Defamation):

Assault: An assault occurs where the defendant intentionally causes the plaintiff to be in reasonable apprehension of an imminent, offensive touching. (*See* ELO Ch.2-V(A).) A could contend that this occurred when B rushed after him when attempting to repossess the radio. B could contend in rebuttal, however, that (1) he apparently was not able to get sufficiently close to A to touch him, and therefore A was never in apprehension of an imminent contact, and (2) under both (i) the storekeeper's privilege (a store owner ordinarily has the right to detain a customer if he/she reasonably believes that the latter has unlawfully taken an item, provided such restraint is conducted in a reasonable manner and for no longer than is necessary to determine if the former's suspicions are correct) and (ii) the right to recapture chattels (where the defendant is in hot pursuit of an item which was unlawfully taken from him/her, the defendant may use reasonable force to reclaim the good), his actions were privileged. (*See* ELO Ch.4-VI(A), (C).) Since B had a reasonable basis for believing that A had stolen a radio, both defenses would be successful, unless the court holds that the former privilege does not extend to the premises surrounding the store.

Defamation: A must show that B made a ***defamatory statement*** (a statement that was false and tended to harm A's reputation) about him, that he communicated that statement to others, and, depending on the jurisdiction, he may have to show that B was at least negligent in making the statement. Since this case involves an oral rather than a written statement, A will sue for slander rather than libel. (*See* ELO Ch.17-III(C).) Here, A will argue that B's statement was false because he did not steal the radio (*i.e.*, he believed the radio was free and thus did not have the *mens rea* required to make his action theft) and therefore he was not a thief. A will also argue that accusations of criminality clearly tend to lower one's reputation. Furthermore, while B did not specifically refer to A by name, it is apparent from the context that all present would have recognized that B's statements were directed to A. (*See* ELO Ch.17-II(D).)

Were B's statements slanderous per se? In a slander action, the plaintiff must ordinarily show some special harm, usually monetary loss, as a direct consequence of the defendant's statements. However, where the words impute the commission of a crime of moral turpitude they are ***slanderous per se*** and special harm is presumed. Calling one a "thief" would seem to satisfy the foregoing standard and therefore it will not be necessary for A to prove special harm to recover for any humiliation and embarrassment he may have suffered as a consequence of B's remarks. (*See* ELO Ch.17-III(D).)

Defenses: Depending on the jurisdiction, B may be able to argue that he did not act with the necessary state of mind to have committed a slander. Some states require that the defendant acted at least negligently in making the defamatory statement. Here, B would argue that he acted reasonably under the circumstances, since A walked out of the store with merchandise he did not pay for. A reasonable person who observed such conduct could conclude that A had stolen the radio. (*See* ELO Ch.17-V(B)(4).)

B will also assert that his statement was covered by the qualified ***privilege of protection of property***. B will argue that he called after A in an attempt to stop him from fleeing with stolen property, or in the hope that passersby would detain the apparent criminal or alert police. (*See* ELO Ch.17-VI(C)(1)(a).)

A will argue that B lost his property protection privilege by acting recklessly and spreading the defamation wider than necessary. A will argue that B could have protected his interests by walking up to him and explaining the situation.

Resolution of this issue may depend on additional factual details of the circumstances surrounding B's conduct.

Damages: A would probably be able to recover for any humiliation and embarrassment associated with the incident (which would seem to be nominal since the persons who heard B's comment probably did not know A). Punitive damages are unlikely since B was merely responding spontaneously to what ostensibly appeared to be the theft of a radio. (*See* ELO Ch.17-VII.)

Carl ("C") v. B (False Imprisonment, Defamation):

False Imprisonment: C would probably assert a false imprisonment (the defendant intentionally confined the plaintiff to a definable area from which there was no reasonably apparent means of escape) action against B. (*See* ELO Ch.2-VI(A).) This tort occurred when B locked Carl in the restroom. Since an intentional tortfeasor is liable for all of the consequences of his/her actions, B would also be liable for the broken leg which C suffered in attempting to escape the restroom.

B might initially assert the *shopkeeper's privilege* (described above). However, C could probably successfully contend that he was not restrained in a reasonable manner (even assuming that he did bear a sufficient resemblance to A to cause B to believe that they were the same individual) since he was abruptly locked in a bathroom without explanation as to why such action was being undertaken. Also, under the shopkeeper's privilege a defendant is liable for any physical harm sustained by plaintiff. Thus, B would be liable for C's injuries.

B could conceivably try to avoid liability for C's injuries by arguing that C consented to his injury by attempting to climb out of the bathroom when he should have realized that it would be impossible to do so. However, while C's judgment may have been poor, he clearly did not consent to being confined in the bathroom in the first place; he was merely doing what most reasonable people would do when confined by some unknown individual for no apparent reason: escape. Through this consent argument, B would really be trying to show that C was contributorily negligent, but the plaintiff's negligence is no defense to an intentional tort. (*See* ELO Ch.11-I(H)(1).)

Defamation: C could try to sue B for defamation, as above (*A v. B*), based on B's statements to the police that C had stolen property from him. Here, however, C's action would fail because he probably could not show that B's statements concerned C; B had mistaken C for A, probably did not know either C or A by name, and presumably told the police merely that he had detained a shoplifter. The police were not on hand to actually see C, so to them it was not apparent that B's statement concerned C. Thus, B's statements were not defamatory of C. (*See* ELO Ch.17-I(A).)

Answer to Question 18

Peter ("P") v. Jim ("J") (Trespass to Chattels, Negligence):

Trespass to Chattels: P could try to recover from J on a trespass to chattels claim, asserting that J intentionally interfered with his use of his wallet by failing to alert him that he had left his wallet on the counter. However, unless additional facts show otherwise, J probably did not have the necessary intent (the intent to do an act which constitutes an interference) since his "act" was one of non-feasance, and P will have to pursue a negligence action. (*See* ELO Ch.3-II(C).)

Negligence:

Did J have a duty to advise P that he had left his wallet? In general, anyone who maintains a business premises must furnish warnings and assistance to business visitors, regardless of the source of danger or harm. (*See* ELO Ch.8-II(B)(2).) Here, P will argue that J therefore had a duty as the operator of a business to warn P that he had forgotten his wallet and to return it to him. Whether J breached this duty may depend on additional facts: how much time had elapsed, how busy it was around the cash register, whether J was on the phone or in the middle of the transaction, whether P appeared to be headed out the door or appeared to be heading back to the table to leave a tip, etc.

Assuming J had a duty, was his inaction the actual cause of P's injuries and losses? A defendant's conduct must be the "but for" cause of the plaintiff's harm. J can be expected to argue that Busco's negligence and David's intentional conduct were the actual cause of P's injuries and losses. However, P should be able to successfully contend in rebuttal that the entire incident with D would have been avoided had J advised P that he had failed to retake his wallet. (*See* ELO Ch.6-I(A)(1).)

Was J's conduct the proximate cause of P's injuries and losses? Where an unforeseeable intervening cause contributes to the plaintiff's harm, some jurisdictions hold that the defendant's conduct is not the proximate cause of the plaintiff's injuries. (*See* ELO Ch.6-IV(A)(1).) J would contend that while it might be foreseeable that someone would steal P's wallet from the counter, it was not foreseeable that the loss of the wallet (being thrown atP, and then falling out of a bus window) and physical injuries (P sustaining a skinned knee when the bus driver pulled away from the curb) would occur as they did. However, P could probably successfully argue in rebuttal that it was foreseeable that another person would take the wallet and that an altercation might arise when P attempted to reclaim it.

Defenses: J would argue that P was contributorily negligent by forgetting to take his wallet as he left the cash register. J would assert that P did not exercise due care and that this failure to act reasonably under the circumstances proximately caused the harm P suffered. A court could probably find that P was contributorily negligent and should therefore be barred from recovery from J. In a comparative negligence jurisdiction, P would be barred completely only if he were more negligent than J. Otherwise, the court would reduce P's recovery according to his share of the fault. (*See* ELO Ch.1-I(D), II(D).)

P v. David ("D") (Conversion, Trespass to Chattels, Assault, Battery):

Conversion and Trespass to Chattels: Conversion and trespass to chattels are both torts based on one person's intentional interference with another's property interest. The difference between the two is one of degree. Here, although D acted in good faith when he took the wallet thinking it was his own, and even though he returned the wallet to P within a matter of minutes, a court could still find that this was a conversion rather than a trespass, since D returned the wallet to P by throwing it at him so recklessly that the wallet was permanently lost. This is such a substantial interference with P's property interest that D will probably be liable for conversion and thus will pay damages for the full value of the wallet and its contents. (*See* ELO Ch.3-II(B), III(D).)

Assault and Battery: P will argue that D committed an assault by intentionally causing him to be in apprehension of an offensive contact when D threw the wallet at him. P will also argue that D committed a battery (the intentional infliction of offensive bodily contact) when the wallet actually hit him.

While D might contend that he was acting in self-defense (*i.e.*, he reasonably believed that P was about to cause an offensive contact upon him, and exercised reasonable force to prevent such contact), the facts do not indicate that P was in close, physical proximity to D when the wallet was thrown, or that D had reasonable grounds to believe that P would actually strike. Thus, this defense should be unsuccessful. (*See* ELO Ch.4-III.)

P will recover nominal damages, damages for mental distress caused by the assault and battery, damages for any physical injury resulting from being hit in the face by the wallet, and possibly punitive damages, if a court finds that D's actions were particularly outrageous. (*See* ELO Ch.2-V(M).)

P v. Busco ("B") (Negligence, False Imprisonment):

Negligence: P would sue B for negligence for the injuries he suffered in his altercation with D. (It does not appear from the facts that the bus driver failed to exercise due care when P attempted to board the bus, so P probably cannot recover from B for his skinned knee.) P will argue that B as a common carrier, has a special relationship with its passengers. Courts have held that bus companies have a ***duty*** to use the utmost care to protect passengers from attacks because passengers have no control over who is on the bus and depend upon the driver to either get help or provide an escape. This duty means that bus drivers and bus companies cannot simply stand by while passengers are in danger; instead, they must either warn violent passengers to stop their behavior, stop the bus, or contact police. (*See* ELO

Ch.8-II(B)(1).) Here, P would assert that B breached this special duty by failing to assist P in any way. The driver could have stopped the bus when D began shouting at P; such action might have dissuaded D from throwing P's wallet, or enabled P to find the wallet if D persisted in throwing it. Furthermore, the driver should have allowed P to leave the bus without insisting on payment, since P had clearly just been subjected to an attack and might have been at risk of another. Thus, B should be liable to P for P's injuries to his face, his mental distress, and possibly for the lost wallet.

False Imprisonment: A false imprisonment ("F.I.") occurs when the defendant intentionally confines the plaintiff to a definable area from which there is no reasonable means of escape. (*See* ELO Ch.2-VI(A).) P would contend that this tort occurred when B's driver did not permit him to leave the bus when he desired to do so. B would probably respond that by boarding the bus, P implicitly consented to being restrained until he paid his fare. However, even if P initially consented to the confinement, where the defendant has a duty to release the plaintiff or help him escape and he does not, there is false imprisonment. (*See* ELO Ch.2-VI(G).) Here, as discussed above (*P v. B*, *Negligence*), B had a duty to help P escape from the bus to protect him from further attacks by D.

Thus, B will be liable to P for false imprisonment. P can recover damages for mental suffering, humiliation, loss of time, and inconvenience.

D v. P (Defamation):

D would bring a defamation action against P for slander based on P's shouting "Stop, thief" at D on a crowded bus. D would have to show that P made a false *defamatory statement* (*i.e.*, a statement tending to lower his reputation) about him and that P communicated the statement to others. (*See* ELO Ch.17-I.) These elements appear to be satisfied. In some jurisdictions, D would also have to show that P acted at least negligently in making the statement. (*See* ELO Ch.17-V(B)(4).) Here, D would argue that P should have realized that he was the one who negligently left the wallet on the counter in the first place and another customer could easily have picked it up by mistake, instead of jumping to the conclusion that D had stolen it. D could probably convince a court that P was at least negligent, if not reckless, in assuming the wallet was stolen and in shouting out accusations of theft before giving D a chance to explain his actions or return the wallet. Although ordinarily in a slander action the plaintiff must prove that he suffered some special harm (usually pecuniary), that requirement is deemed met where the defamatory statement is an accusation of criminal behavior. (*See* ELO Ch.17-III(D)(3)(a).)

P could assert the *qualified privilege of protection of property*. Under this doctrine, where one believes that someone has stolen his property and makes a statement to that effect in order to obtain the return of his property, that statement is privileged. (*See* ELO Ch.17-VI(C)(1)(a).) Since P reasonably believed that D had deliberately taken his wallet (mistaking another person's wallet for one's own is probably a relatively rare occurrence), P's statement was part of his effort to reclaim his property and was thus privileged.

D could argue in rebuttal, however, that P's statement was excessive (*i.e.*, calculated to advise more persons than were reasonably necessary under the circumstances to protect the speaker's interest), since P did not have to yell across the bus (he could have made his way to D and then advised the latter about the mistake which had occurred). Assuming P was not about to leave the bus, it appears to have been unnecessary to shout out that D was a thief. Thus, the privilege was forfeited.

D's recovery in defamation would appear to be nominal, since D apparently suffered no economic losses from P's statements and this situation is not an appropriate one for punitive damages.

Answer to Question 19

Zoe ("Z") v. Resco ("R") (Abnormally Dangerous Activity, Private Nuisance, Defamation, Fraud, Negligent Misrepresentation):

Abnormally Dangerous Activity: Where the defendant has engaged in an ADA, he/she is liable for all personal injury and property damage resulting to the plaintiff from such activity. In determining if conduct should be characterized as an ADA, courts will ordinarily weigh: (1) the magnitude and degree of risk of the harm likely to result from the activity, (2) the inability to eliminate the risk of harm by the exercise of due care, (3) the extent to which the activity is not a matter of common usage in the locale, (4) the extent to which the value of the activity to the community is outweighed by its dangerousness and (5) the inappropriateness of the activity to the place in which it is conducted. (*See* ELO Ch.13-II(C).) Z would argue that the risk involved here was very serious (loss of all infected or exposed cattle), that the risk obviously was not eliminated through the exercise of due care, and that the virus experimentation was highly inappropriate to the area because the cattle and dairy industries were its principal economic activities, and that the value of the activity to the community, although great, was outweighed by the risk it posed and the losses it caused.

R could contend that since (1) experimentation with respect to cattle diseases is an extremely important activity for an area which has a thriving cattle and dairy industry, and (2) the activity was not uncommon to the area when it was begun (the building was erected in an unsettled area, around which the cattle industry grew), its experimentation should *not* be characterized as an ADA. However, Z could probably successfully contend in rebuttal that R was involved in an ADA since (1) the risk is obviously one that cannot be eliminated with due care (the virus escaped without negligence on the part of R), and (2) the experimentation entailed a great risk to surrounding livestock (as evidenced by the fact that it was necessary to slaughter all cattle which were infected by or exposed to the virus). However, in light of the serious losses involved to industries so vital to the community, and because R's experimentation could easily have been conducted somewhere else, R will probably be liable.

R may try to argue that Z was contributorily negligent by establishing a cattle auction market in the area and therefore should not recover. However, even if Z was contributorily negligent (discussed below), such negligence will not bar Z from recovering for R's ADA unless a court found that Z unreasonably assumed the risk of infection of cattle. This finding is unlikely, given the public statement by the president of the virus experimentation company to the effect that there was no danger of infection. (*See* ELO Ch.13-III(C).)

Whether R will be liable for the harm that Z suffered will depend on whether a court finds that that harm resulted from the kind of risk that made the activity abnormally dangerous. Here, the risk was that the virus would escape and infect cattle in the surrounding area. Z would argue that even though he owned no cattle himself, his business was premised on the availability and marketability of cattle in that area, and that the ruin of such a business is one of the things that makes R's activity abnormally dangerous. R will respond that its liability should not extend to such intangible economic harm, since the risk posed by its activity was that of property damage to the nearby cattle. Whether R or Z prevails on this point may depend on how narrow a view the court takes on the scope of liability for ADAs. (*See* ELO Ch.13-III(B).)

> *Conclusion:* R's experimentation probably constitutes an ADA. Whether Z can recover damages for it will depend on whether a court interprets the harm he suffered as within the scope of the risk posed by the ADA.

Nuisance: A private nuisance occurs where the defendant has caused a non-trespassory substantial and unreasonable interference with the plaintiff's use and enjoyment of his/her land. (*See* ELO Ch.15-III(A)(3).) Whether Z can recover on this claim will therefore depend on whether he has an interest in land. If, for example, he merely rented a lot one day a week on which to hold his auctions, he does not have an interest in land and he will not recover, because courts do not allow private nuisance recovery for mere harm to plaintiff's livelihood. If, however, Z held his market on his own land, then he may be able to recover. Z will argue that the virus experimentation was an ADA (as above) and that the escape of the virus to the cattle of the nearby ranches caused his market to become worthless; thereby causing an unreasonable interference with his use of the land. However, R could probably successfully contend in rebuttal that Z's use and enjoyment of his land has not been interfered with simply because a particular business cannot be carried on at it. Additionally, R would contend that (1) there has been no "substantial" interference with R's use of the land (since the escaping virus is a one-time event, and (2) Z assumed the risk of the virus escaping by moving into an area where the experimentation was being carried out. As to the latter contention, however, Z could probably successfully argue in rebuttal that he established the market near R based upon P's statement that there was no possibility of the virus escaping. Z's contention on this point will be strengthened if he already owned the land used for the market before R began its experimentation work. (*See* ELO Ch.15-III(B).)

If Z does not have the requisite interest in land for a private nuisance claim, he could try to recover on a public nuisance theory. He will argue that the escape of the virus and infection on the cattle was an interference with a right common to the general public because the community generally was dependent upon cattle ranching for its economic survival. He will argue that the factors that determine whether R's activity was a public nuisance are met because (1) the neighborhood, a cattle and dairy district, was such that R's activities were inappropriate, (2) the activity itself was an ADA (as discussed above), (3) the experimentation was conducted in close proximity to those most likely to be affected by it, (4) the activity was ongoing and constant, and (5) the damage that resulted from it was substantial. (*See* ELO Ch.15-II.)

For Z to be able to recover damages, he will have to show that the damage he sustained is different in kind, not just degree, from that suffered by the public generally. Thus, Z will have to articulate the harm to the general public as the general loss of revenue and economic hardship imposed on the community as a result of the huge losses of cattle. He will have to distinguish his own harm as the direct interference with his right to buy and sell cattle. Z may have trouble convincing a court that this harm is the result of an interference with a *public* right (*i.e.*, some public right to trade in livestock). (*See* ELO Ch.15-II(B).)

Z does not, however, have to show that he suffered a different kind of harm in order to get an injunction against Resco to stop its experimentation. He can sue for injunction as a member of the general public.

> **Conclusion:** Whether Z can recover from R on a private nuisance theory will depend on whether he has an interest in land and whether he is deemed to have assumed the risk by coming to the nuisance. Z can probably get an injunction against R on a public nuisance theory. Whether he can recover damages for a public nuisance will depend on whether he can show that he suffered a kind of harm different from that suffered by the public generally.

Fraud: Z will sue R for vicarious liability for fraud based on P's statement in the News to the effect that there was "no danger" of the virus escaping.

A fraud occurs where the defendant has intentionally or recklessly made a material misrepresentation of fact for the purpose of causing the plaintiff to rely thereon, and upon which statement the plaintiff has justifiably relied to his/her detriment. (*See* ELO Ch.16-II(A)(1).) Since Prex ("P") had made no investigation prior to his assertion that there was "no danger at all" of the virus escaping, his statement would probably be deemed to be reckless. While R might contend that since P's statement was not addressed specifically to Z, the former had no intention of deceiving the latter, P appears to have intended to cause Z to rely upon his statement (which in fact, Z did), because he made the statement in response to a request by ranchers for him to make a statement to convince Z that it would be safe to establish a market. Even if Z cannot prove that P intended to produce Z's reliance in particular, he can probably show that he is a member of a class of persons whom P had reason to expect would learn of and rely on the misrepresentation, and that the reliance occurred in a transaction that P had reason to expect such a class would engage in because of such a reliance. (*See* ELO Ch.16-II(D)(2)(b).) Z will argue that P had reason to know that a cattle auctioneer based in the area would learn of the statement (since it was published in the area paper) and rely on it. Furthermore, the transaction was clearly one that P would expect cattle auctioneers to engage in: the establishment of a market in local cattle. Z's reliance was clearly justifiable, since the statement was made by the person in the best position to know of the risks posed by R's activities. (*See* ELO Ch.16-II(E).)

R may try to argue that it should not be liable because Z was contributorily negligent by establishing a market so close to R's activities. However, contributory negligence is not a defense to a fraud action, unless the defendant's statement was obviously false and the plaintiff relied on it nonetheless. Here, P's statement was not obviously false, and even if Z had his doubts about the safety of R's operations, he was under no duty to conduct his own investigation. Thus, R should be liable for fraud. (*See* ELO Ch.16-II(E)(2).)

Damages: Z can recover damages for any harm proximately caused by R's misrepresentation. Here, his loss of his cattle market business seems clearly to have been proximately caused by R's misrepresentation, because he would not have suffered the loss if P's statement had been true. The measure of damages will either be reliance (which would put Z in the same position he was in before the misrepresentation) or benefit of the bargain (which would put Z where he would have been if the misrepresentation had been true). (*See* ELO Ch.16-II(I)(2).)

Negligent Misrepresentation: If Z cannot establish that P was at least reckless in making its misrepresentation, he could try to sue R for vicarious liability for negligent misrepresentation based on P's statement. The elements of this action are essentially the same as a deceit action. Z will also have to show that R had a duty to exercise due care in making the statement because the statement was made in the course of R's business and R had a pecuniary interest in the transaction in which the statement was made. (*See* ELO Ch.16-III(B).) Z will argue that P's statement clearly met those requirements because it would affect public perceptions of the company and the safety of its activities, which would in turn affect the company's ability to conduct its research in the area and could affect such things as the company's stock prices. Z will have to show that R breached its duty of due care, which R clearly did by not making any investigation. To recover, Z will have to show that he belongs to a limited group of persons whom R intended to reach with the information, or whom R knew the recipient intended to reach. If Z cannot prove that R intended to reach him (as the facts indicate), he will argue that R intended to reach a class of persons that included all those who were in the cattle and livestock business in the surrounding area in order to assuage their fear. (*See* ELO Ch.16-III(C)(1).)

R will again raise a ***contributory negligence*** defense, which is allowable in a negligent misrepresentation action. This defense will probably fail, however, because a court would probably find that Z acted reasonably under the circumstances by waiting to establish his market until after the president of the company, who should have the best access to relevant safety information, publicly stated that the experimentation posed no risk. (*See* ELO Ch.16-III(D).)

Z will be able to recover reliance damages and consequential damages.

Defamation: Z would sue R for defamation under the doctrine of vicarious liability for P's statement at the press conference. Z would sue for slander because the statement was originally oral, not written. (*See* ELO Ch.17-III(C).)

Z must show that P's statement (1) was false, (2) either tended to lower his reputation or subjected him to hatred, contempt, or ridicule, (3) concerned Z, and (4) was communicated to others. He will also have to show, depending on the jurisdiction, that P was at least negligent in making the statement. (*See* ELO Ch.17-I(A).)

Z can probably show that the statement was false, and certainly being characterized as a "driveling idiot" would tend to lower one's reputation and subject one to ridicule and possibly contempt. However, R may be able to convince a court that the statement was clearly one of opinion and not one implying fact, since it was obviously an *expression of P's opinion* about those who disagreed with him, rather than any real assertion about the level of intelligence of those individuals. (*See* ELO Ch.17-II(F).)

While P might contend that his comment was not *"of and concerning"* Z because the latter was not specifically named, Z could probably successfully contend in rebuttal that it was well known in the community that Z was the individual at whom the comment was aimed. (*See* ELO Ch.17-II(D)(3).)

P clearly communicated the statement to others by making it at a press conference, and Z can probably show that P was at least negligent, if not reckless, in making such a derogatory, untrue remark under circumstances where it was very likely that it would be understood by many as referring to Z.

The plaintiff in a slander action must show that he suffered some special harm (usually a pecuniary loss) as a result of the defamatory statement, unless the statement falls into the category of *slander per se*, where such special harm is presumed. Here, the only possible category of slander *per se* he might be able to use is that of an allegation of unfitness to conduct his business. (*See* ELO Ch.17-III(D)(3).) P's statement is probably not such an allegation, since his remark was generally disparaging and not specifically relevant to Z's fitness to conduct his auction business. Thus, Z will have to show that he suffered *pecuniary harm*, which he will try to do by arguing that he established his cattle market in part out of the desire to avoid further embarrassment after P's statement, and that therefore his financial losses from losing the market when P's statement turned out to be false constitute the necessary special harm. This argument may not succeed, however, because a court could find that Z's loss was not the result of the defamatory statement but of P's misrepresentation and Z's decision to rely on it. Thus, even if Z can establish all of the other necessary elements of slander, he probably cannot recover from R.

Z v. P (Fraud, Negligent Misrepresentation, Defamation):

The result would be the same as in the *Z v. R* case.

Z v. News ("N") (Defamation, Negligence):

Z's suit against N would be essentially the same as its claims against R and P, except that here Z would sue N for having repeated R and P's slander. As above, Z would therefore have to show that he suffered special harm, which he may not be able to do.

In his suit against N, Z also faces the additional obstacles of constitutional requirements since N is a *newspaper*. The level of intent that N must have had will depend on the standard used in the jurisdiction. Under constitutional law, because this case involves a *media defendant* who printed a statement about a private individual in an article on a public matter, Z will have to show that N was at least negligent (*i.e.*, it failed to act reasonably in publishing P's statement about "driveling idiots" without ascertaining that it was false). This will be hard for Z to prove, because, as discussed above under *Z v. R* (*Defamation*), P's statement seems clearly to have been one of *opinion*. It seems hardly reasonable for N to be required to attempt some sort of investigation to ascertain whether all of those in the area who disbelieve P are in fact driveling idiots. If Z did somehow manage to show N had been negligent, Z will not be able to get presumed damages and will have to show actual damage (with the attendant difficulties discussed above, *Z v. R*), unless he can show actual malice (*i.e.*, knowledge of the falsity of the statement or reckless disregard as to its truth or falsity), which will be difficult in this instance given the vagueness of P's statement. (*See* ELO Ch.17-V(B)(4).)

Negligence: Z might try to sue N for negligence, arguing that N failed to exercise due care in publishing P's statement there was "no danger at all" of the virus escaping from its facilities without investigating to see if the statement were true. Such a suit would probably fail, however, because N probably acted reasonably under the circumstances by publishing the statement of the president of the company without further investigation, since the president should have the best available information about the company. Furthermore, since the statement was attributed to P, the newspaper was not itself asserting the statement as true; rather, it was merely reporting a company spokesman's public statement.

Answer to Question 20

Polly ("P") v. Norm ("N") (Defamation, Intentional Infliction of Mental Distress):

Defamation: P will sue N for slander (because his statement was oral, not written) for his statement that "one of the top leaders at this college is a high school dropout who was once arrested for peddling dope." (She will not base her action on the allegation of lesbianism because that charge probably does not refer to her. See below.) (*See* ELO Ch.17-I(A).)

Were N's statements defamatory? A defamatory statement is one which is false and exposes the subject to hatred, contempt or ridicule to a considerable and respectable class of the community or which tends to lower one's reputation. P will have to show that it is not true that she dropped out of high school or that she peddled drugs. (*See* ELO Ch.17-II(E).) Assuming that she makes this showing, she will then argue that an allegation that a college student is a high school dropout would tend to lower her reputation, because such a fact might suggest that she used false information on her college application. The allegation about a drug-related arrest would certainly lower her reputation, since it is an allegation that she engaged in criminal activity. (*See* ELO Ch.17-II(A).)

Were N's statements "of and concerning" P? A defamatory statement must clearly pertain to (*i.e.*, be "of and concerning") the plaintiff. N's first statement probably does *not* refer to P, since the group alluded to (all of the leaders in the nation) is far too numerous. N's last two statements, however, refer to "one" of the "top leaders" at the college. The facts are not clear as to (1) whether the term "leaders" would be understood as referring to the officers of the Women's Lib club, and (2) how large (or small) that group is (5, 10?). N would argue that his statement did not refer to the Women's Lib club and did not refer to Polly by name. However, Polly only has to show that his statement was reasonably interpreted by at least one recipient as referring to her. Assuming, that (1) the club is the only feminist group on campus, and (2) there are only a few (*i.e.*, three) officers, P could probably prevail on this issue. It might be mentioned that P's response to N's statements would not make his comments applicable to her (the defendant's statement must be analyzed by itself). (*See* ELO Ch.17-II(D).)

Ordinarily, the plaintiff in a slander action must show that she has suffered some special harm, usually *pecuniary*. Here, however, N's statement included an allegation of criminal behavior, and this will constitute *slander per se*. Thus, P does not have to make a showing of special harm and may recover presumed damages (*i.e.*, a sum representing the harm that ordinarily stems from a similar defamatory statement). (*See* ELO Ch.17-III(D).)

Intentional Infliction of Mental Distress: The intentional infliction of mental distress occurs where the defendant engaged in outrageous conduct for the purpose of causing (or which was substantially certain to cause) the plaintiff severe emotional distress, and the latter actually suffered such distress. (*See* ELO Ch.2-VII(A).) Here, P probably could not prevail in such an action, because N's conduct probably does not rise to the necessary level of recklessness and outrageousness. First, there is no evidence in the facts that N even knew P, much less knew that she was in the audience. Further, regardless of whether people in the audience interpreted his comments as referring to P, N did not name P in his statement, address it directly to her, or describe the person he was referring to so specifically that everyone would know he was referring to P. While his comments need not have been that specific to constitute defamation, a higher degree of specificity would be needed before his actions would be conduct so extreme and beyond the bounds of decency as to constitute the tort of intentional infliction of mental distress. Even if N's comments were more specifically aimed at P, she still might not recover, since mere insults are not enough for liability, and a court could conclude that N's comments, while more damaging than insults (indeed, they are defamatory), are simply not outrageous enough. (*See* ELO Ch.2-VII(C).)

P v. Spector ("S") (Defamation, Invasion of Privacy, Intentional Infliction of Mental Distress):

Defamation: P would sue S for libel, since S's defamatory statement appeared in written form. P would argue that S's statement that she struck N and made him bleed was false (which it was) and that it clearly tended to lower her reputation, since it depicts her as a very violent individual who has committed a crime.

With respect to the statement that N accused her of having been convicted of selling drugs, P could argue that the statement was not true (*i.e.*, he did not specifically accuse *her*) and that this statement was clearly damaging to her reputation, because it would make people in the community think she was a criminal. However, this argument might be a tricky one for her to make, since in order to recover from N for defamation she has to argue that his statement about drug-peddling *was* made in reference to her. Thus, P will be better off arguing that this statement is libel because it was not true that he accused her of a conviction, rather than an arrest, or that S's statement was a repetition of N's original slander (see above) and that S should be liable for repeating it. (*See* ELO Ch.17-II.)

A ***media defendant*** cannot constitutionally be liable in defamation unless its publication was at least negligent (some jurisdictions require actual malice - knowledge of the statement's falsity or recklessness as to its publication). Here, whether S was negligent may depend on additional facts. The facts state that S interviewed several persons who were present at the event, but it is not clear what they told the reporter. Perhaps the reporter distorted or exaggerated what she had been told, either out of some personal grudge against P or to make the story "juicier" and thereby get attention for herself. Furthermore, the facts do not make it clear who the people interviewed were; perhaps they were individuals who were politically opposed to members of the Women's Lib club and thus had a reason to give false information. If the reporter knew that, she should have sought out other sources of information that were more objective. Similarly, if these were individuals who were standing at the back of the room and could not see or hear events occurring near the stage, the reporter should have sought out people who were better positioned to hear the talk and observe the fracas. Thus, it is not clear from the facts whether S acted reasonably under the circumstances. (*See* ELO Ch.17-V(B)(2).)

Damages: Although ordinarily P would not have to prove actual damages for the libellous statement(s) (since the defamatory nature of the statement is clear from the statement itself) or special damages for the repeated slanderous statement (it is slander *per se* because it involves an accusation of criminal behavior), presumed damages cannot constitutionally be awarded against a media defendant absent a showing of actual malice, at least where the statement concerns a public figure or a private individual in a matter of public concern. (*See* ELO Ch.17-VII(A)(2).) Here, P would argue that she is not a public figure and that the defamatory statement was not about a matter of public concern. As a college student and secretary of an obscure campus club, she probably is not a public figure. However, N is a public figure (so a story about him probably is one of public concern), and a fight on campus probably is a matter of public concern, so P will have to show actual malice. Whether she will succeed will depend on additional facts, as described above. Even if P can only show that S was negligent and cannot get presumed damages, P can show actual damages (*i.e.*, her postponed graduation and consequent lost income, her psychiatric treatment expenses, her mental distress, etc.). (*See* ELO Ch.17-VII.)

Invasion of Privacy: P will try to sue S for invasion of privacy on the grounds that S placed her in the public eye in an offensive false light. While S clearly placed her in the public eye by naming her, and clearly portrayed her in a false light (certainly with the statement about her striking N, and probably in the drug-peddling statement as well), P may not prevail if she cannot show that S acted with actual malice. This constitutional requirement may be relaxed, however, where the plaintiff is a private individual, so P may be able to convince a court that she need only show negligence to recover. Whether she can prove either negligence or actual malice will depend on additional facts, as above. (*See* ELO Ch.18-I(E).)

Intentional Infliction of Mental Distress: P will contend that S intentionally or recklessly inflicted severe mental distress on her by its publication of the false statements about her. To prevail, however, P would probably have to show that S acted deliberately and with knowledge of the falsity of the statements, because this tort requires that the defendant's conduct be so extreme and outrageous as to be beyond the bounds of decency. From the facts provided, it is unlikely that P would be able to make such a showing. (*See* ELO Ch.2-VII.)

Answer to Question 21

1. Theories upon which White might base a cause of action against News.

Defamation: White could ***not*** successfully sue News for defamation since the facts indicate that the proposed story is true; and ***truth is an absolute defense*** to such an action. (*See* ELO Ch.17-II(E).)

Invasion of Privacy (Publicity of Private Life): White might try to bring an action for invasion of privacy for News' publication of details of his private life.

White would have to show that the publicizing of such details would be highly offensive to a reasonable person. White will argue that his conviction for murder and subsequent imprisonment were very painful events for him, that he has spent the last thirty years trying to put these events behind him, and that a reasonable person would find it offensive to be forced to recall these events in such a highly public way (*i.e.*, receiving attention from the public and the media, who will surely try to contact him once the story comes out).

White will also have to show that the details published are truly private; that is, that they are not contained in any public record. White will probably not be able to make this showing; see discussion of News' defenses below.

White will also try to argue that his private life is not of legitimate public concern. He will argue that he has returned to private life and that these events happened long ago and can be of no legitimate public interest at this point in time. This argument will also probably fail (see below). (*See* ELO Ch.18-I(D).)

Intentional Infliction of Mental Distress: The tort of intentional infliction of mental distress occurs where the defendant has engaged in outrageous conduct which is substantially certain to cause (and does in fact cause) the plaintiff severe emotional distress. White will argue that he is especially sensitive because of the vows of his religious order (since he is under a vow of silence, he will be subjected to intense pressure to break that vow by the renewed public attention) and because of his ill health. White will argue that News was aware of his special sensitivity because News was warned of it by White's doctors. White will have to show that he suffered severe emotional distress, and possibly physical harm as well (depending on the jurisdiction). (*See* ELO Ch.2-VII(D).)

2. Defenses available to News against a suit for an injunction.

Invasion of Privacy: News will argue that the details it intends to publish about White's private life would not be offensive to a reasonable person. News will argue that a reasonable person would be glad to have an account of her exoneration for a crime she did not commit made public, and that White is simply overly sensitive as a result of his membership in a religious order that values silence and privacy. On this point, the court should rule in White's favor (see White's arguments above).

News will argue that the material that it wishes to publish is all available in the public record, and that therefore there is no invasion of privacy involved here. The court should rule in News' favor, since there is no action for invasion of privacy based on publicity of one's private life when the material publicized is already public. (*See* ELO Ch.18-I(D)(1).)

News will argue that the material it seeks to publish is of legitimate public concern (1) because White is a public figure, and (2) because the public has an interest in having information about the workings of the justice system, particularly when the justice system fails (even if only temporarily). News should prevail on this point, because White was in the public eye in a highly publicized series of events, and that fame (or notoriety) made him a public figure, even if it was against his will and even if he has since fled from such attention. Furthermore, criminal cases and legal proceedings generally are matters of legitimate public concern. (*See* ELO Ch.18-I(D)(3).)

Intentional Infliction of Mental Distress: While the facts indicate that White will, in fact, suffer emotional distress if the article is published, it is doubtful that the conduct of News would be considered outrageous enough that News should be liable. Generally, conduct that gives rise to such liability is outrageous in the extreme, such as a practical joke that involves telling someone that their spouse has died, or threatening someone with physical injury, or humiliating someone in the course of a sustained prank and in front of a large number of people. If the publication of a somewhat embarrassing but true story about a matter of public concern were considered outrageous conduct, mass media entities would be severely limited in the choice of subjects which could be presented to the public. Thus, this contention by White should fail. (*See* ELO Ch.2-VII(C).)

Answer to Question 22

The facts are silent as to why the Masons' ("M") mobile home was mistakenly repossessed (*i.e.*, did Finance Company misstate the information pertaining to Ms' trailer to Repo, or did Repo's employees take the wrong mobile home despite an accurate description)? If the former, then Finance Company ("F") was probably negligent, and would be directly liable to the Ms' for the foreseeable consequences resulting from its error. If, however, the mistake was made by Repo's employees, then a question arises as to whether F is responsible for their conduct. For purposes of analysis, we'll assume that Repo's employees were furnished accurate information by F.

Is F liable for the conduct of Repo's agents? There are two bases upon which F could be **vicariously liable** for the acts of Repo's employees.

First, an employer is liable for the conduct of his/her employees occurring within the scope of their employment. Whether one is an employee or not depends upon whether he/she was under the employer's "control." F could contend that Repo was not under its control since (1) Repo, not F, had control over the physical details of the work performed, (2) Repo used its own equipment and employees, and (3) F apparently gave Repo no instructions with respect to how the repossession was to occur. While the Ms could argue in rebuttal that F advised Repo (1) what to do (repossess a mobile home), (2) where the vehicle was located, and (3) where to bring the item after it had been confiscated, a court would probably find that this amounted merely to control over the general manner in which the work was to be performed, rather than the more specific type of control necessary to make someone the employee of another. Thus, Repo will probably be found to be an independent contractor, and its employees will not be found to be employees of F. (*See* ELO Ch.12-II(B)(1).)

Second, the plaintiffs could argue that F should be liable for the acts of Repo even if it is an **independent contractor** because repossession is work that poses a high degree of dangers to others unless special precautions are taken. The plaintiffs would argue that repossession entails peculiar risks that are different from the common risks to which people are generally exposed as a result of the ordinary, common forms of negligence. The nature of repossession work (*i.e.*, the physical taking of property from someone who does not want to relinquish it) poses the risk of physical injury and emotional distress as a result of the acts of the repossessors and the risk of tortious interference with the possessors' property rights. Plaintiffs will argue that these dangers could have been reduced or eliminated if special precautions had been taken; for example, Repo's employees could have brought with them copies of the papers governing Stranger's financing arrangement, which would have enabled the Ms to show that they were not Stranger, thus alerting Repo that it had the wrong mobile home. Plaintiffs should prevail on this issue. (*See* ELO Ch.12-III(B)(3).)

Ms v. F:

The Ms could sue F for the following torts.

Assault and Battery: An assault occurs where the defendant intentionally causes the plaintiff to be in reasonable apprehension of an imminent, offensive touching. A battery occurs where the defendant intentionally causes an offensive contact upon the plaintiff. The intent required for these torts is the defendant's knowledge with substantial certainty that the result (*i.e.,* the apprehension or the contact) will occur from his action. (*See* ELO Ch.2-V(B).) Here, even though the repomen probably did not intend to harm Bill in any way, they (and thus F) will still be liable to him for assault and battery, since they saw him on the trailer steps and thus should have known that pulling the trailer away would cause him to fall. Bill was thus in apprehension of an offensive bodily contact before he fell, and he suffered an offensive bodily contact when he hit the ground. Even though the repomen never actually touched Bill, he can recover for the contact that they caused indirectly. (*See* ELO Ch.2-IV(D)(1).)

The fact that Repo's personnel were mistaken as to B's right to retain the trailer would be irrelevant, since mistake alone is no defense to intentional conduct.

Bill can recover damages for his mental suffering and for his broken leg (*e.g.,* his medical bills, pain and suffering, hedonistic damages, etc.). He may be able to recover punitive damages if a court finds that the repomen's conduct was extreme and outrageous. (*See* ELO Ch.2-II.) Given that the repomen apparently made no effort to confirm that they had the proper trailer and in light of the distress, inconvenience, and loss that would foreseeably ensue from such a mistake, a court could find that their conduct was indeed extreme and outrageous. Even though the scope of liability for intentional torts is very broad, Jane will not be able to recover for her mental distress on the basis of this tort, since she was not in apprehension of an offensive bodily contact and did not suffer an offensive contact. She may be able to recover for loss of consortium.

Trespass: A trespass occurs where the defendant intentionally intrudes upon the plaintiff's land. Since Repo's employees must have traversed upon the land which the M's were leasing for their mobile home, a trespass occurred. The repomen's mistaken belief that they had a right to enter onto the land does not relieve them of liability; as long as they intended to enter the land and were not privileged to do so, they have committed a trespass. (*See* ELO Ch.3-I(C)(1).)

As trespassers, the repomen (and thus F, as per above discussion of vicarious liability) will be liable for virtually all consequences of their trespass, no matter how they occurred. Bill can thus recover for $5,500 for property damage (to repair the dent on the trailer and to replace personal possessions) and damages for his personal injuries (medical expenses, pain and suffering, hedonistic damages). Some courts even allow recovery for mental distress suffered by family members as a result of trespass; thus, Jane could recover for her mental suffering and her medical expenses. (*See* ELO Ch.3-I(D).)

Trespass to Chattels/Conversion: A trespass to chattels occurs where the defendant has intentionally caused a minor interference with the plaintiff's ownership or control of a good. (*See* ELO Ch.3-II(B).) A conversion occurs where the defendant causes a substantial interference with the plaintiff's right to possession or control of an item. The difference between the two torts is one of degree. (*See* ELO Ch.3-III.) The factors a court will consider in determining which tort has occurred are the extent and duration of the defendant's dominion over the good, the defendant's good faith, harm done to the property, and the inconvenience and expense to the plaintiff. Here, the defendant's dominion over the trailer was complete, although the facts do not indicate when the trailer was returned. Although mistake is not a defense to conversion, the defendant did appear to act in good faith under the belief that it had a right to repossess the good. The harm done to the trailer was significant monetarily (to repair it would cost $500), but insignificant in terms of function and appearance. The inconvenience and expense to the Ms is presumably substantial, since they had to find new accommodations while the trailer was out of their possession. If the trailer was returned right away, a court could conceivably find the defendant(s) liable for trespass to chattels, and thus plaintiffs could recover for the fair rental value of the trailer and for damages to it. If, however, the court finds that a conversion occurred (especially if the defendants delayed in returning the trailer), the defendants would be liable for the market value of the trailer ($65,000). Even if they are liable for a conversion, defendants would probably be able to mitigate their damages by returning the trailer, and plaintiffs would only recover for their actual damages. Defendants are clearly liable in conversion for the other personal property that was missing when the trailer was returned ($5,000), even if they did act in good faith, since the property is now lost to the Ms forever. (*See* ELO Ch.3-III(G).)

Invasion of Privacy (Intrusion on Solitude): An invasion of privacy occurs where the defendant has intruded into an area in which the plaintiff reasonably believed that he/she would have solitude. The place that was invaded must be private, and the intrusion must have been one that would be highly offensive to a reasonable person. Here, one's home is clearly private, and it would be highly offensive to a reasonable person to have one's home towed away illegally. Thus, when Repo's employees abruptly towed away the M's home, this tort probably occurred. The Ms would thus be entitled to recover any reasonably foreseeable damages arising from the repossession. (*See* ELO Ch.18-I(C).)

Intentional Infliction of Mental Distress: The tort of intentional infliction of mental distress occurs where the defendant intentionally or recklessly inflicts severe mental or emotional distress by his or her extreme and outrageous conduct. The Ms could contend that unexpectedly moving someone's home away from them is conduct which the defendant knew, or should have realized, would cause the owners severe emotional distress. Whether Bill can recover on this basis will depend on whether a court finds that the repomen's conduct was extreme and outrageous. Even if the repomen knew that some emotional distress would occur, that is not enough to make their conduct extreme and outrageous. A court might consider the fact that their actions were not premeditated in order to cause distress (*i.e.*, they did not know that Bill was the wrong possessor, and they did not know that he would refuse to leave the trailer). A court could find that because the repomen believed that they were acting legally, their conduct was not extreme and outrageous. However, a court could also find that it was extreme and outrageous for them not to confirm that they had the right trailer in the face of Bill's protest. (*See* ELO Ch.2-VII.)

Even if a court finds that the repomen's conduct was extreme and outrageous, Jane will probably not be able to recover damages for her mental suffering on this basis because she was not present to witness the repomen's conduct. Thus, the repomen could not have had the requisite intent with respect to Jane; they did not know she existed, and thus could not have reasonably anticipated that she would suffer emotional distress.

Negligent Infliction of Emotional Distress: Alternatively, Jane ("J") might assert a cause of action for negligent infliction of severe emotional distress, contending that as a consequence of Repo's unreasonable conduct she suffered emotional distress. However, the majority view is that the plaintiff can only recover for mental distress resulting from contemporaneously observing physical injury to family members, and some jurisdictions further require that the plaintiff must have been in the zone of danger. Since J did not see B being injured or the mobile home towed away, it is unlikely that she can recover for the mental distress resulting from these incidents. (*See* ELO Ch.8-IV(B).)

Answer to Question 23

Ellen ("E") would probably assert the following causes of action against Disco ("D"): intentional infliction of severe emotional distress, invasion of privacy (appropriation of name or likeness, and possibly, objectionable, false public light) and fraud.

Intentional Infliction of Severe Emotional Distress ("IISED"): The tort of IISED occurs where the defendant has intentionally engaged in outrageous conduct for the purpose of causing, or which is substantially certain to cause, the plaintiff severe emotional distress. E would contend that the elements of this tort are satisfied by reason of D's conduct in deliberately misleading E as to the existence of a door prize and publicizing E as the award's winner for the selfish purpose of promoting D's new store. (*See* ELO Ch.2-VII(A).) D would argue in rebuttal that (1) its conduct, while not completely ethical, cannot be characterized as "outrageous", and (2) in many jurisdictions, humiliation or embarrassment, alone, is not sufficient to constitute "severe" emotional distress (*i.e.*, there must be proof of some type of physical harm having been suffered). E could contend in rebuttal that (1) D should have realized that E (a 15-year-old) would become a veritable "laughing stock" when the public learned that the purported door prize was merely a promotional effort, and (2) given the publicity surrounding the incident, the degree of embarrassment and grief which she had suffered exceeds that which the typical person could reasonably be expected to endure. However, without some type of physical impairment E would probably ***not*** be successful against D under this theory.

Misrepresentation: A ***fraud*** occurs where the defendant intentionally or recklessly misrepresents a material fact with the intent to induce the plaintiff's reliance, and where the plaintiff has justifiably relied on the misrepresentation to her detriment. (*See* ELO Ch.16-II(A)(1).) Here, Disco's advertisement and Mana's statements clearly misrepresented material facts by announcing its intention to award a door prize and by purporting to award such a prize, when in fact Disco never intended to award any prize at all. Mana clearly intended E to rely on his oral statements to her, because he wanted E to allow him to take publicity photos. Even if E cannot show that Disco specifically intended to induce her to rely on its advertisement, Disco will be liable for those statements because they were incorporated in a commercial document (*i.e.*, a public advertisement). E's reliance was clearly justifiable, since she had no reason to doubt the truth of the ad or of Mana's statements. However, E may have trouble showing that she relied to her detriment. Although she suffered emotional detriment, most courts require that the detriment sustained by the plaintiff be reflected in some type of pecuniary loss. D would argue that E has not suffered any pecuniary loss as a consequence of its misrepresentation (*i.e.*, E has only been denied a ***gift***). E may be able to persuade a court to award her damages if she frames her injury in monetary terms. If the court awards her reliance damages, she can recover for her expenses in travelling to

Disco's store on two occasions. If the court awards her expectation damages, she may recover for the value of the promised trip to Paris. If she recovers either reliance or expectation damages, she may be able to tack on consequential damages for the embarrassment she suffered as a result of the fraud and the publicity about it. She may also be able to recover punitive damages, if a court finds that Disco's conduct was malicious. (*See* ELO Ch.16-II(I).)

Invasion of Privacy (Appropriation of Likeness, False Light): An invasion of privacy occurs where the defendant has appropriated the plaintiff's name or likeness, in other than an incidental manner, for the former's financial benefit. (*See* ELO Ch.18-I(A).) Since D utilized E's picture to promote the opening of its new store, E would assert that the elements of this tort are satisfied. D would probably argue that (1) E consented to her picture being taken, and consent is a defense to this tort, and (2) the local newspaper published E's picture (rather than D) and that therefore the picture was used for news reporting purposes rather than for commercial purposes. E could probably successfully contend in rebuttal that: (1) any purported consent was vitiated by the fact that it was fraudulently obtained by D, and (2) D took the pictures expressly for publicity purposes (see Mana's statements to E), and presumably forwarded them to the newspaper so that they would be published and thus attract customers for the store. E should prevail, and thus be able to recover from D for invasion of privacy. E can recover damages for her embarrassment and mental suffering, damages for the economic value of the use of her photograph, and possibly punitive damages.

E could also conceivably assert an invasion of privacy action against D for causing her to be placed in a false public light, since she was portrayed in the newspaper as a winner of a trip from Disco, when in fact she was not. However, the publication must ordinarily be objectionable to a person of ordinary sensibilities. Since being the winner of a door prize would probably ***not*** be highly offensive to a reasonable person, this contention should fail. (*See* ELO Ch.18-I(E).)

Answer to Question 24

Bank v. Ben ("B") (Disparagement) (Defamation):

Disparagement: The tort of disparagement (sometimes known as "injurious falsehood") occurs where the defendant has intentionally or recklessly made a false statement about the plaintiff's business, with the result of (and in some jurisdictions, for the purpose of) causing the plaintiff economic loss. Bank could assert that this tort occurred as a consequence of B's statement that one of its trust department employees was misusing trust funds (which was spoken in front of 14 customers in a loud voice). B would argue that he made it clear in his statement that he did not believe it was true, and that since he did not assert its truth, it could not constitute a false disparagement. If this jurisdiction requires that he acted out of spite or to interfere with the plaintiff's business, he would argue that these elements are not satisfied; indeed, as a beneficiary of a trust administered by Bank, he clearly has an interest in seeing Bank succeed. Finally, there is no indication from the facts that Bank has suffered any economic loss as a result of B's comment (*i.e.*, loss of customers). (*See* ELO Ch.18-III(B).)

In the event, however, that Bank was successful with respect to the foregoing issues, B might assert the **common interest privilege** as a defense to the former's action. Under this theory, where the party speaking and the party to whom the statement is communicated have a common interest, the statement is **not** actionable if made in good faith and in other than an excessive manner. B could contend that he, as a trust fund beneficiary, and Bank, as the administrator of that trust, had a common interest in making certain that funds were not misused. However, (1) it is unclear as to whether B had a "good faith" basis for his assertion that funds were being misused (*i.e.*, had a previous customer or someone associated with Bank advised B that funds were being misused, or was B simply re-stating a rumor?), and (2) B's statement was probably excessive (*i.e.*, communicated to more people than which was reasonably necessary to protect the interest involved) since it was made in front of 14 persons (instead of communicated directly to Bank's president in the privacy of his/her office). Thus, the common interest privilege probably could **not** be successfully asserted in this instance. (*See* ELO Ch.17-VI(C)(3).)

Defamation: Bank could contend that B slandered it by suggesting that its trust officers were misusing funds in a sufficiently loud voice that 14 persons overheard him. Such a statement would tend to impugn Bank's reputation in the community. The fact that B stated that he did not believe the allegation would not preclude liability. While the facts do not indicate that Bank suffered special damages (*i.e.*, economic loss resulting from its diminished reputation), B's statement is probably **slanderous per se** both because it imputes criminal behavior to Bank and because it implies that Bank is not fit to **conduct** its business. Thus, Bank could recover presumed damages, which are damages for the harm that would ordinarily result from a similar defamatory statement. (*See* ELO Ch.17-III(D).)

The discussion of the common interest privilege (above) would be applicable in this instance also.

Arthur v. B (Defamation):

A's suit against B for defamation would be essentially the same as the **Bank v. B** case discussed above.

B would contend, however, that the statement was *not of and concerning* A, since the latter was never mentioned by name. A could contend, however, that the group alluded to was sufficiently small (*i.e.*, four people) so that B's statement applied to everyone in the class. Although B would assert in rebuttal that his comment did not refer to the entire class (he stated that "one of" Bank's trust employees was misusing funds, as opposed to all of them), A should prevail since the reputations of each of Bank's trust officers was probably impugned by B's statement. (*See* ELO Ch.17-II(D).)

As above, the fact that B indicated that he did not believe the statement to be true would ordinarily be no defense to A's action.

Finally, the discussion of the common interest privilege above would be equally applicable in this instance also.

Bill v. Jane ("J") (Negligent Misrepresentation):

One is liable for negligent misrepresentation where he/she negligently misrepresents a material fact upon which the plaintiff justifiably relies to his/her detriment. The defendant must have been under a duty to exercise due care with respect to the plaintiff (*i.e.*, the information was furnished in a business context in a transaction in which the defendant had a pecuniary interest). Furthermore, the plaintiff must belong to a limited group of persons whom the defendant intended to reach with the information, or whom he knew the recipient intended to reach. (*See* ELO Ch.16-III.)

Bill would argue that J, as a representative of the bank, made the misrepresentation in a business context, and that J had a pecuniary interest in the transaction because she could attract Ed as a customer for the bank by giving him this advice. Bill will argue that J breached this duty to exercise due care created by the business context, because she acted unreasonably by repeating incomplete information obtained in a casual, social context. Bill will argue that it was justifiable for Ed to rely on J's advice, since she was a representative of the bank and the bank presumably answers questions of this sort routinely. Bill will also argue that as an intended heir, he clearly belongs to a limited group of people whom J should have known Ed would intend to reach with the information.

J will argue that the misrepresentation was not given in a business context, since Ed was not a customer of the bank (he was merely accompanying Ben). She will also argue that she had no pecuniary interest in the transaction, because giving Ed advice on making a will did not create possibilities for further business transactions between him and Bank in the way that a free first consultation with an attorney would. J will also argue that Ed's reliance on her statement was not justifiable, since she made the statement totally outside of her usual business (she is a secretary, not an attorney), and thus she should not be liable. Finally, she will assert the *defense of contributory negligence*, arguing that Ed did not act reasonably under the circumstances by relying on advice about will preparation from a secretary; he should have consulted an attorney. (*See* ELO Ch.16-III(D).)

Bill probably will not prevail against J since she is a secretary and not an attorney, which means that Ed probably did not justifiably rely on her advice (unless additional facts show that she appeared to be a trust officer, on whom it is probably justifiable to rely for advice on the requirements for a valid will). Even if his reliance was justifiable, he was probably contributorily negligent by failing to consult a lawyer. Thus, Bill might be able to seek all or some of his damages (depending on whether this is a contributory or comparative negligence jurisdiction) from Ed's estate based on Ed's negligence.

Bill v. Bank (Negligent Misrepresentation):

Bill would also sue Bank for J's negligent misrepresentation on a *respondeat superior* theory. Bill would contend that Bank was vicariously liable for J's statements to him since an employer is ordinarily liable for the torts of its employees committed in the scope of their employment. If J's statement did constitute a negligent misrepresentation, then Bank will be liable as well, since the statement was clearly made in the scope of J's employment at the bank (*i.e.*, while she was at work and to someone seeking advice from Bank). (*See* ELO Ch.12-II(A).) However, as discussed above, it is unlikely that Bill could succeed in his negligent misrepresentation action against J (and therefore his lawsuit against Bank would also fail).

Bill or Jane v. Larry (Negligent Misrepresentation):

Neither Bill nor Jane (Jane might sue if she, *e.g.*, loses her job as a result of this incident) can recover from Larry for negligent misrepresentation because his statement to J probably falls into the category of a "curbstone opinion", an opinion casually given to a social acquaintance in an informal setting. Here, Larry gave the opinion to J outside of the course of his usual professional work, and so he should not be liable for it. (*See* ELO Ch.16-III(B)(1)(a).)

Furthermore, with respect to Bill, Larry probably did not have reason to know that Jane would repeat the information to customers at the bank who would then use that information in preparing their wills. Thus, Larry would not be liable to Bill even if he did make a negligent misrepresentation. (*See* ELO Ch.16-III(C)(1).)

Larry would also have the defense of contributory negligence available to him in the event that he was found to have made a negligent misrepresentation. He would argue that J did not act reasonably under the circumstances by purporting to give legal advice when she had no legal training and by relying on information obtained in a social context. He would argue, as above, that Ed was negligent in not consulting a lawyer.

Answer to Question 25

Mrs. Bird ("B") v. Able ("A") (Intentional Infliction of Mental Distress, Invasion of Privacy):

Mrs. B would sue Able on a vicarious liability theory, asserting that he should be liable as an employer for the torts committed by the private detectives whom he hired. A would argue that the private detectives are not his employees because they were not under his control; instead, they are independent contractors and thus he should not be liable for their torts. Mrs. B will argue that even if they are not his employees, he should be liable for their torts because the work he hired them to do poses a high degree of danger to others, and that the danger that it poses is not that of the common risks to which people are generally exposed as a result of ordinary negligence. Instead, surveillance of private individuals can be performed recklessly, or maliciously for purposes of harassment (as it was here), so that it causes intense mental distress and invasion of privacy. Mrs. B should prevail on this issue. (*See* ELO Ch.12-III(B)(3).)

Intentional Infliction of Mental Distress:

The tort of intentional infliction of mental distress occurs where the plaintiff has intentionally or recklessly engaged in outrageous conduct for the purpose of causing, or which is substantially certain to cause, the plaintiff severe emotional distress. B could contend that A's conduct in having her shadowed, tape-recorded and viewed (via binoculars) in her home satisfied the foregoing standard. Although A might argue in rebuttal that his conduct was not "outrageous" since (1) the tape-recording was merely to determine if there were any factual inaccuracies in her statements, and (2) in a hotly contested public issue such as a zoning amendment it is not unusual for one side to attempt to "dig up dirt" on the other, and thereby discredit the latter's position. Additionally, B could have easily avoided being seen in her home by drawing the window shades. Nevertheless, a court could find that A's conduct was extreme and outrageous, since it used tactics that were clearly personally harassing and verging on threatening in a dispute over zoning policy. A court could also find that A acted intentionally, since A used those tactics in order to upset Mrs. B to the point where she would stop opposing A's position. Furthermore, a court could find that A acted recklessly, since it is foreseeable that a reasonable person would suffer severe emotional distress as a result of being spied on and followed by strangers. Mrs. B can recover for her mental distress and for her psychotherapy expenses. (*See* ELO Ch.2-VII.)

Invasion of Privacy (Intrusion on Solitude):

One who intrudes into an area which the plaintiff would reasonably believe to be private or confidential is liable for invasion of privacy. B would argue that surveillance of her home via binoculars from adjoining buildings constituted an invasion of her solitude. While a reasonable person would find such surveillance highly offensive, A could probably successfully contend that one has no reasonable expectation that persons from adjoining buildings will not attempt to view them with instrumentalities that are readily available to the public. (*See* ELO Ch.18-I(C).)

A v. Cross ("C") (Defamation):

A could contend that C's remark that his proposal (and therefore A himself) was "idiotic" and "stupid" was defamatory (*i.e.*, impugned A's reputation). A could additionally argue that C's statement that A must have been "flying on something" is also defamatory, since it suggests that A had been intoxicated (*i.e.*, via alcohol or drugs). However, C could probably successfully contend in rebuttal that his statements were in the nature of *opinion* and were directed to A's proposal to amend the City's zoning ordinance (rather than a clear statement that A was unintelligent or is ordinarily under the influence of drugs or alcohol). Where an allegedly defamatory remark is made in the context of a public controversy, courts ordinarily allow for some degree of exaggeration. Therefore, C's statements would probably *not* be considered defamatory. (*See* ELO Ch.17-II(F).)

A v. XYTV (Defamation):

Even if C's comments were found to be defamatory, XYTV would probably *not be liable* for repeating them. Because XYTV is a *media* defendant, A is subject to the constitutional limitation of having to prove that XYTV was at least negligent in not ascertaining the falsity of C's statements. The interview was broadcast live, so XYTV did not have an opportunity to verify C's statements. Imposing liability in these circumstances would be tantamount to imposing a rule of *strict liability on broadcasters* for statements made by people not subject to the control of the broadcaster (*i.e.*, not an employee) in live broadcasts. Such a result would be unconstitutional. (*See* ELO Ch.17-V(A).)

C v. A (Interference with Advantageous Relations):

C could sue A for intentional interference with (1) existing contractual relationships, or (2) prospective advantage. *Interference with existing contracts* occurs where the defendant, knowingly and for an improper purpose, induces another to breach an existing contract with the plaintiff. Interference with prospective advantage occurs where the defendant, knowingly and for an improper purpose, has intentionally interfered with a prospective contract which the plaintiff had a substantial likelihood of obtaining. (*See* ELO Ch.18-III(C)-(D).)

C might lose with respect to the tenants who terminated their tenancies at will, since most courts will not hold a defendant liable for inducing one party to terminate a terminable-at-will contract. However, if a court finds that A's means were improper (*i.e.*, the use of threats and a boycott), A will lose the terminable-at-will privilege. If A is liable, C can recover for the pecuniary loss he suffered as a result of A's interference (*i.e.*, the lost rent). The fact that the contract was terminable at will may reduce C's damages (if, *e.g.*, A can show that the tenants were unhappy with their tenancies and would have terminated anyway).

With respect to the tenants whose leases will expire soon, A probably would be liable for **interfering with prospective business relationships** since it probably can be shown that most of these entities would have renewed the leases in the absence of A's threats. While a privilege is recognized for situations where the defendant is merely attempting to acquire the business for him/herself, in this instance A was attempting to undermine C's advocacy against altering the existing zoning ordinance. (*See* ELO Ch.18-III(D)(1).) While A might contend in rebuttal that dissuading someone from a position which would cause him to lose a financial opportunity is a proper purpose, this argument would probably fail. Therefore, C should be able to recover for any losses resulting from the loss of tenancies caused by A's threats. C would, however, presumably be obliged to avoid damages to the extent that it were possible to acquire new tenants for any premises subsequently vacated. While C could also seek punitive damages, these might not be awarded since A's threats to the suppliers may, to some extent, have been a response to C's uncomplimentary remarks on the television broadcast.

Multiple-Choice Questions

Questions 1-4 are based on the following fact situation:

Motorco is a manufacturer of motor vehicles. A federal regulation requires that all motor vehicles manufactured for sale in the United States be equipped with a seat belt for each passenger and prescribes specifications for the belts. Motorco equipped all its cars with seat belts. It purchased all the bolts used in its seat belt assembly from Boltco and it tested samples from each shipment received.

Dunn purchased a motor vehicle manufactured by Motorco. While operating the car, with Price as a passenger in the front seat, Dunn collided with another vehicle. The collision was caused solely by Dunn's negligence. Price had his seat belt fastened, but one of the bolts which anchored the belt to the frame broke. Price was thrown through the windshield, sustaining various injuries. Dunn, whose belt was fastened and held, was killed when, following the collision, the car went off the road, slid down an embankment, and overturned.

Subsequent to the accident, tests of the bolt that broke showed stress in the metal itself. Motorco's records showed that tests of samples taken from the shipment in which the defective bolt was contained had revealed no defective bolts.

1. If there is a guest statute in the state where the accident happened, then in any action by Price against Motorco, that guest statute has which of the following effects?

    (A) It bars recovery by Price.
    (B) It bars recovery by Price unless he can prove that Dunn was culpable of more than ordinary negligence.
    (C) It bars recovery by Price unless he can prove that Motorco was culpable of more than ordinary negligence.
    (D) It is not relevant.

2. In a negligence action by Price against Motorco, the proof needed to establish a *prima facie* case is

    (A) Only that the bolt was defective.
    (B) That the bolt was defective and had not been inspected by Motorco.
    (C) That the bolt was defective and was inspected by Motorco.
    (D) That the bolt was defective, that it should have been inspected, and that the defect would have been discovered if Motorco had exercised reasonable care in the inspection of component parts .

3. In a negligence action by Price against Motorco, the negligence of Dunn will be deemed:

(A) Within the risk created by the action of Motorco.

(B) The sole proximate cause of Price's injuries.

(C) The sole legal cause of Price's injuries.

(D) An independent, superseding cause of Price's injuries .

4. In a negligence action by Price against Motorco, a defense that is likely to prevail is that

    (A) Motorco exercised due care in testing the bolts.

    (B) Dunn's negligence was the legal cause of Price's injuries.

    (C) Price was a passenger in Dunn's car.

    (D) Boltco, as the manufacturer of the bolts, has the sole responsibility for any defects therein.

5. One night Paul and David were having a heated argument in Paul's office on the 40th floor of an office building. David became angry and left, slamming the office door violently behind him. The force of David's action caused the lock to jam and Paul was unable to open the door or to leave his office until a locksmith was able to come the next day.

    If Paul asserts a claim against David based on false imprisonment, will Paul prevail?

    (A) Yes, because David's act caused Paul to be confined.

    (B) Yes, if David was negligent in slamming the door.

    (C) No, because Paul was in his own office.

    (D) No, if David did not intend to jam the lock.

6. Daniel owned a restored "classic" automobile made in 1922. To discourage tampering with the car, Daniel installed an electrical device designed to give a mild shock, enough to warn, but not to harm, persons touching the car. Paul, a heart patient with a pacemaker, saw Daniel's car and attempted to open the door so that he could sit and inspect the inside. Paul received a mild shock which would not have harmed an ordinary individual but which caused his pacemaker to malfunction, resulting in a fatal heart attack.

    If Paul's estate asserts a claim against Daniel for the wrongful death of Paul, will the estate prevail?

    (A) No, because Daniel was not using excessive force to protect his car.

    (B) No, because Paul was a trespasser.

    (C) Yes, because Daniel's act was a substantial factor in causing Paul's death.

    (D) Yes, because Paul had no reason to suspect the presence of the electrical device.

Questions 7-8 are based on the following fact situation:

Paul was nine years old and a third-grade student in Lincoln School. While playing in the school yard during the recess period, Paul started an unprovoked fight with David, ten years old and a student in the fourth grade. David kicked Paul in the leg to drive him away. As a result of the kick, Paul suffered a fracture of the tibia.

Through an appropriate legal representative, Paul, has asserted claims for damages against David and against the school.

7. Will Paul prevail on his claim against David?

   (A) Yes, because David kicked Paul.
   (B) Yes, if David outweighed Paul.
   (C) No, unless David used excessive force.
   (D) No, if Paul's bones were unusually brittle.

8. Will Paul prevail on his claim against the school?

   (A) Yes, because the fight took place on school premises.
   (B) Yes, because the fight took place during the recess period.
   (C) No because Paul was the person who actually started the fight.
   (D) No, unless the school district failed to use reasonable care in supervising the school premises.

9. Boater owned a power boat which he was operating on Lake Tutu, a large body of water, on a clear, calm day. He approached Sailer whose sailboat was disabled by a broken rudder. Sailer asked Boater to tow his sailboat to shore but Boater refused because he feared the tow might damage the paint on his power boat.

   Sailer was unable to bring his sailboat in and became severely ill from exposure before he was rescued. Sailer now asserts a claim against Boater for damages based on Boater's refusal to provide assistance. Will Sailer prevail?

   (A) Yes, because Boater's failure to rescue Sailer worsened the situation.
   (B) Yes, if the probability of harm to Sailer outweighed the probability of damage to Boater's property.
   (C) No, unless there was some special relationship between Sailer and Boater.
   (D) No, if Boater reasonably believed that towing Sailer's sailboat might damage the paint on Boater's power boat.

10. Owner took his television set to Repairer for repair. Repairer sold the set to Buyer. Buyer believed that Repairer owned the set.

If Owner asserts a claim based on conversion against Repairer and Buyer, Owner will prevail against

(A) Repairer but not Buyer, because Buyer was a good faith purchaser.

(B) Both Repairer and Buyer, because each exercised dominion over the television set.

(C) Buyer but not Repairer because Repairer no longer has possession of the television set.

(D) Buyer but not Repairer because Repairer had lawful possession of the television set.

Questions 11-12 are based on the following fact situation:

Al lived in a home adjacent to a large stretch of open fields. One afternoon Al took his dog, on leash, for a walk across the fields. Unknown to Al, Burt was also in the field, engaging in target practice with his revolver.

Burt was hidden from Al's view by a small clump of trees. As Al walked with his dog, past the clump of trees, Burt fired at a target that he had pinned up to one of the trees. The sound of the explosion frightened Al's dog, which broke the leash and ran. The dog bit the first person he saw. This happened to be Charles, who was walking in the field about 100 feet from Al.

11. If Charles asserts a claim for damages against Al, will Charles prevail?

    (A) Yes, because Al owned the dog.
    (B) Yes, because the dog escaped from Al's control.
    (C) No, unless the dog had previously bitten some other person.
    (D) No, unless Al was negligent in not restraining the dog.

12. If Charles asserts a claim against Burt for damages for the dog bite, will Charles prevail?

    (A) Yes, because Burt's firing the gun caused the dog to run away.
    (B) Yes, because firing a gun is an abnormally dangerous activity.
    (C) No, because injury to Charles from a dog bite was not a foreseeable consequence of Burt's act.
    (D) No, because the breaking of the leash was an independent, intervening force.

13. Joe and Tom saw Bill's new automobile parked on a street. They decided to take the automobile for a joyride. Joe drove the automobile a few blocks before he turned the wheel over to Tom, who drove the car into a truck. The collision totally destroyed Bill's car.

If Bill obtains a judgment against Joe based on conversion and Joe pays the judgment, may Joe compel Tom to reimburse him for any part of the amount paid to Bill?

(A) Yes, on a theory of implied indemnity.

(B) Yes, because Tom was a joint tortfeasor.

(C) No, unless Bill had joined Tom as a party defendant in the action.

(D) No, because Bill's judgment was based on conversion.

NO CONTRIBUTION FOR INTENTIONAL TORTS

Questions 14-17 are based on the following fact situation:

Driver was operating his auto at a negligently excessive speed. As a result, he lost control and hit Walker, a pedestrian on the sidewalk along the road. Pat, age 13, arrived at the scene several minutes latter. Pat saw that Walker was in obvious need of medical attention, so she ran into the ground floor lobby of Highrise, a nearby apartment building owned by Realty, to telephone for help. There was no telephone in the lobby, so Pat dashed through a door marked "Stairs" and up a concrete stairway leading to the second-floor landing. She tripped over a skateboard which was lying on the second-floor landing, fell and fractured an ankle. Prior to the accident, neither Realty's resident manager nor the maintenance staff employed by Realty at Highrise had known that the skateboard was on the landing.

14. If Pat asserts a claim against Driver based on negligence and Driver does not raise the issue of contributory negligence, will Pat prevail?

RESCUERS

(A) Yes, because Pat's attempt to telephone for help was foreseeable.

(B) No, because Driver could not have foreseen the skateboard.

(C) No, because Pat was not in the zone of impact danger.

(D) No, because the presence of the skateboard on the landing was a superseding cause.

15. Assume Pat lived in Hightower. If Pat asserts a claim against Driver based on negligence, and Driver claims Pat was contributorily negligent, which of the following facts should be taken into account by the jury and court in determining whether Driver will prevail on the issue?

I.   Pat was 13 years of age.

II. Walker was in obvious need of medical attention.

III. Pat lived in Highrise and knew that items were sometimes left in the hallways and stairwells of the apartment house.

(A) I, II and III.

(B) I and II but not III.

(C) II and III but not I.

16. Assume Pat did not live in Hightower. If Pat asserts a claim against Realty based on negligence and Realty does not raise the issue of assumption of risk, the likely result is that Pat will

(A) Prevail, because Realty's employees had a duty to discover and remove the skateboard.

(B) Prevail, because Realty's failure to provide a public telephone in the lobby created an unreasonable risk to its tenants.

(C) Not prevail, if a tenant of Highrise had left the skateboard on the landing just prior to Pat's fall.

(D) Not prevail, because Pat was a trespasser on Realty's property when she fell.

17. If Pat asserts a claim against Realty based on negligence for failing to remove the skateboard and if Realty claims that Pat assumed the risk, will Realty prevail on that issue?

(A) Yes, because Pat dashed recklessly onto the second-floor landing.

(B) Yes, if Pat should have seen the skateboard.

(C) No, because Pat was 13 years of age.

(D) No, because Pat did not see the skateboard.

Questions 18-20 are based on the following fact situation:

Jeff, who was 17 years old, was given a new speedboat by his wealthy parents. The internal controls of the boat had been defectively manufactured. They caused the boat to go backwards when the direction lever was moved toward the "Forward" position, and forward when it was moved toward the "Reverse" position. This fact was known to Jeff and his parents, who learned to use the boat despite the defect. A state law prohibited minors (anyone under the age of 18) from operating a speedboat without the presence and supervision of an adult,. But Jeff decided anyway to make a short trip to a nearby island by himself. He placed the key in the ignition, and then decided to purchase a sandwich and soda at a diner one block from the dock. Unfortunately, Jeff neglected to remove the ignition key before leaving the boat.

Mark, a 16-year-old who had been watching Jeff, decided it would be fun to take the boat for a brief jaunt. He turned the ignition key to start the vessel and moved the lever to the "Forward" position. The boat lurched backwards, causing a huge dent in a boat owned by Jill, damage to Jeff's boat and injuries to Mark

18. If Jill sues Jeff for the damage to her craft, the fact that Jeff violated the statute

- (A) IS one factor in determining Jeff's liability.
- (B) Establishes Jeff's liability as a matter of law.
- (C) Establishes Jeff's liability as a matter of law, unless his conduct was excusable.
- (D) Is irrelevant in determining Jeff's liability.

19. If Mark sues Jeff for his personal injuries, Jeff would most likely assert that Mark

- (A) Had committed a criminal act.
- (B) Assumed the risk of operating the boat.
- (C) Acted unreasonably in operating the boat without permission.
- (D) Jeff's breach of duty did not cause Mark's injuries.

20. If Jeff sues Mark for damage to his boat, Jeff will most likely recover:

- (A) Because Mark did not have an adult with him.
- (B) Because Mark intentionally took the boat.
- (C) Because Mark's conduct is punishable as a crime. *(CAN RECOVER CIVIL & CRIM)*
- (D) Because Mark, despite his age, is held to the standard of care of a reasonable person. *(NOT NEGLIGENT CONDUCT)*

21. John bought a package of bologna from Don's Supermarket. It was packaged by Packo, which delivered the sealed packages in airtight plastic. John made a sandwich with the bologna for his wife Nancy. When Nancy bit into the sandwich, she was seriously injured by a small nail embedded in the bologna.

If Nancy sues Don on a negligence theory, she will most likely

- (A) Recover, on the theory of *res ipsa loquitur.*
- (B) Recover, on the theory that Packo was negligent and Don is liable for the negligence.
- (C) Not recover, because Packo actually sealed the bologna.
- (D) Not recover, because John (not Nancy) purchased the bologna.

Questions 22-23 are based on the following fact situation:

John was driving through a rural area on his way to a job interview. Suddenly, a moose started to run across the road. John quickly applied his brakes, but struck the animal anyway. He had been driving within the speed limit. Ellwood, a local resident who saw the accident, walked over to look at the moose. He told John, who had stopped his vehicle and gotten out, that it was already dead. John said, "Well, there's nothing we can do" and drove away. Ellwood walked away. Ten minutes later, Phil drove along the road, also within the speed limit. Phil struck the slain moose, causing damage to his car and injury to himself.

22. If Phil sues John, who will prevail?

    (A) John, because he was driving within the speed limit when he hit the moose.

    (B) John, because he was under no legal duty to remove the moose from the road.

    (C) Phil, because he did not assume the risk of hitting the moose.

    (D) Phil, if he was not contributorily negligent.

23. If Phil sues Ellwood, who will prevail?

    (A) Ellwood, because it was John who hit the moose.

    (B) Ellwood, because John never specifically asked Ellwood for assistance in removing the moose.

    (C) Phil, because Ellwood, having witnessed the accident, was obligated to remove the moose from the road.

    (D) Phil, because he was driving within the speed limit when the accident occurred.

Questions 24-26 are based on the following fact situation:

For Son's seventh birthday, Father bought Son a small bicycle at Hardware. The bicycle was manufactured by Bikeco.

A week later, Son asked Sis, his 11-year old sister, to get out his new bicycle so he could show her how well he could ride it. Sis went to the garage, sat on the bicycle seat and began to "walk" the bicycle between the two family cars and out of the garage.

As Sis neared the doorway of the garage, the rod on which the seat was mounted snapped, causing Sis to fall backward over the bicycle and to suffer severe head injuries. Friend, standing a few feet from Sis, was horrified to see what happened to Sis, but she suffered no other harm.

Most bicycle manufacturers make the supporting rods for seats from a metal which is much stronger than the metal used by Bikeco. The use of the stronger metal increases the cost of manufacture by about $1.50 a bicycle.

24. If Sis asserts a claim against Bikeco based on strict liability in tort the likely result is that Sis will

(A) Recover, if use such as hers was foreseeable.

(B) Recover, because Bikeco can spread the risk of loss.

(C) Not recover, if the bicycle was intended for use by small children.

(D) Not recover, because the bicycle was purchased for Son.

25. If Sis asserts a claim against Hardware based on strict liability in tort, is it likely that Sis will prevail?

(A) Yes, if the bicycle was defective.

(B) Yes, but only if Hardware could have discovered the defect by a reasonable inspection.

(C) No, because Hardware sold the bicycle in exactly the same condition as that in which it was received.

(D) No, because Sis was not in privity with Hardware.

26. If Friend asserts a claim against Bikeco based on mental distress, is it likely that Friend will prevail?

(A) Yes, if the bicycle was inherently dangerous.

(B) Yes, because Friend was within a few feet of Sis when she was injured.

(C) No, because Friend was not using the product when the accident occurred.

(D) No, because although Friend was horrified, she suffered no other harm.

27. Cattle Company paid $30,000 for a tract of land ideally suited for a cattle feed lot. The tract was ten miles from Metropolis, then a community of 50,000 people, and five miles from the nearest home. Six years later, the city limits has extended to Cattle Company's feed lot and has a population of 350,000. About 10,000 people live within three miles of the cattle feeding operation.

Cattle Company uses the best and most sanitary feed lot procedures to keep down flies and odors. Despite these measures, an action has been filed by five individual homeowners who live within half a mile of the Cattle Company feed lot. The plaintiffs' homes are currently valued at $25,000 each. Recently, flies in the plaintiffs' area have become ten times more numerous than in other parts of Metropolis. The flies and odors are identified as a substantial health hazard.

If plaintiffs assert a claim based on private nuisance, plaintiffs will

(A) Prevail, because Cattle Company's activity unreasonably interferes with plaintiffs' use and enjoyment of their property.

(B) Prevail, because Cattle Company's activity is being carried on in a negligent manner.

(C) Not prevail, because Cattle Company has operated the feed lot for more than 5 years.

(D) Not prevail, because Cattle Company uses the most reasonable procedures to keep down flies and odors.

28. Susie Blake, a working woman, always carried her lunch to eat in the office. One Saturday afternoon she went to Roger's Market, a local self-service grocery, and bought a can of corned beef. The can had printed on its label "A Product of West Beef Company." The company was a reputable supplier of beef products. On Sunday evening, Susie prepared a sandwich for her lunch the next day, using the can of corned beef she had bought on Saturday. When Susie bit into her sandwich at lunch time the next day, a large sliver of bone concealed in the corned beef pierced her gum, broke off one of her teeth, and lodged deep in the roof of her mouth. This accident caused her severe pain and medical expenses of $700.

Susie brought two claims for damage: one against Roger's Market and the other against West Beef Company. The claims were tried together. At the trial, Susie proved all of the above facts leading up to her injury, as well as the elements of her damage. West Beef Company, one of the defendants, proved that it had not processed and packed the meat, but that an independent supplier, Meat Packers, Inc., had. West Beef Company further proved that it had never previously obtained defective meat products from Meat Packers, Inc., and that it had no way of knowing that the can contained any dangerous material. Roger's Market, the other defendant, proved that it had no way of knowing the contents of the can were likely to cause harm, and that it had sold the products of West Beef Company for a number of years without ever having been told by a customer that the products were defective. Both defendants agreed by stipulation in open court that Meat Packers, Inc. had been negligent in packing the corned beef containing the sliver of bone.

If Susie's claim against West Beef Company is based on the theory of strict liability in tort, Susie will

(A) Recover, because the can contained a sliver of bone when the defendant sold it.

(B) Recover, because any breach of warranty chargeable to Roger's Market would be imputed to the defendant.

(C) Not recover, because there was not privity of contract between her and the defendant.

(D) Not recover, because any breach of warranty was that of Meat Packers, Inc. and not that of the defendant.

29. Householder resented the fact that joggers and walkers would sometimes come onto his property along the sidewalk and just outside his fence, in order to enjoy the feel of walking or running on grass. He put up a sign, "No Trespassing," but it did not stop the practice. He then put up a sign, "Beware of Skunk," and bought a young skunk which he intended to tie to the fence. He took the skunk to Dr. Vet to have its scent gland removed. Unfortunately, Dr. Vet did not perform the operation properly, and the scent gland was not removed. Householder was unaware that it had not been removed.

One day Walker was out for a stroll. When she came to Householder's property, she walked on the grass alongside the sidewalk onto Householder's property. The skunk came up behind Walker and sprayed her with its scent. The smell was overpowering, and she fainted. She struck her head on the sidewalk and suffered serious injuries.

The probable result of Walker's claim against Householder is that she will

(A) Recover, because the skunk was a private nuisance.

(B) Recover, because the skunk was not a domesticated animal.

(C) Not recover, because Walker was a trespasser.

(D) Not recover, because Dr. Vet's negligence was the cause of her injury.

Questions 30-31 are based on the following fact situation:

Actor, a well-known film star, was photographed by a freelance photographer, while sitting at a sidewalk cafe, drinking beer and with a bottle of Foamus Light Beer on the table in front of him. The picture was reproduced in Magazine, a publication containing stories and articles about the film industry, in connection with a story about the eating and drinking tastes of film stars. The label on the beer bottle was clearly visible in the picture.

The following month, advertisements for Foamus Light Beer appeared in other publications and carried a reproduction of the page from Magazine on which Actor's picture appeared, with the heading "Drink the beer that movie stars drink."

30. If Actor asserts a claim against Magazine, will Actor prevail?

(A) Yes, if Actor had not authorized any use of the picture.

(B) Yes, because Magazine was using Actor's picture for its commercial purposes.

(C) No, because Actor's picture was taken in a public place.

(D) No, if Actor's career was advanced by the publicity.

31. If Actor asserts a claim against Foamus Light Beer based on the advertisements in the other publications, will Actor prevail?

(A) Yes, if Actor had not consented to having his picture taken.

(B) Yes, if Actor had not consented to Foamus Light Beer using Actor's picture for commercial purposes.

(C) No, because Actor's picture had already appeared in Magazine.

(D) No, if Actor was already a public figure.

32. Alma, a well-known literary critic, wrote a review of the latest book written by Bessy, a well-known author. In the review, Alma said that Bessy did not use the English language effectively and that the political and social views expressed in the book were "inane." Bessy has not suffered any pecuniary loss.

If Bessy asserts a claim against Alma based on defamation, Bessy will *not* recover

(A) Because Bessy is a well-known author.

(B) Because Alma's literary criticism is an expression of opinion.

(C) Because Alma's remarks could be regarded as implied assertions of fact.

(D) Because Bessy did not suffer any out-of-pocket loss.

33. Caster, who conducted an evening news broadcast on television, reported on one of his evening broadcasts that Teacher, an instructor in a private school in the community, was being discharged for incompetence. The fact was that Teacher was not being discharged for incompetence but was leaving to accept a better position at another school.

If Teacher asserts a claim against Caster based on defamation, Teacher will not prevail if Caster

(A) Used reasonable care to investigate the statement prior to his broadcast.

(B) Honestly believed the statement to be true at the time of the broadcast.

(C) Promptly retracted the statement upon learning of its falsity.

(D) Had no ill-will toward Teacher.

34. Purchaser paid Vendor $50,000 for a deed to a parcel of land in reliance on Vendor's statement that the land was free from encumbrances Vendor knew that the land was subject to a recorded and unsatisfied mortgage of $15,000. Immediately after the closing, Purchaser was offered $60,000 for the land.

If Purchaser asserts a claim for damages against Vendor, will Purchaser prevail?

(A) Yes, because Purchaser has been damaged.

(B) Yes, unless a reasonable person in Purchaser's position would have discovered the mortgage before purchase.

(C) No, because the land was worth more than the purchaser paid for it.

(D) No, if Vendor is willing to return Purchaser's money and cancel the transaction.

Questions 35-36 are based on the following fact situation:

Mrs. Ritter, a widow, recently purchased a new uncrated electric range for her kitchen from Local Retailer. The range has a wide oven with a large oven door. The crate in which Stove Company, the manufacturer, shipped the range carried a warning label on the oven door that the stove would tip over if a weight of 25 pounds or more were placed on the door. Mrs. Ritter has one child — Brenda, aged 3. Brenda was playing on the floor of the kitchen while Mrs. Ritter was heating water in a pan on top of the stove. The telephone rang and Mrs. Ritter went into the living room to answer it. While she was gone Brenda decided to see what was cooking in the pan. She opened the oven door and leaned on it with all her weight (28 pounds) to see what was in the pan. Brenda's weight on the door caused the stove to tip over and fall forward. Brenda fell to the floor and the hot water in the pan spilled over her, burning her severely. Brenda screamed. Mrs. Ritter ran to the kitchen and immediately gave her first aid treatment for burns. Brenda thereafter received medical treatment.

Brenda's burns were painful. They have now healed and do not hurt, but she has ugly scars on her legs and back. Brenda's claim is asserted on her behalf by the proper party.

35. If Brenda asserts a claim based on strict liability against Stove Company, she must establish that

(A) The defendant negligently designed the stove.

(B) Stoves made by other manufacturers do not turn over with a 25-pound weight on the oven door.

(C) The defendant failed to warn the Ritters that the stove would turn over easily.

(D) The stove was defective and unreasonably dangerous to her.

36. If Brenda asserts a claim based on strict liability against Local Retailer, she must establish that

(A) Local Retailer did not inform Mrs. Ritter of the warning on the crate.

(B) The stove was substantially in the same condition at the time it tipped over as when it was purchased from Local Retailer.

(C) Local Retailer made some changes in the stove design or had improperly assembled it so that it tipped over more easily.

(D) Local Retailer knew or should have known that the stove was dangerous because of the ease with which it was tipped over.

37. Bill liked to dance. One evening he went to his usual hangout—a local disco. As he entered, he heard what sounded to him like a gunshot. Everyone stopped dancing for a moment and looked around. Someone yelled, "You got me, Bart. See you on the other side." As everyone else knew, the statement was made by someone in jest. But Bill believed that someone had fired a gun and panicked. He ran towards the exit as fast as he could, colliding into several people who were trying to get in. Joan, one of the persons whom he inadvertently knocked down, suffered a broken arm when she fell to the floor. The "shot" was actually caused by the backfire of a car outside the disco.

Based upon the foregoing, if Joan sues Bill for battery, it is most likely that:

(A) Joan will prevail because the impact upon her was substantially certain to occur as Bill ran to the exit.

(B) Bill will prevail because he did not intend to injure anyone as he fled.

(C) Bill will prevail because he honestly believed that a gun had actually been fired.

(D) Bill will prevail because an injury to Joan or anyone else was not reasonably foreseeable.

38. Joe lived in a home in Central City. While looking out his window one day, Joe saw Bart dealing in drugs to the local teenagers. Intending to frighten Bart away, Joe bought a toy gun. The gun looked very real. When Joe saw Bart again in front of his home, he approached Bart and said, "Get away from my house. If you don't, you'll be sorry." As he made the statement, Joe opened his overcoat so that Bart could see the toy gun. Bart sensed that Joe was bluffing, but afraid that Joe might call the police, Bart walked away. As he left, Bart yelled to Joe, "Okay, Hondo, I'm out of here."

Based upon the foregoing, if Bart sues Joe, it is most likely that:

(A) Bart will prevail because Joe has committed an assault.

(B) Bart will prevail because Joe has committed an intentional infliction of emotional distress.

(C) Joe will prevail because Bart was engaged in illegal conduct.

(D) Joe will prevail because Bart was not afraid of him.

39. Arthur is a student at Podunk Law School. He often types his briefs in a room at the law school designated for typists. One evening, about two hours before

the law library was to close, Arthur felt unusually tired. Alone in the typing room, he lay down on the floor behind his desk and fell into a deep sleep. The janitor opened the door to the room and looked to see if anyone was left, but failed to see Arthur lying on the floor. He locked the door behind him. Arthur awoke suddenly about 2:00am and turned the lights on, only to find that the door was locked. Realizing that he would have to stay in the library all night, Arthur fell back to sleep again. When he awoke the next morning, he found that he had several animal bites on his legs and arms. He assumed he'd been bitten by a rat.

Based upon the foregoing, if Arthur sues the school for false imprisonment, it is most likely that:

(A) Arthur will prevail because he was confined to the room against his will.
(B) Arthur will prevail because the janitor was negligent in failing to walk through the typing room to look for students.
- (C) The school will prevail because the janitor never saw Arthur.
(D) Arthur will prevail because he suffered physical injury as a consequence of the confinement.

40. Max had to take a bus to Crescent City to pick up a new car. Unknown to Max, the bus line had received several bomb threats the previous day. As Max attempted to board the bus, the driver announced that every passenger had to submit to a "pat down" search by security personnel. Anyone refusing to do so would not be permitted on the bus. Max had been abused as a child and was unusually sensitive to touching. However, he reluctantly submitted to the "pat down." Nothing was found on Max, and he was permitted to board the bus. Ten minutes later, he became ill and vomited.

If Max sues the bus line for battery, it is most likely that:

(A) Max will prevail because he was prevented from boarding the bus without submitting to the "pat down."
(B) Max will prevail because he suffered physical harm as a consequence of the "pat down."
(C) The bus line will prevail only if its judgment in requiring the "pat down." was reasonable.
(D) The bus line will prevail because Max consented to the touching.

41. Bill and Joe were partners in a retail carpet business. One day, as Bill was parking his car about one block from their store, he saw two burly men beating Joe up. Impressed by the brawn of the attackers, Bill did not interfere. But he was very upset by the incident and now becomes violently ill whenever he recalls the attack. Bill's wife, Anne, has also been upset by the fear that the

men may come after Bill. Joe's attackers were recently identified. They are two customers who believe that Joe overcharged them for an oriental rug.

Based upon the foregoing, if Bill sues Joe's attackers for intentional infliction of severe emotional distress, it is most likely that:

(A) Bill will prevail under the transferred intent doctrine.

(B) Bill will prevail because he actually suffered physical harm as a consequence of the attack.

(C) Bill will not prevail unless he and Joe were related.

(D) Bill will not prevail because he was not a person upon whom the customers intended to inflict emotional distress.

42. Tim planned to shoot Frank from the fourth floor of an apartment building as Frank drove by the building. Tim shot his rifle at Frank but missed. The rifle had a very effective silencer and the shot was not heard by anyone. The bullet hit a grassy area behind Frank, and Frank drove on, unaware that he had been shot at. Before Tim could re-aim, Frank had disappeared from sight. A week later, the police found the bullet and notified Frank of the attempt to kill him. Frank became hysterical and has suffered nagging stomach pains and crippling anxiety.

Based upon the foregoing, if Frank sues Tim:

(A) Frank will prevail if he alleges assault.

(B) Frank will prevail if he alleges battery.

(C) Frank will prevail if he alleges intentional infliction of severe emotional distress.

(D) Frank will not prevail.

43. Jack and Dan were hostile neighbors. One afternoon, Jack decided to picnic in a nearby forest. Following a path through the forest, he lost his way and walked through Dan's land. Hungry, tired and overheated, Jack stopped at an opening in the forest, tore some branches off a Linden tree and picked some apples and peaches, which he proceeded to eat. Jack never knew he had entered Dan's land; he believed that he was on public land. While Jack was eating the fruit, Dan appeared and informed Jack that he was on Dan's land. Dan sued Jack for trespass. Jack has several expert witnesses who will testify that Dan's land was not diminished in value by Jack's actions.

If Dan sues Jack for trespass:

(A) Dan will prevail because Jack entered upon his land.

(B) Dan will prevail because Jack caused damage (however minor) to Dan's land.

(C) Jack will prevail because he did not intend to enter upon Dan's land.

(D) Jack will prevail if Dan cannot prove any loss to the fair market value of his land.

44. Albert and Bill were neighbors. Albert installed a basketball net over the front door of his garage and would often "shoot baskets", sometimes as late as 10:00 p.m. Bill complained to Albert several times about the noise and the late hours. One night, Bill decided to water his lawn and plants before going to bed. Angry with Albert, he deliberately directed his hose at Albert's driveway and net, hoping that the water would prevent Albert from shooting baskets. Albert saw the puddles of water on his driveway but decided to shoot baskets anyway. After a few minutes, he slipped and fell and was unable to get up. His wife called a doctor, who diagnosed his injury as a multiple fracture of the left leg.

If Albert sues Bill for his injury:

(A) Albert can recover for trespass.

– (B) Albert can recover for negligence.

(C) Albert can recover under the nuisance doctrine.

(D) Albert cannot recover, since Bill never actually entered upon Albert's land.

45. Howard stole a television set from Randy's home. He took the set to the local flea market, where he sold it to Jessie for $50. Jessie took it home, confident that the set was lawfully his. In carrying the set into his house, Jessie accidentally scraped it against the door. This cut a deep groove along the side of the set. As it happened, Jessie and Randy were good friends and one evening Jessie invited Randy to his home. Jessie turned on the television set and Randy realized that this was the set that had been stolen from him. Randy picked the set up and told Jessie that he was going to take it home with him. Jessie responded, "No way," and stood in front of the set with his fists raised. Anxious to avoid a fight, Randy turned and left.

If Randy sues Jessie for conversion:

(A) Randy will prevail because Jessie damaged the television set.

(B) Randy will prevail because Jessie bought the set intending to own it.

(C) Jessie will prevail because he paid for the set in good faith without notice that the set had been stolen.

(D) Jessie will prevail if he can show that Randy failed to exercise reasonable care in protecting the set from being stolen.

46. Exco Company sent its employee, Joe, to repossess a motor home purchased by Owner. When Joe arrived, Owner objected and stated that he was current in his payments. Owner thought this was the case, although he had absentmindedly forgotten to pay the last two installments. As Joe was about to tow the motor home off, Owner defiantly mounted the steps to the doorway. Joe advised Owner, "You had better get off, or you might fall." Despite this warning, Owner remained on the steps. As Joe started to drive off, Owner slipped off and fell to the ground. Owner sustained a broken hip as a consequence of the fall.

If Owner sues:

(A) Exco will prevail because Owner owed two installments to the defendant.
(B) Exco will prevail because Owner assumed the risk of falling off the steps.
(C) Owner will prevail because Exco had no right to remove the motor home.
(D) Owner will prevail because he believed in good faith that he was current in his payments.

47. Anthony was playing basketball at a public schoolyard. Leo, who was the same size as Anthony, ran up to Anthony and grabbed his basketball. When Anthony attempted to retrieve the basketball, Leo pulled a knife with a four-inch blade from his belt. Leo took a single step toward Anthony, but Anthony suddenly pulled a pistol from underneath his sweatshirt, and shot Leo. Anthony had no license to carry a concealed weapon, or to own a gun. Leo required extensive and expensive surgery, but ultimately lived.

Based on the foregoing, if Leo sues Anthony for battery, it is most likely that:

(A) Leo will prevail because Anthony had no right to use deadly force in defense of property. ✓
(B) Leo will prevail because Anthony never shouted "Stop."
(C) Leo will prevail because Anthony's possession of the gun was illegal.
(D) Anthony will prevail because he was entitled to utilize deadly force under the circumstances.   KNIFE = SERIOUS BODILY INJURY ; FORCE = REASONABLE

48. Xavier and Chuck were watching a football game in a bar. It soon became obvious that they were cheering for opposing teams and they began to taunt each other. Finally, their bickering became so intense that they decided to "go outside" and settle things in a "manly" way. They both intended a fist fight. Once outside of the bar, Chuck formally challenged Xavier and raised his fists in a "boxing" pose. Xavier let loose with a left jab that struck Chuck in the chin. Chuck did not know — and Xavier did not tell him — that Xavier had boxed for his college boxing team. Chuck fell to the ground but got up quickly. He was not significantly injured by Xavier's jab.

If Chuck sues Xavier for battery, it is most likely that:

(A) Chuck will prevail because he was unaware that Xavier was a boxer.

(B) Chuck will prevail if we assume that fistfights in a public area were illegal in this jurisdiction.

(C) Xavier will prevail because Chuck consented to being hit by Xavier.

(D) Xavier will prevail because Chuck initiated the fight by raising his fists.

49. Aaron and Eddie hated and taunted each other. One day, Eddie accosted Aaron's girlfriend and made lewd and lascivious remarks about Aaron. When Aaron heard about this, he went after Eddie and lunged at him. Aaron was 4" taller and 22 pounds heavier than Eddie. Unknown to Aaron, Eddie was a prominent karate expert who taught advanced self-defense techniques at a local karate gym. Eddie was able to block all of Aaron's punches, and to kick Aaron in the right leg. Although Eddie only intended to disable Aaron, the blow caused Aaron serious arterial injury. Eddie did not know that Aaron had previously had a major operation upon that leg.

If Aaron sues Eddie for battery, it is likely that:

(A) Aaron will prevail because his attack upon Eddie was justified by Aaron's comments.

(B) Aaron will prevail because Eddie used unreasonable force in protecting himself.

(C) Eddie will prevail because he was defending himself from serious bodily harm.

(D) Eddie will prevail because Aaron had no legal right to attack Eddie.

50. Darren was told that Sam was secretly dating his (Darren's) girl. Darren was furious at the news and decided to attack Sam with a knife. He happened to see Sam the next day as Sam was leaving a supermarket. Sam is a prominent karate expert, who is trained in aggressive, self-defense techniques. Darren lunged at Sam with his knife, but Sam blocked Darren's move and simultaneously punched Darren in the stomach. Darren fell to the ground, but Sam stood his ground instead of running away. After a few seconds, Darren recovered his breath and lunged at Sam again. Sam again blocked Darren's blow. This time, he kicked Darren in the left knee, breaking it.

If Darren sues Sam for battery, the likely result is:

(A) Darren will prevail because Sam could have escaped and avoided the second attack by Darren.

(B) Darren will prevail if Sam could have seized Darren's knife without serious risk to himself.

(∅) Sam will prevail if Darren was illegally carrying the knife.

(D) Sam will prevail because his conduct was privileged.

Questions 51-52 are based upon the following fact situation:

The State of Utopia has a law which provides that hotels, motels and other establishments that have accommodations for eight or more overnight guests, must have at least two fire exits per floor. The Argyle Hotel was built before the statute was enacted. It has one fire exit. The statute contained a five year "grace" period for construction of additional fire exits to satisfy the law. Ten years later, the Argyle still has not complied with the law.

Recently, there was a fire at the Argyle. The fire was an accident for which the Hotel was not immediately responsible. When the firefighters arrived, they were informed that a 70-year-old invalid (Martha) lived on the second floor. Gordon, one of the firefighters, immediately ran up the steps to Martha's apartment, broke down the door, and found her weeping in a corner. She resisted Gordon's efforts to carry her away. After five minutes of assuring her that "everything would be all right," Gordon finally lifted Martha to his right shoulder and walked to the doorway. The entire hallway was now engulfed in flames. Unable to use the hallway, Gordon went to the nearest window, and jumped onto a first-floor awning. The awning broke their fall but Martha still suffered a broken leg.

51. If Martha sues the Argyle for her injuries, it is most likely that:

   (A) Martha will prevail because the Argyle was negligent *per se.*
   (B) Martha will prevail because she was injured as a direct result of the Argyle's failure to construct the prescribed number of fire exits.
   (C) The Argyle will prevail because the entire hallway was engulfed in flames.
   (D) The Argyle will prevail because Martha failed to respond immediately to Gordon's rescue efforts.

52. If Gordon was also injured and sued the Argyle, it is most likely that:

   (A) Gordon will prevail because the Argyle was negligent *per se.*
   (B) Gordon will prevail because the Argyle was liable in failing to have an adequate number of fire exits.
   (C) The Argyle will prevail because Gordon was injured in the course of his duties.
   (D) The Argyle will prevail because Gordon was contributorily negligent in jumping upon the awning with Martha on his right shoulder.

53. Paula and Paul have been dating for a year. Paula's brother John has been making uncomplimentary remarks reflecting on Paul's sexual prowess. When

Paul learned of the remarks, he angrily confronted John and began to scream at him. Unwilling to tolerate Paul's attack on him, John pushed Paul backward as hard as he could. After staggering about five feet, Paul regained his balance. Paul proceeded to attack John, wrestling him to the ground. Zigby, a passerby, tried to separate the two, but was struck in the face. As a result of the blow, Zigby's nose was broken and two of his teeth were dislodged. Zigby doesn't know which of the two hit him.

If Zigby sues Paul, it is most likely that:

(A) Zigby will recover because Paul started the fight.

(B) Zigby will prevail regardless of who started the fight.

(C) Paul will prevail because Zigby cannot prove who actually struck him.

(D) Paul will prevail because Zigby was a gratuitous volunteer and had assumed the risk of injury.

54. Louis was a burly night watchman at a truck storage facility. The facility had been robbed in the previous week. As Louis sat in his guardhouse, the electronic system indicated that someone was scaling the wire fence surrounding the facility. Louis did not know that the person scaling the fence was John. John, who lived nearby, had gone outside for his evening jog. He soon realized that he was being closely followed by two rough-looking men. When John increased his speed, the men actually began running after him. In an attempt to escape from the men, John scaled the wire fence at the northeast corner of the facility and dropped to the other side.

Alerted by the alarm, Louis went to see what was happening at the fence. When Louis arrived, John was running away from the two men, who stood on the other side of the fence. Louis did not see the men and ordered John, who was about 20 feet away, to stop. John hesitated, but then continued running away from the fence and from Louis. Louis drew his gun, and shot John in the leg.

If John sues Louis for battery, it is most likely that:

(A) John will prevail because Louis was not privileged to shoot him.

(B) John will prevail if he could not reasonably see that Louis was a security guard.

(C) Louis will prevail because he was privileged to use reasonable force under the circumstances.

(D) Louis will prevail because the two men pursuing John were primarily responsible for the injuries to John.

55. Steven owned a luxurious mansion in the State of Utopia. While driving by the mansion one morning, George noticed that a fire had broken out in the woods

and was moving toward Steven's large garage. Proud of his record as a war and police hero, George ran to the garage, hoping to save any cars inside. He found eight vintage Cadillacs in the garage. The keys for the cars were hanging near the door. Working at top speed, George was able to drive all the cars out before the garage was engulfed in flames. He did not — and could not — know that he had driven the cars not onto Steven's land, but onto Laura's carefully landscaped lawn. The lawn was served by an expensive sprinkler system installed just beneath the surface. In his desperation to save the cars, George had caused over $8,000 in damage to Laura's lawn and sprinkler system.

If Laura sues George for her $8,000 loss:

(A) George will prevail because he had no way of knowing that he was on Laura's land.
(B) George will prevail under the private necessity doctrine.
(C) Laura will prevail because George failed to act reasonably under the circumstances.
(D) Laura will prevail because George trespassed upon her land.

56. Anne and Emma were half-sisters (they had the same father, but not the same mother). They were also neighbors on an affluent street in Beverly Hills. One day, Anne saw burglars entering Emma's home and reported the incident to the police. The police responded and arrested the intruders. Anne believed that Emma was not sufficiently appreciative of her bravery and alertness and of her success in saving Emma's money and jewelry. A few days later, as Anne was walking past Emma's home, she saw Emma's one-year-old daughter splashing frantically in her small wading pool. Although the child appeared to be in trouble, and Anne was in a position to help the infant without any risk of harm to herself, she thought instead, "not my problem." When Anne arrived home approximately a minute later, she relented and did call the police. When the paramedics arrived, they found that the child had already drowned.

If Emma sues Anne for failing to come to her child's aid, it is most likely that:

(A) Emma will prevail because Anne failed to act reasonably under the circumstances.
(B) Emma will prevail because she and Anne have a consanguinary relationship.
(C) Anne will prevail because she was under no duty to rescue the child.
(D) Anne will prevail because she fulfilled her legal obligation by calling the police.

57. For his son's twelfth birthday, Dad gave him a small, motor-powered "race car." By law, this vehicle could only be used in driving areas specifically designated by the city for that purpose. One day the boy came home from school to find no one at home. He went looking for the car and found it in the garage. With some difficulty, he was able to dislodge the race car from its container. He took it outside and and began driving it on the sidewalk. Jane, an 80-year-old neighbor, was struck by the car, fell to the ground and broke her leg.

If Jane sues Dad for her injuries:

(A) Jane will not prevail because the boy was engaged in an activity reserved for adults.

(B) Jane will prevail because Dad should have been more careful in securing the "race car." ✓

(C) Dad will prevail because parents are not strictly liable for the torts of their children.

(D) Dad will prevail if a normally agile adult would have been able to avoid contact with the car.

58. Bill wanted to cut a number of strong branches which hung dangerously from trees growing on his property. He purchased a power saw from The Hardware Store, a local business. The saw was manufactured by The Roo Company. The store manager was careful to tell Bill to read the instruction booklet which came with the saw. But because Bill had often worked with power tools before, and this particular saw seemed easy to operate, Bill did not read the instructions. The first time he used the power saw, the blade flew off and severely injured Joe, Bill's neighbor.

The instruction booklet emphasized that the blade was very powerful, that it was essential to operate it with both hands and that some things should not be cut with it. However, Bill was utilizing the power saw in a proper manner when the blade flew off.

Neither Bill nor the store manager knew that that while the saw was being put onto a truck for delivery to the hardware store, it had fallen 15 feet to the ground. The blade was loosened in the fall and was delivered to the store in that condition.

If Joe sues The Roo Company for his injuries, it is most likely that:

(A) Joe will prevail because Bill was negligent in failing to read the instruction booklet.

(B) Joe will prevail because the power saw was in an unreasonably dangerous condition when it left Roo's possession.

(C) Joe will not prevail because Bill was the purchaser and Joe was a mere bystander.

(D) Joe will not prevail, if The Hardware Store failed to make a reasonable inspection of the power saw.

59. One winter evening, Bill and Mary were at a party in a rural area of Minnesota. They found that they lived within a short distance of each other. Mary did not have a car and Bill asked if he could drive her home. Mary said "All right." Mary did not know that the rear lights of Bill's car were not working.

When Bill began driving erratically, Mary ordered him to stop. Bill complied. Mary accused Bill of being drunk. Bill denied it and said, "You can stay here if you want; when I get home, I'll send a cab to pick you up." Afraid she would suffer hypothermia, Mary told Bill to go on but ordered him to drive more carefully. Five miles farther on, Bill lost control of the vehicle and crashed against a rock wall. Mary was severely injured. The jurisdiction recognizes contributory negligence.

If Mary sues Bill for her injuries:

(A) Mary will prevail if Bill was intoxicated and a "guest" statute is not applicable to this situation.

(B) Mary will prevail because Bill's vehicle was in a dangerous condition due to the lack of backlights.

(C) Bill will prevail because Mary assumed the risk of riding with him while he was intoxicated.

(D) Bill will prevail because Mary was contributorily negligent in returning to the vehicle though she was aware of Bill's condition.

60. John and Mary met at Sue's birthday party. John offered to drive Mary home and Mary accepted his invitation. John drove off with a flourish and within a few seconds was twenty miles over the speed limit. Mary told John that she did not believe in exceeding the speed limit. John responded, "Get out if you don't like it." Afraid to get out in the dark, Mary decided to remain in the vehicle. John stopped at the next stop light, but his car was struck from behind by Harvey. Harvey had been looking at a billboard of scantily clad women, and failed to notice that John had stopped for the light. Mary sustained serious injuries in the crash.

If Mary sues both John and Harvey for her injuries, contending that they both acted in a negligent manner:

(A) Mary will prevail against both.

(B) Mary will prevail only against Harvey.

(C) Both defendants will prevail because Mary had assumed the risk by remaining in the car after complaining of John's negligent driving.

(D) The defendants will prevail if there is a typical "guest" statute in this jurisdiction.

61. Art, who weighed 220 pounds and lifted weights, obtained a job as a security guard at Marcy's Department Store. During his second day at work, a teenager named Desmond entered the store with a sweatshirt wrapped around his waist. The sweatshirt seemed to bulge excessively in several places. Art walked over to Desmond and asked the teenager to accompany him to the security office. Desmond agreed. Several people saw Art, who was wearing a uniform, leading Desmond away and wondered what Desmond had done. Once inside the office, Art told Desmond that he wanted to look at the sweatshirt and asked Desmond to remove it. Desmond did, and Art found that the bulges were simply knots that Desmond had made in wrapping the sweatshirt around his waist. Art informed Desmond that he was "free to leave."

Based upon the foregoing, if Desmond sues Art and Marcy's for false imprisonment, it is most likely that:

(A) Desmond will prevail because people seeing Art lead him away would believe that Desmond had been arrested.

(B) Desmond will prevail because Art's imposing figure and stern tone constituted a "confinement."

(C) Desmond will prevail if Art closed the door of the security office when he confronted Desmond.

(D) Art and Marcy's will prevail because they were exercising the shopkeeper's privilege.

62. Jane, who is 72-years old, went to see Dr. Smith for a skin infection. The doctor prescribed Donatol for Jane's condition. Dr. Smith's writing was the usual doctor's illegible scribbling. Jane took the prescription to Maxwell, her local druggist. Maxwell was busy trying to fill a number of orders for customers who were waiting in line. He asked Ann, his clerk, to read Jane's prescription to him. Ann did her best, but read the drug as Ponatol. Ponatol is a drug typically prescribed for persons who have experienced excessive sunburn. It is never prescribed for elderly persons. Jane took the drug, and was promptly hospitalized with nausea and severe stomach cramps. She has now recovered after five days in the hospital.

If Jane sues Maxwell for her injuries:

(A) Jane can recover under a negligence theory.

(B) Jane can recover under a products liability theory.

(C) Jane can recover under an abnormally dangerous activity theory, since the pharmacy industry is highly regulated.

(D) Jane cannot recover against Maxwell.

63. Best-Buy Car Sales ("Seller") is a car vendor who sells cars manufactured by Fordico, Incorporated ("Fordico"). Seller sold Susie Flake ("Buyer") a new Fordico vehicle which contained the appropriate number of seat belts. However, Buyer found that the driver's seat belt did not fit comfortably. Buyer was somewhat overweight, and the seat belt felt too tight. When Buyer took the car back and complained to Seller about this condition, Seller stated, "I'll fix it ASAP. I can make the belt a little looser." However, Seller loosened the strap too much, and Buyer was severely injured in a collision caused by Bob Olsen's negligent driving.

Based upon the foregoing, if Buyer sues Fordico for her injuries, it is most likely that:

(A) Buyer will prevail under a products liability theory.

(B) Buyer will prevail under a negligence theory.

(C) Buyer will not prevail because she assumed the risk.

(D) Buyer will not prevail because Seller modified the car's seat belt.

64. Tess was a 38-year-old woman who weighed 100 pounds. She purchased a rocking chair from Romo Department Store ("Romo"). The chair was manufactured by Zero Manufacturing Company ("Zero"). Melba, a neighbor of Tess, was asked by Tess to come to her home. Melba sat in the new rocking chair. Melba weighs 62 pounds more than Tess. After Melba had rocked back and forth for about six minutes, the chair suddenly collapsed, seriously injuring her. Tess immediately called the paramedics. When they arrived, they helped Melba out of the chair, but in the process, they inadvertently worsened her injuries.

Based upon the foregoing, if Melba sues Romo:

(A) Melba will prevail, if Romo had failed to make a reasonable inspection of the chair before delivering it to Tess.

(B) Melba will prevail because the rocking chair was defective.

(C) Romo will prevail because Melba did not purchase the rocking chair.

(D) Romo will prevail because Zero manufactured the rocking chair.

65. Oscar purchased a new car from Ajay Motors ("Ajay") on a Monday. The next day Oscar began to speed through a red light, but then changed his mind. He stopped abruptly just short of the intersection. During the quick stop, Oscar noticed that one of the tires was wobbly. Oscar telephoned Ajay. The chief

mechanic at Ajay said that the tire "probably" needed a little tightening, and that Oscar should bring it in "as soon as possible." Oscar said that he would, but then decided to drive it until the following Saturday (when he could take the car to Ajay's without losing any "work" time).

The next day, as Oscar was driving home from work, the tire fell off the car, causing the vehicle to come to a screeching halt. Joe, who was a passenger in the vehicle, struck his head on the window on the right hand side of the vehicle. He required six stitches to seal the wound, and has been having headaches for the past three months.

Based upon the foregoing, if Joe sues Ajay for his injuries:

(A) Joe will prevail because Ajay's chief mechanic negligently minimized the risk involved.

(B) Joe will prevail because the car was in an unreasonably dangerous condition.

(C) Ajay will prevail because Oscar was primarily at fault in not returning the vehicle immediately to Ajay.

(D) Ajay will prevail, if Ajay merely sold the vehicle delivered to it by the manufacturer without making any material alteration.

66. John had a Doberman Pinscher named Rusty. The dog had often exhibited vicious tendencies. It had even once bitten the mailperson. To reduce the risk that others might be bitten, John usually kept Rusty chained to a stake in his backyard. One day John saw a large snake in the backyard and took Rusty inside to keep kim from being bitten. To keep the dog from escaping, he tied the dog's leash to a leg of the kitchen table.

Later that day, Ralph, a friend of John, walked into John's home to return a book he had borrowed. Ralph knew Rusty well and was always sure to stay clear of him. This time, Ralph did not notice Rusty and tripped over the dog. When Rusty stirred and barked, Ralph ran as fast as he could to the door. He had no way of knowing that the dog was tied to the table and could not pursue him. In his haste, Ralph banged his leg into the wall abutting the doorway and broke his knee.

If Ralph sues John for his injuries:

(A) Ralph will prevail under the "dangerous animal" doctrine (i.e., Rusty was a vicious dog).

(B) Ralph will prevail because John was negligent in putting the dog inside his home without warning Ralph.

(C) John will prevail because he was not responsible for Ralph's injuries.

(D) John will prevail because Ralph was trespassing at the time of his injuries.

67. John made his living growing prize-winning tulips. He often won prizes of $1,000 or more at flower shows throughout the state. John purchased a new lawn mower from The Hardware Store. The item was manufactured by Dynatron, Incorporated. The lawn mower worked fine for two weeks. But after that time, John always had difficulty shutting the motor off. The mower would sputter and shake violently before shutting down.

One month after the purchase, John was mowing his lawn when he heard his telephone ring. He turned off the motor switch and began to walk toward his home to answer the phone. The lawn mower suddenly started to move across the lawn on its own. Before it stopped, it had chewed up all of John's beautiful tulips. John estimated his loss at $25,000.

If John sues Dynatron for his property damage:

(A) John will prevail because Dynatron manufactured the lawn mower.
(B) John will prevail, if Dynatron should have discovered the problem prior to its sale of the mower to The Hardware Store.
(C) Dynatron will prevail because John did not suffer physical injury.
(D) Dynatron will prevail because John assumed the risk of damage to his property by using the lawn mower with knowledge of a defect.

68. Bill stopped at a local gas station. He asked the attendant to fill the tank with gas while he visited the washroom. Joe, Bill's devil-may-care friend, happened by and saw Bill's car. As a practical joke, Joe tried the back door, found it open, and threw a foul-smelling pile of rags into the vehicle. Bill returned to the car, and started off down the road. Smelling the rags behind him, Bill turned to see what was producing the odor. As he did so, he lost control of the wheel and struck an expensive parked car owned by Oscar (injuring himself, as well as damaging his car and Oscar's parked vehicle).

If Owner sues Bill for the damage to his car:

(A) Owner will prevail because Bill was negligent in leaving the back door of his car unlocked, permitting Joe to get access. ✓
(B) Oscar will prevail because Bill acted unreasonably in turning around while driving.
(C) Oscar will not prevail because Joe's conduct was an intentional, superseding cause.
(D) Oscar will not prevail because Bill had acted reasonably.

69. Curtis and Paul were driving down a four-lane road, Curtis, who was ahead of Paul, was driving five miles over the speed limit. Curtis decided to use his car phone and slowed down to dial. At the very same moment, Paul took his eyes off the road to adjust the dial on his radio. He bumped into the rear of Curtis's car, pushing it into the rear of another car driven by Tracey. Tracey's face hit the steering wheel, resulting in serious injury to her and causing her to undergo extensive plastic surgery.

Paul's lawyer advised him that he and Curtis were joint tortfeasors. (You may assume his analysis was correct.) When Tracey threatened to sue Paul, Paul quickly settled Tracey's claim for $50,000. Tracey wrote to Curtis asking a similar amount, but has not commenced an action against him. Tracey believes that Curtis is insolvent and judgment-proof. Paul knows that Curtis recently inherited $200,000 and has sued him for $25,000. The relevant statute states: "When two or more defendants are adjudged to be jointly and severally liable, each has a proportionate right of contribution from the others."

With respect to Paul's suit against Curtis, it is most likely that:

(A) Paul will prevail because Curtis was negligent *per se* by exceeding the speed limit.

(B) Paul will not prevail because no contribution rights exist.

(C) Paul will not prevail because Tracey never recovered a judgment against either defendant.

(D) More facts are needed to determine whether Paul will prevail.

70. Arnold watched almost the entire O.J. Simpson trial on television. He was enraged by the conduct of the trial attorneys. A prominent politician, Arnold was often invited to speak before various civic groups. At a Breakfast Club luncheon attended by approximately 30 people, Arnold railed against all attorneys, asserting that they were "a band of overcharging, unscrupulous rascals who do whatever it takes to win, regardless of ethics." Malcolm, a trial lawyer who advertised on television and who was sitting in the group, became increasingly uncomfortable. As Arnold's diatribe continued, several of the other attendees who knew Malcolm looked in his direction and smirked.

If Malcolm sues Arnold for defamation:

(A) Malcolm will prevail because a reasonable inference by the attendees was that Arnold's statements applied to Malcolm.

(B) Malcolm will prevail because any reference to attorneys as a group constituted a defamation of every attorney individually.

(C) Malcolm will not prevail because Arnold's remarks pertained to all attorneys, not to trial attorneys.

(D) Malcolm will prevail only if he proves that he lost clients as a consequence of Arnold's statements.

71. While driving his car and talking with Rex, his passenger, Albert went through a red light. Eddy was approaching the same intersection from the right. Eddy

increased his speed to "beat" the light. Although Eddy "hit" his brakes when he saw Albert, he was unable to avoid the collision. Eddy and Rex were not hurt at all, but Albert did sustain several painful bruises and significant damage to his car. Assume that this jurisdiction adheres to contributory negligence principles.

If Albert sues Eddy for his injuries and property damage:

(A) Albert will prevail because Eddy had the last clear chance.
(B) Albert will prevail because he was hurt and Eddy was not.
(C) Albert will not prevail because he was contributorily negligent.
(D) Albert will not prevail because Eddy acted reasonably under the circumstances.

72. Joseph was an extremely jealous husband. At a high school reunion, he saw Bill, a childhood friend, talking with Joseph's wife, Josephine. Bill was now the manager of a local department store. As Joseph and Josephine were driving home, Josephine casually mentioned that Bill had invited her to "stop by" if she ever passed the store. The more Joseph thought about Bill's invitation, the more enraged he became.

The next day, Joseph took part in an office discussion about a local politician who was being accused of seducing a number of women. Unable to contain himself, Joseph said, "You know it's not only politicians and office holders who take advantage of susceptible women. There's a guy I know who works at a local department store. I thought he was my friend, but he's nothing but a rotten womanizer. He's after my wife, just the way he's been after every woman in town. He's as rotten and depraved as a skunk." That night, a friend who had heard Joseph's remarks and had seen both Joseph and Bill at the reunion called Bill to tell him about Joseph's diatribe.

If Bill commences an action against Joseph for defamation:

(A) Bill will prevail because Joseph's statements subjected him to hatred, contempt or ridicule.
(B) Bill will prevail because Joseph's statements were factually inaccurate.
(C) Bill will not prevail because a reasonable person would not have associated Joseph's statements with Bill.
(D) Bill will not prevail because Joseph's remarks were merely verbal.

73. Debbie was injured when her co-worker, Karen, negligently bumped into her, causing Debbie to fall down a stairwell. Debbie's disability insurance policy entitled her to receive income lost as the result of an accident at work.

Debbie sued Karen in negligence for her personal injuries and lost income. Karen's attorney objected to any judgment based lost income, but the court entered a judgment against Karen for monetary damages which included pain, mental suffering, and lost income.

If Karen's attorney argues on appeal that Debbie's disability proceeds should be set off against the judgment:

(A) Karen will not prevail because Debbie's disability proceeds derive from a collateral source.

(B) Karen will not prevail because Debbie is merely being indemnified for her losses by the insurer.

(C) Karen will prevail because Debbie would otherwise receive a double recovery.

(D) Karen will prevail because insurance proceeds are ordinarily offset against a plaintiff's recovery.

74. Bruce, David and Mark were drag racing down a public street one evening, when one of them lost control of his car. Drag racing violates a local statute. The three cars collided in a burning mass. Carl, an off-duty police officer who happened to be walking by, suffered severe burns when he attempted to pull Mark from his vehicle. Carl sued all three for his personal injuries, pain and suffering. He obtained a $120,000 judgment against them. The defendants were adjudged to be joint and severally liable. (Assume this is a contributory negligence, rather than comparative negligence, jurisdiction.)

Carl proceeded to recover the entire amount of the judgment from Mark. If Mark seeks to recover $80,000 from Bruce and David:

(A) Mark is entitled to contribution from Bruce and David, each in the amount of $40,000. *No APPORTIONMENT IF CONTRIBUTORY NEG*

(B) Mark is entitled to indemnity from Bruce and David, each in the amount of $60,000.

(C) Mark is entitled to contribution from Bruce and David in proportion to their fault.

(D) Mark is not entitled to contribution from Bruce or David if he was the one who lost control of his car.

75. Veronica and Betty live in the State of Travail, a "straight" comparative negligence jurisdiction. One snowy afternoon, their cars collided when they were driving home from work. Veronica suffered personal injuries and property damages in the amount of $30,000. Betty incurred injuries and property damage equal to $10,000. After settlement negotiations had failed, Veronica sued Betty, claiming that Betty's negligence had caused the accident.

Betty counterclaimed against Veronica under the same theory. After a highly acrimonious three-day trial, the jury found that Veronica was 60% at fault, and Betty was 40% at fault.

The amount which Veronica can collect from Betty is:

(A) $12,000.

(B) $6,000.

(C) $18,000.

(D) Nothing, because Veronica was more than 50% at fault.

76. Compco manufactured a computer which was distributed by MiddleManCo. The computer was defective when it left Compco's plant. It was eventually sold to Barney by The Computer Warehouse, a large retail store. In setting up his computer, Barney followed all of the instructions exactly as written. When Barney used the computer for the first time, it blew up in his face, causing him serious injury. He decided to sue The Computer Warehouse only. He obtained a $400,000 judgment against the retailer.

If The Computer Warehouse sues Compco and MiddleManCo for indemnity for the full amount of the judgment against it:

(A) The Computer Warehouse will be entitled to indemnity from Compco or MiddleManCo for the full amount of Barney's judgment against it.

(B) The Computer Warehouse will be entitled to indemnity from Compco, but not MiddleManCo.

(C) The Computer Warehouse will be entitled to indemnity from Middle-ManCo, but not Compco.

(D) The Computer Warehouse will not prevail against either defendant under an indemnity theory.

77. Kim and Stacey were driving in town when their cards collided. Both were negligent. In the collision, Stacey's car was pushed onto the sidewalk and struck Patti, a pedestrian. Patti sued Stacey, but not Kim. Kim and Patti were friends, and Patti did not want to inconvenience or recover from Kim. Patti obtained a judgment in the amount of $200,000 against Stacey.

If Stacey subsequently sues Kim for contribution:

(A) Stacey is not entitled to contribution from Kim because Kim and Stacey were equally culpable.

(B) Stacey is not entitled to contribution from Kim because Stacey's car was the one which actually struck Patti.

(C) Stacey is entitled to contribution equal to 1/2 of the judgment against her.

(D) Stacey is entitled to contribution from Kim, if comparative negligence principles are applicable and Kim was more than 50% at fault.

78. Pete was fumigating Bill's house against termite infestation. He was proceeding in a reasonably competent manner. Despite his care, fumes leaked out of Bill's home into the yard of Bill's neighbor, Bob. Bob was planting flowers at the time. He inhaled the fumes and became slightly ill. Later that day, Kevin, Bob's son, came home from college. Bob told Kevin that Pete's house was being fumigated. Kevin could smell the fumes, but nevertheless, Kevin lit a match to start a cigarette. This resulted in a mighty explosion that caused substantial damage to the house of another neighbor, Carol.

If Carol sues Pete for the damage to her home:

(A) Carol will prevail because a peculiar risk associated with fumigation is the volatility of the gas utilized.

(B) Carol will prevail because the fumes which escaped were a contributing cause in her damage.

(C) Carol will not prevail because she incurred only property damage.

(D) Carol will not prevail because Pete's liability was extinguished by Kevin's intervening recklessness.

79. Amy was a retired F.B.I. agent. One day, she was firing her rifle at a makeshift range which she had constructed in her backyard. Amy's home was located in a New York City suburb. A bit out of practice, Amy's first shot missed the target completely. The bullet entered the home of her neighbor, Jocelyn. Jocelyn is a prominent zoologist who breeds a particular type of poisonous snake. Aware that it is illegal to keep or breed this snake, Jocelyn keeps the snakes in a big glass tank. The bullet from Amy's rifle shattered the tank and several snakes escaped. One of them bit Amy the next morning as she walked in her yard. The bite caused Amy serious injury, just short of death. This jurisdiction adheres to contributory negligence principles.

If Amy sues Jocelyn for (1) engaging in an abnormally dangerous activity, and (2) negligence:

(A) Amy will succeed under an abnormally dangerous activity theory.

(B) Amy will succeed because Jocelyn's illegal activity constituted negligence *per se*.

(C) Amy will not recover under either theory, if it is determined that she was contributorily negligent by firing the rifle.

(D) Amy will not recover under either theory, if Jocelyn told her that the snakes had escaped.

80. Danco Incorporated, a multi-state construction company, undertook some blasting along a country highway. Danco's workers posted a large, conspicuous sign, advising motorists to utilize another roadway because of the danger of flying rocks. Carl, who was driving along the highway, failed to notice the sign when he passed it. He was looking down at the dashboard, trying to change radio stations. Carl was struck by debris from the next blast. He sustained serious injuries and sued. This jurisdiction adheres to contributory negligence principles. In Carl's suit against Danco to recover for his injuries and lost income:

    (A) Carl will prevail because Danco failed to undertake adequate safety measures.

    (B) Carl will prevail because Danco was engaged in an abnormally dangerous activity.

    (C) Danco will prevail because Carl assumed the risk of injury from the blast.

    (D) Danco will prevail because Carl was contributorily negligent in failing to see the warning sign.

81. Susan, a famous TV soap opera actress, takes her docile poodle Froo-Froo with her wherever she goes. Although she appears on camera regularly with Susan, Froo-Froo has never bitten anyone. Too busy and self-centered to do what ordinary people do, Susan has never obtained a license for Froo-Froo (although she was required to do so under applicable state law). One day, while Susan was at her favorite manicurist, Froo-Froo was sitting meekly at Susan's feet, next to Susan's large satchel bag. Cindy (another patron) decided to peek into Susan's bag to see what a prominent television starlet carried in her bag. As Cindy reached into the bag, Froo-Froo bit her on the hand. It took almost three minutes before Susan could get Froo-Froo to release her grip on Cindy's hand. Cindy went into "shock." Subsequent medical exams revealed that Cindy's hand was permanently paralyzed.

    If Cindy sues Susan for the injuries she sustained:

    (A) Cindy will not prevail because Froo-Froo had not previously exhibited a propensity to bite human beings.

    (B) Cindy will not prevail because she was injured while engaging in an improper act.

    (C) Cindy will prevail because Froo-Froo was an abnormally dangerous animal.

    (D) Cindy will prevail because Susan's failure to obtain a license for Froo-Froo constituted negligence *per se*.

82. Wecut Company manufactured a line of power saws. One of the saws was sold to The Marx Brothers, a distributor of power tools. The Marx Brothers resold

it to Tom's Hardware Store, which sold it three months later to The Blue Company, a builder of commercial buildings and mini-malls. Steve, one of Blue's employees was using the saw on a Blue Company construction site, when it malfunctioned, causing him serious injury. Steve was using the saw carefully and properly. There is no evidence that the power saw was negligently manufactured. In fact, Wecut has an excellent reputation for careful craftsmanship.

If Steve joins Wecut Company, The Marx Brothers and Tom's Hardware in a law suit:

(A) Only Tom's Hardware Store is liable to Steve under a products liability theory.

(B) Only Wecut Company is liable to Steve under a products liability theory.

(C) Wecut Company, The Marx Brothers and Tom's Hardware Store are all liable to Steve under a products liability theory.

(D) Wecut Company is liable to Steve under a negligence theory.

83. Andrew purchased a new car from Just Cars For You, a local retailer of unusual sports cars. The vehicle was manufactured by The Fordico Company. After driving the car for one week without problems, Andrew sold it to his neighbor Charles, a prominent personal injury attorney. Charles was so anxious to buy the car that he paid Andrew $3,000 more than Andrew had paid. Unfortunately, two days later, the car abruptly malfunctioned, causing a collision which resulted in serious personal injuries and an enormous loss in income to Charles.

If Charles sues Andrew:

(A) Charles will recover for a breach of implied warranty of merchantability.

(B) Charles will recover under a products liability theory.

(C) Charles will recover under a negligence theory.

(D) Charles will not recover under any theory.

84. Alex began to experience constant and severe pain in his lower back. He visited Dr. Miriam Frank, a highly recommended physician, Dr. Frank gave Alex a packet of pills manufactured by Drugco. Although Dr. Frank usually sent her patients to a pharmacy for the drugs she prescribed, the packet she gave to Alex had been given to her by a contact person for Drugco as part of its nationwide effort to promote the drug. Soon after he took the pills, Alex's eyesight failed, and he became partially blind. Alex's attorney can introduce proof sufficient to support a finding that there was a causal connection between the pills and Alex's partial blindness.

If Alex sues Dr. Frank and/or Drugco:

(A) Alex can recover against Dr. Frank on a products liability theory.

(B) Alex can recover against Drugco on a products liability theory.

(C) Alex cannot recover against Dr. Frank on a breach of implied warranty of merchantability theory.

(D) Alex can recover against Drugco on a breach of implied warranty of merchantability theory.

85. Brett bought a toy rocket at Jolson's Toy Store for his 7-year-old son, James. The rocket contained methane cylinders that caused it to fire and lift several feet off of the ground. The rocket became James' favorite toy, and he played with it constantly. One month after the purchase, James invited Margaret, a neighborhood playmate, to join him in playing with the rocket. Margaret was using the toy in the way it was intended when it suddenly exploded and caused serious permanent injury to her hands and arms.

It is most likely that:

(A) Margaret's guardian can recover against James' parents for negligence.

(B) Margaret's guardian can recover against Jolson's Toy Store under a products liability theory.

(C) Margaret's guardian cannot recover against Jolson's Toy Store under a breach of implied warranty of merchantability theory.

(D) Margaret's guardian cannot recover against either Jolson's Toy Store or James' parents.

86. To impress his many rich and famous friends, John purchased an eight-seat airplane. He also hired a professional pilot to fly it. John then invited all of his "football buddies" to go with him to the Super Bowl. By using his influence, John had been able to get six 50-yard-line seats for the "big game." On the way to the Bowl, the plane's engine malfunctioned and it crashed. John and all his friends were killed instantly. John had purchased the plane from Equinox Leasing, a company that ordinarily leased, but sometimes sold, small airplanes.

If the executors of the estates of John's friends sue Equinox Leasing on a products liability theory:

(A) They will prevail even though the friends were merely passengers in the airplane.

(B) They will prevail unless Equinox can prove by clear and convincing evidence that the pilot contributed to the accident by failing to maneuver the airplane correctly when the engine began to fail.

(C) They will not prevail because Equinox did not ordinarily sell aircraft.

(D) They will not prevail if Equinox can prove that it inspected and tested the plane before selling it to John.

87. Marlene purchased some Mountain High mouthwash at the Acme Supermarket. The bottle had a conspicuous warning that advised purchasers to "Keep This Product Away From Children At All Times." After using the mouthwash one morning, Marlene placed the bottle on her bedroom table and went downstairs to prepare breakfast.

Marlene's three-year-old son wandered into the bedroom, grabbed the mouthwash bottle and quickly swallowed its entire contents. The boy died of poisoning and internal bleeding within a few hours.

If Marlene sues Acme Supermarket under a products liability theory, it is most likely that:

(A) Marlene will prevail because because she could not reasonably foresee that the child would swallow the mouthwash.

(B) Marlene will prevail because it was foreseeable that consumers might neglect to keep the product out of the reach of children.

(C) Marlene will not prevail because her negligence was an intervening, supervening cause.

(D) Marlene will not prevail if Acme Supermarket merely resold the item in exactly the same condition as it was received from the manufacturer or distributor.

88. Primacorp designed and produced a defective automobile, which it sold to Floyd's Car Corral ("Floyd's"), a retailer. Later, Primacorp discovered its design error and immediately contacted Floyd's, via a certified letter. Primacorp instructed Floyd's to return the vehicle to Primacorp's plant, so that Primacorp could remedy the defect. Within two hours after receipt of the certified letter, but before the car could be returned, one of Floyd's salespersons, anxious to make a sale and collect his commission, sold the car to Mrs. Boom. The salesperson intended to advise Mrs. Boom of the recall eventually but hoped that she would enjoy the car so much she would not ask to get her money back. Unfortunately, Mrs. Boom was injured the very next day, when the design defect caused the car to malfunction and crash.

If Mrs. Boom sues Floyd's to recover for battery:

(A) She will prevail because Floyd's ignored the recall notification from Primacorp.

(B) She will prevail because Floyd's was a commercial supplier of motor vehicles.

(C) She will not prevail because Floyd's salesperson did not intend to cause Mrs. Bloom any injury.

(D) She will not prevail if she was exceeding the speed limit at the time she was injured.

89. One evening, Peter invited Josh to his home for a "friendly" game of cards. While they were playing, Josh suspected that Peter was dealing himself aces from the bottom of the deck. Frustrated after losing five straight "hands," Josh suddenly called Peter a "lying cheat." Peter replied that he wasn't cheating, and that Josh should "watch his mouth." Unwilling to press the matter further for the moment, Josh told Peter that he was sorry; but that he would be "watching him closely" for the rest of that night. As it happens, Peter is the soul of rectitude and had not been cheating. The next day, Peter told several of his co-workers what Josh had said about him. They became extremely upset that Josh had accused Peter of cheating.

If Peter sues Josh for defamation and invasion of privacy (false, public light), it is most likely that:

(A) Peter will not prevail because Josh's remark was made only to Peter.

(B) Peter will not prevail because Josh apologized to Peter almost immediately.

(C) Peter will prevail on the defamation count, but not on the invasion of privacy count.

(D) Peter will prevail on the invasion of privacy count, but not on the defamation count.

90. Aura, the 20-year-old daughter of Paul and Paula Ranka (a well-known actor-actress couple), was planning to be married. The Rankas decided that they wanted the ceremony to be a very private one. They refused to allow any reporters and decided to have the affair at their palatial estate in Bel Air. They made it very clear to their twenty invited guests that they wanted things kept "private," and that no photographs would be permitted. Reporters and photographers were prohibited from entering the premises.

Arnie, one of the invited guests, was badly in need of funds. He made a secret arrangement with Exposed, a lurid celebrity magazine, to tape-record the affair and to permit the magazine to publish his impressions. In return, Arnie was handsomely compensated. When the article about Aura's "secret" wedding was published by Exposed, the Rankas were absolutely furious and sued

In a suit by the Ranka family against Exposed magazine for invasion of privacy, it is most likely that:

(A) The family will prevail because they they had expressly advised Arnie that they wanted the affair to be kept private and had prohibited the media from entering the premises.

(B) The family will prevail because Arnie secretly utilized a tape recorder in collusion with Exposed.

(C) The family will not prevail because Exposed is legally entitled to cover newsworthy events in any manner.

(D) The family will not prevail because weddings are considered to be social and public events.

91. Xavier Company ("Xavier") manufactures television sets. It sold one hundred sets to Yattle, Inc., a major distributor of radios and television sets. Yattle subsequently sold twenty of these televisions to Zerio Stores, a major retailer. The televisions were sold to Zerio by Yattle in the identical and unopened cardboard boxes in which they had been received from Xavier.

Amy bought one of the sets from Zerio. Shortly thereafter, Amy invited her boyfriend, John, to her home to watch some of their favorite programs. While Amy was out of the living room preparing some lemonade, the set exploded. As a result of the explosion, several metal pieces were imbedded in John's face and neck, causing him significant personal injuries.

If John sues Yattle under a products liability theory:

(A) John cannot recover from Yattle because Yattle was not at fault.

(B) John cannot recover from Yattle because he was a mere bystander.

(C) John can recover from Yattle, but Yattle can obtain indemnity from Zerio.

(D) John can recover from Yattle, but Yattle can obtain indemnity from Xavier.

Multiple-Choice Answers

1. **D** Many states have adopted guest statutes. The effect of these is to lower the level of care owed to her own passengers by a driver. Guest statutes differ from state to state, but, generally, they require gross negligence or wilful conduct by the driver, not ordinary negligence, before liability to the passenger is imposed. (*See* ELO Ch.5-VI(B).) In any event, all guest statutes deal only with the liability of the driver to her own passenger, not to a claim by that passenger against a third party who may have caused or contributed to the accident. Here, Price is suing the manufacturer of the vehicle rather than Dunn, the driver of the vehicle. The guest statute is irrelevant to Price's claim against Motorco. The correct answer is Choice **D**. Choice **A** is wrong because Price is not barred from recovering against Motorco. Choice **C** is incorrect. It will not be necessary for Price to prove that Motorco was guilty of more than ordinary negligence. That is the standard of proof required against Dunn by the statute, not against Motorco. Choice **B** is incorrect because the relevant degree of culpability by Dunn will not be determined by the guest statute but by the rules of negligence and contributory negligence in effect in this jurisdiction.

2. **D** A manufacturer acts negligently when it fails to act with due care, *i.e.*, it fails to act reasonably under all the relevant circumstances. There is nothing in these facts to suggest that Motorco was subject to strict liability. Price must prove more than that the bolt was defective. For this reason, Choice **A** is incorrect. Price *must show* not only that the bolt was in fact *defective, but also* that Motorco had *failed* to exercise reasonable care in inspecting the parts used to assemble the seat belt. Choice **B** is incorrect because it understates the amount of proof required. It's not enough to show that the bolt was not inspected. Price must also show that the bolt was in fact defective and that the defect would have been discovered on inspection. Choice **C** is incorrect because, again, Price must also show that Motorco failed to exercise reasonable care in making its inspection of the bolt. Only Choice **D** states correctly all the elements of proof required of Price. (*See* ELO Ch.14-I(C)(1).)

3. **A** The terms "proximate cause" and "legal cause" are different names for the same basic legal concept — the concept that liability attaches to a person whose negligence is responsible for an injury which is reasonably foreseeable from his act. (*See* ELO Ch.6-II(A).) Proximate cause does *not* exist when an unforeseeable, intervening cause results in an injury which was not likely to occur as a consequence of the defendant's negligence. Dunn's negligence was an intervening cause of Price's injuries (*i.e.*, it occurred subsequently to Motorco's actions), but it was *not unforeseeable* (*i.e.*, negligent driving by an owner or user of a motor vehicle must

always be anticipated); furthermore, the type of harm (physical injury resulting from a collision) is exactly what is likely to occur as a *consequence* of a defective seat-belt bolt. Choice **D** is incorrect because even though Dunn's negligence was an independent cause of Price's injuries, it was foreseeable and, therefore, not a *superseding cause*. Choices **B** and **C** are incorrect because, in a negligence action by Price against Motorco, the negligence of Dunn would *not* be looked upon as the "sole" proximate or legal cause of Price's injuries, since Dunn and Motorco's conduct both operated as proximate or "legal" causes of Price's injuries. Remember, "legal cause" is another term for "proximate cause."

4. **A**   If a defendant can show that it exercised due care, *i.e.*, that it acted reasonably under the circumstances, it will ward off a claim of negligence. (*See* ELO Ch.5-IV(A).) On these facts, Motorco's best defense is that it exercised due care in testing the bolts. As an assembler of components manufactured by others, it will have done everything reasonable by testing the bolt before it integrates it into the seat belt. The correct answer is Choice **A**. Choice **C** is not correct because guest statutes concern only the relationship between a driver and his own passengers, not third parties who may have contributed to the accident. Choice **B** is incorrect because it's not enough for Motorco to show that Dunn was negligent. It must also show either that it itself was not negligent or that Dunn's negligence was an independent, supervening cause. Finally, Choice **D** is incorrect because Boltco does not have the sole responsibility for defects in the bolt. As the assembler of components including the bolt, Motorco has a responsibility to exercise reasonable care in checking every component which goes into its finished product.

5. **D**   The tort of false imprisonment occurs when the defendant has *intentionally caused* the plaintiff to be confined to an area which has definite physical boundaries and from which there is no reasonable means of escape. (*See* ELO Ch.2-VI(A).) There is *no indication* on the facts that D *intended* to lock Paul in his office, nor is it reasonable to anticipate that a lock will jam when a door is slammed shut. The correct answer is Choice **D**. Choice **C** is incorrect because intentional confinement to any definable area will result in liability. It doesn't matter that Paul was in his own office. The point is that he was held within limits beyond which he could not move. Any other construction would mean that false imprisonment could not occur if a person were confined to his own home or his own car. Choice **B** is incorrect because false imprisonment, which is an intentional tort, does not include negligence as one of its elements. Finally, Choice **A** is incorrect because although David intended to slam the door,

he did not intend to confine Paul by his actions. An intent to confine is an essential element of the tort of false imprisonment. (*See* ELO Ch.2-VI(B).)

6. **D** There are two basic requirements for the use of force in the defense of property. The force must be only as much force as is necessary to protect the property. And the owner of the property must first make a verbal demand that the potential intruder stop, unless it appears that harm will occur immediately, or that the demand will be ignored. Rest. 2d § 77(c). (*See* ELO Ch.4-V(A).) When mechanical devices are used, only the same degree of force may be used as if the owner were present and acting himself. (*See* ELO Ch.4-V(D).) On these facts, Daniel had no right to install the electrical device unless he also provided some reasonable means of notifying trespassers of its existence. The correct answer is **D**. Daniel failed to provide any notice that would have caused Paul to suspect the presence of the device. Choice **A** is wrong because although the force may not have been excessive under ordinary circumstances, it did prove fatal to Paul who was not furnished with the requisite notice. Choice **B** is wrong because a trespasser is entitled to notice before subjecting himself to the owner's threatened use of force. Choice **C** is incorrect because although Daniel's act was a factor in Paul's death, it would not have imposed liability on Daniel if Daniel had given proper notice to Paul and Paul had persisted in trying to enter the car.

7. **C** A person is entitled to use reasonable force to prevent a threatened harmful or offensive contact with his person. This is true whether the threatened contact is intentional or the result of negligence. David had the **right to defend himself** from Paul's attack and will not be liable to Paul as long as he **did not use excessive force**. (*See* ELO Ch.4-III(C).) On these facts, which indicate that Paul began an unprovoked fight, there is nothing to indicate that David used excessive force. Choice **D** is incorrect legally. It is not a defense that the plaintiff had some unusual disability which could not be anticipated. A tortfeasor takes his victim as he finds him, infirmities and all. (*See* ELO Ch.6-III(D)(1).) Choice **A** is incorrect. David had the right to kick Paul if he reasonably believed that was necessary to repel Paul's attack upon him. Finally, Choice **B** is incorrect because the fact that David outweighed Paul would not, in itself, establish that David's kick was not reasonably necessary to repulse Paul. So long as David reasonably believed the kick was necessary to beat off Paul's attack, the self-defense privilege would be sustained.

8. D In some situations involving a special relationship between the plaintiff and the defendant, the courts have imposed liability when the defendants fails to act to to protect the plaintiff against injury from a third person. The school/student relationship is one of these special relationships. A school may be liable in negligence for injuries caused by the conduct of others when it fails to fulfill its duty to exercise reasonable care in the ***supervision*** of a third person or in the ***protection of the plaintiff.*** (*See* ELO Ch.8-II(B)(7).) On these facts, the school district would ***not*** be liable unless it failed to exercise ***reasonable*** care with respect to the supervision of the school yard, and there is nothing in these facts to indicate that failure. It does not appear that the fight between Paul and David could have been anticipated, nor that it could have been prevented or even stopped. A fight can be over in seconds, before anyone has a chance to intervene. Choice **C** is incorrect because the facts do not show any reason for the school to anticipate that Paul would start the fight. Choice **A** is incorrect because although a fight on school grounds may impose a duty on the school to intervene, there is nothing on these facts to indicate that the school failed to observe that duty. Finally, Choice **B** is incorrect. Although a school may have a greater responsibility when many students congregate during a recess, the facts do not show that the school could have prevented or anticipated an unprovoked attack by Paul.

9. C A person ordinarily has no duty to come to the aid or rescue of another, unless some special relationship exists between them. Since there is nothing in the facts to indicate that Boater and Sailer had any type of special relationship between them, Boater was ***not legally obligated to respond*** to Sailer's requests for assistance. (*See* ELO Ch.8-II(A).) Choices **B** and **D** are incorrect because Boater had no obligation to assist Sailer, even if the probability of harm to Sailer outweighed the probability of harm to Boater, and even if Boater's belief that rendering assistance to Sailer would damage his own boat was not reasonable. Choice **A** is incorrect because Boater was not responsible for creating Sailer's predicament; he would have been liable for worsening the situation if he had begun to assist Sailer and then discontinued his aid. (*See* ELO Ch.8-II(B)(5).)

10. B Defendant is liable for a conversion to the rightful owner when he exercises ***substantial dominion and control*** over the owner's personal property. Both Repairer and Buyer exercised dominion and control over Owner's television set in an ***unauthorized*** manner. (*See* ELO Ch.3-III(D).) The fact that Buyer was unaware of the true ownership of the television would not preclude a suit for conversion by owner. In most states, even a bona fide purchaser would be deemed a converter on these facts. (*See* ELO Ch.3-III(E)(1)(a).) Buyer would, however, have a right of indemnity against Repairer for any judgment against Buyer, because Buyer is entitled to rely on Repairer's title. Choice **A** is incorrect because the mere fact that one is a good faith purchaser of an item does not preclude liability for conversion. Choice **C** is incorrect because Repairer committed a conversion when he sold the television set to Buyer. Finally, Choice **D** is incorrect because, while Repairer initially had lawful possession of the television set, his sale to Buyer constituted a conversion.

11. **C**   Injuries from a domestic animal do not give rise to strict liability unless the animal has shown signs of being dangerous and the owner is aware of the animal's dangerous tendencies. (*See* ELO Ch.13-I(B)(1)(a).) These facts do not disclose that Al's dog had ever bitten anyone. Al was not guilty of ordinary negligence, because he had the dog on a leash, and the dog broke the leash in response to an unexpected explosion. Because Al's liability could be based only on strict liability, Al will not be liable on these facts for the harm caused by his pet. Choice **A** is not correct because mere ownership of a domestic animal does not make one liable for all harm caused by the animal. Choice **B** is not correct. If it were correct, it would impose strict liability for any harm caused by one's pet while the pet was beyond its owner's immediate control, which is inconsistent with rules respecting domestic animals. Choice **D** is incorrect because Al was not negligent; he acted reasonably under the circumstances by walking his dog on a leash. In any event, any possible negligence by Al was not the proximate cause of Charles' injuries. Al could not reasonably foresee that someone would discharge a gun in an open field.

12. **C**   On these facts, this is probably the best answer. We are not told whether the open fields at issue are on public land or private land. We are told only that it was a "large stretch." Under this circumstances, Burt could reasonably argue that there was no basis on which to foresee that a dog on a leash would escape and bite a stranger. Nor was there any reason for him to suspect that anyone else — let alone someone with a dog — was in the area. Choice **B** is incorrect because although firing a gun may be a dangerous activity under most circumstances, it is not necessarily dangerous in an open field when no one else is visibly present. Choice **A** is incorrect because Burt could not reasonably anticipate that the dog was in the area, or that he would break loose from a leash, or that he would bite a stranger who was not visible to Burt. Choice **D** is incorrect because, although the breaking of the leash was an independent, inter-

vening force, it was not reasonably foreseeable by Burt and was not, therefore, a superseding cause that would cancel Burt's negligence, if any. Rest. 2d § 442A. (*See* ELO Ch.6-IV(A),(B).)

13. D An intentional tortfeasor is ordinarily not entitled to indemnity or contribution from his fellow tortfeasor. Because *conversion is an intentional tort*, Joe may *not* obtain indemnity or contribution from Tom. (*See* ELO Ch.7-IV(C)(1).) The correct answer is Choice **D**. Choice **C** is incorrect because the right to indemnity or contribution does not depend on the plaintiff's choice of defendants. In any case, even if Tom had been joined as a defendant, Joe would not be entitled to indemnity or contribution from his fellow tortfeasor. Choice **A** is wrong because Joe cannot recover in indemnity, implied or otherwise. Choice **B** is wrong precisely because Tom was a joint intentional tortfeasor.

14. A The law encourages rescuers by imposing liability upon negligent tortfeasors who create circumstances to which a rescuer is likely to respond. The intervention of the rescuer is *deemed* a foreseeable consequence of the negligence. Choice **A** is therefore the correct answer. (*See* ELO Ch.6-III(D)(2), IV(D)(1)(b).) Choice **B** is incorrect. Cases involving rescuers are exceptions to the general rule that the specific consequence must be foreseeable to impose liability for negligence. This is a matter of public policy which is designed to encourage rescuers. Choice **C** is incorrect because the rescuer need not be in the zone of danger. As a practical matter, he will often be outside the zone. Choice **D** is incorrect because it's immaterial whether the skateboard was a superseding cause or merely an additional contributing cause. Pat was proceeding as any rescuer would on these facts.

15. A The standards for determining contributory negligence are the same as for negligence. A person is negligent if she fails to act with due care (*i.e.*, reasonably under the circumstances). In determining if Pat failed to act in a reasonable manner, *all three of the listed factors are pertinent.* (*See* ELO Ch.5-IV(B)(6).) The fact that she was 13 years old would be relevant in that she would be held only to the standard of a child of like age, experience and intelligence. This is a lower standard than for adults under the same circumstances. The fact that Walker was in obvious need of medical attention would justify her in dashing with less care than normally through Highrise. Finally, her awareness that objects were often left in the hallways would be offered by Driver to prove his contention that Pat failed to act reasonably under the circumstances (*i.e.*, was contributorily negligent). (*See* ELO Ch.11-I(C), (D)(1).)

16. C This question assumes that Pat did not live in Hightower. This would make her either a trespasser or an invitee. If Realty had a duty to Pat at all, it was a *duty to warn* Pat of known dangers, but *not to inspect*. Thus, if the skateboard were left just before Pat's fall, then Realty would not have breached its duty, particularly since Choice **C** assumes that Realty did not know the skateboard was there. (*See* ELO Ch.9-IV(A).) Choice **D** is incorrect. The fact that Pat was a trespasser would not necessarily relieve Realty of all responsibility to her. Because Pat was only thirteen, Realty had a duty to her greater than to adults. Under these facts, however, that duty was probably met by Realty. Choice **A** is incorrect because Realty's employees probably did not have a duty to Pat to discover and remove the skateboard, especially because there is no showing that an unreasonable time had elapsed between the time the board was placed on the landing and the time Pat fell. Finally, Choice **B** is incorrect because Realty probably did not have a duty to maintain a public telephone in the lobby of the apartment building. Most apartment houses do not instal public telephones in the lobby.

17. D An assumption of risk defense to a negligence cause of action is available if the plaintiff knew the risk and assumed it voluntarily. Because Pat was *not aware* of the skateboard until she tripped over it, she could not have possibly assumed the risk of it. (*See* ELO Ch.2-III(C)(2).) The correct answer is Choice **D**. Choice **C** is incorrect because a minor can assume a known risk. Choice **B** is incorrect because, even if Pat should have seen the skateboard (which appears dubious), that fact might constitute contributory negligence, but not assumption of risk. Finally, Choice **A** is incorrect because, even though Pat was running, her actions were reasonable if you consider that she was attempting to obtain medical attention for one in obvious need of it. Even if it was not reasonable for Pat to run, she was not aware of the skateboard and Realty cannot rely upon an assumption of risk defense.

18. C Breach of a "safety" statute ordinarily constitutes negligence *per se* when: (1) the plaintiff was *within* the class of persons intended to be protected by the statute, (2) the statute *sought to prevent* the type of harm suffered by the plaintiff, (3) the defendant's *violation* of the statute is not excusable, and (4) there is a *causal relationship* between the statutory violation and the plaintiff's harm. Here, Jill was clearly within the class of persons the statute meant to protect (*i.e.*, swimmers and boaters). The statute was designed to prevent physical injury and property damage from the operation of boats by youthful and inexperienced boaters. Leaving a key in the ignition is one of the very acts an inexperienced operator might do. The facts are similar to those involving keys left in parked cars. (*See* ELO Ch.5-VIII(D)(2)(a).) Choice **A** is incorrect because Mark's violation is negligence *per se*, not merely one factor evidencing negligence. Choice **B** is incorrect because under some circumstances even a person who violates a safety statute may be able to show that his violation was excusable. (*See* ELO Ch.5-VIII(D)(3).) Choice **D** is incorrect because as discussed above, the violation is not only relevant, it is determinative.

19. A   Ordinarily, ***no duty of care is owed*** by the victim to anyone who commits a ***criminal act against him.*** Because Mark was committing a crime against Jeff's property (malicious mischief or larceny), Jeff would have had no duty of care towards him. (*See* ELO Ch.5-II(A)(2)(a).) Choice **C** is incorrect because it is framed in negligence terms, instead of in terms of intentional tort. Choice **B** is incorrect because Mark could not be said to assume a risk of which he was not aware. It's not reasonable to expect anyone to know that a boat would go backward when directed to go forward. Finally, Choice **D** is incorrect. It is not likely to be an argument on which Jeff will rely because Jeff did not owe any duty to Mark.

20. B   Intentional interference with another person's use or possession of a chattel is trespass to chattel, and the defendant will be liable for ***actual damages to the chattel.*** (*See* ELO Ch.3-II(B).) If the harm to the property is sufficiently great, the tort may rise to the tort of ***conversion*** instead of trespass to chattel, and the defendant will be liable for the item's full value. Both torts require an intentional act by the defendant — true here. Mark has at least committed a trespass to chattel (if not a conversion) because he took the boat intentionally, and Jeff will be able to recover for any damage to it. Choices **A** and **D** are not correct because they "sound in" negligence and thus will not affect Mark's liability for his intentional tort. Choice **C** is not correct because the same conduct can give rise to both criminal and civil liability. Recovery for one does not preclude recovery for the other.

21. C   These facts raise the issue of a retailer's liability for a sealed package which has been sold to him by the packer. The correct answer is Choice **C**. The retailer is liable only if he had a duty to inspect the goods and had a reasonable chance of finding the defect. No court would expect a retailer to open prepackaged bologna to look for a nail. On the contrary. opening the package might itself constitute negligence because it would expose the ham to contamination. (*See* ELO Ch.14-I(C)(3).) Choice **A** is incorrect because, while the doctrine of *res ipsa loquitur* might impose liability on Packo, it would not apply to Don because Don was not in exclusive control at the critical time — *i.e.*, when the bologna was packaged. (*See* ELO Ch.5-X(B)(3).) Choice **D** is incorrect because horizontal privity is generally no longer required in suits involving defective products. Finally, Choice **B** is incorrect because nothing in these facts suggests that Don had any special relationship with Packo which would make Don liable for Packo's negligence.

22. **C**   Negligence is unreasonable conduct in the face of a foreseeable risk to others by the person who creates the risk. Even though John *did not act negligently* in hitting the moose *initially,* he *did act unreasonably by leaving it in the middle of the road where it would foreseeably pose a great risk of harm to others.* Because Phil was injured as a consequence of this risk, he can successfully sue John for damages. (*See* ELO Ch.5-III(A)(1)(a).) On these facts, Phil did not assume the risk of the moose in the road. Choice **D** is incorrect because the facts do not indicate whether or not Phil was contributorily negligent — did he take his eyes off the road, for example. Without the facts, we cannot say that this will be a factor in recovery by Phil. Choice **A** is incorrect because, while John was not at fault in hitting the moose, he was nevertheless under a duty to remove it from the road. Finally, Choice **B** is incorrect because John did have a duty to remove the risk of harm to others which he had accidentally created by striking the moose.

23. **A**   When one is responsible for creating a risk to others (whether intentionally or accidently), she has a *duty to make a reasonable effort to remove the risk before someone is foreseeably damaged by it.* The converse is also true. Because Ellwood was not responsible in any manner for the death of the moose or for its presence in the road, he was under no obligation to assist in its removal. Choice **B** is incorrect because, even if John had asked Ellwood for assistance in removing the animal, Ellwood would have been under no legal obligation to cooperate. (*See* ELO Ch.8-II(A)(2).) Choice **D** is incorrect because the fact that Phil may have acted reasonably under the circumstances does not affect or enlarge Ellwood's liability. Finally, Choice **C** is incorrect because Ellwood's duty was not increased either by his having witnessed the accident or by his knowledge that the moose was left in the road.

24. **A**   The commercial manufacturer of a *defective item* (*i.e.,* one which is unreasonably dangerous in light of its anticipated and normal use) is liable for *any* personal injuries or property damage suffered by a purchaser or user of the item as *a consequence of such defect.* This doctrine is known as *strict tort liability.* Since Sis was using the bicycle in a *reasonably foreseeable manner* when she was injured by the defective product, she should be able to recover against Bikeco based on strict liability. (*See*

ELO Ch.14-III(B),(C).) Here, a court would probably find the bike was defectively designed and constructed because it was unreasonably flimsy, and because the cost of constructing it properly was small when compared to the resulting risk. (*See* ELO Ch.14-IV(B).) Choice **B** is incorrect because it is merely restates the rationale which the courts have used to support the strict liability doctrine, not a basis for supporting Sis' right to recover on these facts. Choice **C** is incorrect because a commercial supplier is liable for personal injuries to any user caused by a defective product so long as the item was used in a reasonably foreseeable manner. It was certainly foreseeable that an eleven-year old child might temporarily ride a bicycle sold to a seven year old. Choice **D** is wrong because strict liability extends to any foreseeable user or consumer of the product, not only the purchaser or the intended user.

25. A   The ***commercial supplier*** of a defective item (*i.e.*, one which is unreasonably dangerous in light of its anticipated and normal use) is liable for any personal injuries or property damage suffered by a purchaser or user of the item as a consequence of such defect. Because Hardware is a commercial supplier, ***it will be liable in strict liability in tort*** to Sis if the bicycle was defective (*i.e.*, in an unreasonably dangerous condition) at the time of sale. (*See* ELO Ch.14-I(C)(2).) Choice **B** is incorrect because strict products liability does not require a failure by the defendant to act reasonably (*i.e.*, one may be liable under strict liability in tort even though he has acted reasonably under the circumstances). Choice **D** is incorrect because strict liability in tort does not require privity between the commercial supplier and the injured party. Finally, Choice **C** is incorrect because each commercial supplier in the chain of distribution may be liable to the injured user (even though the item was merely re-sold in its original form). (*See* ELO Ch.14-VII.)

26. D   To recover for ***mental distress suffered*** as a consequence of ***observing an injury to another***, the plaintiff ***must have suffered some physical injury herself***. Although Friend was horrified by the unpleasant sight of seeing Sis injured severely, she can ***not*** recover for her mental distress as a consequence unless she can show that she has also suffered some type of physical injury. Some courts also require that the plaintiff be in the zone of danger or be a close relative of the injured party. Choice **C** is incorrect because the fact that Friend was not using the item would not, by itself, preclude a recovery for mental distress. If she had been injured by Sis as she fell, she would have been able to recover even though she sad not herself used the bike. Choice **A** is incorrect because the source of harm need not be inherently dangerous for the plaintiff to recover for mental distress. Finally, Choice **B** is incorrect because, even if Friend was in the zone of danger, she probably cannot recover under a mental distress theory unless she actually sustained some type of demonstrable physical harm. (*See* ELO Ch.8-IV(B)(3).)

27. **A**   A *private nuisance* occurs when the defendant has intentionally, negligently or through an ultrahazardous activity, caused an unreasonable and substantial interference with the plaintiff's use and enjoyment of his land. sold in its original form). (*See* ELO Ch.15-III(A).) The flies and noxious odor around plaintiffs' homes as a consequence of Cattle Company's activities probably constitute an *unreasonable interference* with the plaintiffs' use of their property. Choice **C** is incorrect because the mere fact that the Cattle Company has been operating for more than 5 years would not, in itself, constitute a defense to plaintiffs' private nuisance action, especially since the plaintiffs are not the only people whose interests are at stake. Approximately 10,000 others live nearby. Choice **B** is incorrect because the Cattle Company was not negligent (it was using the "best and most sanitary" equipment). In any event, a private nuisance can occur even if the defendant is not negligent. The claim of nuisance is supported by the fact that the nuisance is intentional (this does not mean that the defendant intends the consequences of its use, but only the continued use itself). Finally, Choice **D** is incorrect because the fact that Cattle Company uses reasonable procedure does not relieve it of liability. Cattle Company's continuation of its activities, especially once it became aware of the impact of its activities on the plaintiffs, make its conduct intentional, and thus Cattle Company is liable for a private nuisance. (*See* ELO Ch.15-III(D).)

28. **A**   A commercial supplier who sells a *defective* and unreasonably dangerous item in the ordinary course of its business is liable for any personal injury or property damage resulting from the defect, whether or not the commercial supplier was negligent in the design or production of the product. (*See* ELO Ch.14-III(B).) The corned beef was *defective and unreasonably dangerous* by reason of the fact that it contained the sliver of bone. The fact thatWest Beef Company may have exercised *reasonable care* in purchasing the product from Meat Packers is *irrelevant* in a products liability action based on a *strict liability theory*. Answer **B** is legally incorrect because a vendor's breach of warranty is not imputed backward to the distributor or manufacturer. Choice **C** is incorrect because privity of contract is not required in strict liability suits. Finally, Choice **D** is incorrect because Susie is suing in strict liability, not for breach of warranty. West Beef is liable in strict liability even though it was not itself negligent.

29. B   A person who keeps a wild animal is ***strictly liable for all damage*** done by it if the damage results from a dangerous propensity that is typical of it. A skunk is considered a wild animal because it is ***not*** one which is customarily used in the service of mankind. Even though Householder ***thought*** the skunk's propensity to spray an offensive scent had been eliminated, Householder is still strictly liable for all damage resulting from the original propensity. (*See* ELO Ch.13-I(B)(1).) He ***may*** be able to assert an assumption of risk defense against Walker, but he will have to prove that she was more than inattentive or careless — *i.e.*, that she read the second sign and voluntarily proceeded past the skunk. (*See* ELO Ch.13-III(C)(1),(2).) Choice **A** is not correct because a private nuisance must interfere with another's property interest, and Walker's harm is based on personal injury, not damage to property. Choice **C** is not correct because there is an exception to the general freedom from liability to trespassers when the landowner knows that a portion of her land is frequently used by trespassers as a crossing or path. (*See* ELO Ch.9-IV(B)(1).) Although the landowner can usually satisfy this exception with a warning, the warning may not be enough when it is apparent that the trespassers will not respect the warning, as is the case here (trespassers ignored the first sign he erected, so he should have foreseen that the second would not be respected either). Choice **D** is incorrect because Householder will be strictly liable, and thus antecedent causation is not relevant.

30. C   Magazine utilized Actor's picture within a general story about the eating and drinking tastes of film stars. Movie actors expect that newspapers and magazines will run stories of this kind. The use of Actor's photo was merely ***incidental*** to the overall subject matter of the article. Furthermore, Actor could not reasonably argue that his privacy or solitude had been invaded when he was drinking beer in a public place. (*See* ELO Ch.18-I(C)(1).) Choice **D** is incorrect because the impact of a publication upon the subject's career or profession is not pertinent to the issue of invasion of privacy. Choice **B** is incorrect because the publication of the Actor's photo by Magazine was only incidentally for commercial purposes. To hold otherwise would result in a ban on publication of the photo of any public figure in a newspaper or magazine of general circulation. Finally, Choice **A** is incorrect because no consent is required when the plaintiff's likeness is used incidentally to a broader subject or in connection with a news event.

31. B   One who uses another's ***name or likeness*** for one's financial benefit or gain is liable for the tort of invasion of privacy. In this instance, Foamus is blatantly utilizing Actor's likeness ***for its commercial and financial***

benefit. The use is not incidental to a proper purpose but clearly for the sole benefit of Foamus, without the authorization or consent of Actor. (*See* ELO Ch.18-I(B).) Choice **A** is incorrect because the mere fact that Actor had not consented to having his picture taken is not enough to make Foamus liable: it is Foamus' use of the picture in selling beer without his consent that creates liability. Film actors are photographed all the time. Often, they have no control over the photographer. Choice **C** is incorrect because the fact that the photo had appeared Magazine did not constitute permission in Foamus to use the photo for its own gain. Finally, Choice **D** is incorrect because Actor's status as a public figure is not authority in others to make use of his likeness or to profit from his fame.

32. **B**   *Pure expressions of opinion can never be defamatory.* Alma's criticism of Bessy is an *opinion* about the quality of Bessy's work, *rather than a statement of fact* about Bessy, herself, or about facts contained in her work. (*See* ELO Ch.17-II(F).) Literary criticism is probably the best example of opinion which is not actionable. Choice **C** is incorrect on the facts which do not show any statements by Alma constituting assertions or implications based on fact. Implied assertions of false facts can be actionable, but that is not the case here. Choices **A** and **D** are incorrect because the threshold elements of a cause of action for defamation are not met (since Alma's statement was one of opinion, not fact) and therefore whether Bessy can show out-of-pocket loss or her status as a well-known author is irrelevant.

33. **A**   To recover against the media for defamation, a public figure must show either knowledge of falsity or reckless disregard of the truth. A private citizen on the other hand, need show only that the medium acted unreasonably in ascertaining the facts. But if the medium can establish that it acted reasonably, even a private person cannot recover for defamation. (*See* ELO Ch.17-V(B)(4).) The correct answer is Choice **A**. If Caster, a media defendant, exercised reasonable care in investigating the statement which he broadcast, a defamation action can *not* be successfully sustained against him (*even though* his statements were incorrect). Choice **B** is incorrect because the medium's belief with respect to the truth is not the measure of liability. It must make a reasonable investigation into the truth. Choice **D** is incorrect because Caster's ill will toward Teacher, if it exists, will be relevant on the issue of damages, not liability, which will depend on the extent to which Caster investigated the truth of his statements. Choice **C** is incorrect because a retraction will not necessarily bar Teacher's recovery. It will in some states but not in others, depending on the statute or case law in force. (*See* ELO Ch.17-VII(B).)

34. B The elements of a cause of action for ***misrepresentation*** are (1) a misrepresentation of a material fact, (2) scienter, (3) intent to induce reliance, (4) justifiable reliance, and (5) damage to the plaintiff stemming from the reliance. (*See* ELO Ch.16-II(A)(1).) Here, Vendor ***intentionally made a misrepresentation*** that the land was free from encumbrances in order to induce Purchaser to buy the land. However, despite Purchaser's damage, the correct answer is Choice **B**. Purchaser's reliance on the misrepresentation was not justified because a reasonable person would have discovered the mortgage before the closing of the transaction (*i.e.*, through a routine inspection of the title to the land). Choice **A** is incorrect. Although Purchaser has been damaged, he cannot recover because he had constructive notice of the mortgage. Choice **C** is not correct. Though the value of the land itself may have increased, Purchaser's interest is worth $5,000 less than the price he paid. Choice **D** is not correct because the choice between equitable and legal remedies is up to the plaintiff, not the defendant. It's up to the plaintiff to choose whether to sue for rescission or for damages.

35. D The question calls for analysis of the Choices on the basis of strict liability rather than ordinary negligence. The manufacturer of a product will be ***strictly liable*** if the product wa defective ***at the time of sale*** and unreasonably dangerous to a consumer or foreseeable user. (*See* ELO Ch.14-III(B).) The correct answer is Choice **D**. It states the rule of law applicable in strict liability cases. Choice **C** is incorrect because a defective product cannot be made non-defective through use of a warning nor will a warning relieve the manufacturer of liability for a defective product. Choice **A** is incorrect because proof of negligence is not required in strict liability cases. Finally, Choice **B** is incorrect because although the conduct of other manufacturers may be relevant to the "defect" issue, it is not dispositive.

36. B A commercial supplier who sells a ***defective*** and unreasonably dangerous item in the ordinary course of its business is ***strictly liable*** for any personal injury or property damages resulting from consumption or use of the item. Because the facts do not show otherwise, we must assume the stove was defective when it left Local Retailer's hands. Local Retailer is therefore liable for any physical injuries arising from the product's use, ***so long as the injury did not result from changes made to the product after purchase by someone other than Local Retailer.*** (*See* ELO Ch.14-III(H)(4).) The correct answer is Choice **B**. Choice **A** is incorrect because a warning about defects in the product will not relieve the retailer of liability if the product is sold by him with the defect. Choice **C** is incorrect because a retailer can be strictly liable even if he was not at fault in any way for the design or assembly of the product. (*See* ELO Ch.14-I(C)(3).) Finally, Choice **D** is incorrect because strict liability does not require that the retailer know or have constructive knowledge that the product is dangerous.

37. A Intent in tort law is a difficult concept. A person intends to commit an act either when he means to carry out the act or when he knows with substantial certainty that his movements or actions will result in the act. (*See* ELO Ch.2-I(B) and Example). When Bill ran off a crowded dance floor and through the exit, it was substantially certain that he would collide with another patron. Joan can recover against Bill for battery. The correct answer is Choice **A**. Choice **B** is incorrect, since Bill's lack of intent to injure anyone is not controlling. As long as his actions were substantially likely to result in contact with another patron, he is liable. Choice **C** is incorrect because Bill's reason for his actions is irrelevant. What is relevant is that he acted in a way which was substantially certain to result in contact with another patron. Finally, Choice **D** is incorrect because an injury to Joan or to someone else was reasonably foreseeable under the circumstances of a crowded dance floor and Bill's actions. (*See* ELO Ch.6-III(C)(1).)

38. D An assault occurs when the defendant intentionally causes the plaintiff to apprehend that he is in imminent danger of an offensive touching. The intent of the defendant and the apprehension of the plaintiff must co-exist. If the plaintiff is not put in apprehension of an imminent contact, there is no assault. (*See* ELO Ch.2-V(A)-(B).) On these facts, Bart believed Joe was bluffing and did not fear an offensive touching. The best answer is Choice **D**. Choice **C** is incorrect because it's immaterial to the issue of Joe's assault that Bart may have engaged in illegal conduct. Choice **B** is incorrect, because Bart will not be able to show that he suffered emotional distress; the facts tell us that he did not believe Joe would harm him. (*See* ELO Ch.2-VII(D).) Finally, Choice **A** is incorrect because, as discussed above, Bart did not apprehend that Joe would actually make an offensive contact upon him, and a necessary element of assault was therefore lacking.

39. C A false imprisonment occurs when the defendant has intentionally confined the plaintiff to an area with defined physical boundaries from which there is no reasonable means of escape. (*See* ELO Ch.2-VI(A),(D).) The intent to confine is an essential element of the tort. Because the janitor was unaware that Arthur was in the typing room, he did not have the requisite intent and the school is not liable for false imprisonment. The correct answer is Choice **C**. Choice **D** is incorrect.

Physical injury is not an element of false imprisonment. Arthur may be able to recover damages against the school on the theory of negligence, but not for false imprisonment. Choice **A** is incorrect; Arthur was indeed confined to the room against his will, but the janitor did not intend the confinement. Finally, Choice **B** is incorrect because negligence in causing confinement will not support an action for false imprisonment.

40. D. Consent by the plaintiff is a valid defense to a claim based on an intentional tort. (*See* ELO Ch.4-II(A).) Because Max voluntarily consented to the "pat down" search, he cannot recover for battery. Faced with the demand that he submit to the search, Max could either accede to the demand or decline to board the bus. The choice was voluntary. The correct answer is Choice **D**. Choice **C** is incorrect because the defendant does not have to prove that it was reasonable in requiring the "pat down." So long as Max submitted to the search voluntarily, the bus line has a valid defense. Choice **A** is incorrect because Max was not "compelled" to submit to the search. Although he had planned to board the bus, the decision to consent to the "pat down" was voluntary. Finally, Choice **B** is incorrect. The fact that Max subsequently suffered physical harm by becoming ill is irrelevant to whether the defendant committed a battery and to whether Max consented to the battery.

41. D The tort of intentional infliction of severe emotional distress occurs when the defendant, through outrageous conduct, causes the plaintiff severe emotional distress. The plaintiff may recover if he can prove the defendant intended the distress, knew with a certainty that the distress would occur, or acted recklessly. (*See* ELO Ch.2-VII(B).) The transferred intent doctrine does not ordinarily apply to this tort. The reason is to prevent litigation by people who happen to see an outrageous act and claim to be distressed. (*See* ELO Ch.2-VII(B)(2).)The correct answer is Choice **D**. Choice **C** is incorrect. Under the majority rule, even a relative may not recover on the theory of transferred intent. Only a member of the immediate family may recover under the doctrine. (However, the Restatement 2d does extend the doctrine to anyone who is in the vicinity of the act and who suffers bodily harm.) (*See* ELO Ch.2-VII(B)(2)(c).) Choice **A** is incorrect because it misstates the law of transferred intent as it applies to the tort of Infliction of Mental Distress. Finally, Choice **B** is incorrect; it is not necessary that a plaintiff who is entitled to sue for infliction of mental distress prove physical harm; nor does physical harm entitle a plaintiff to sue for emotional distress. (*See* ELO Ch.2-VII(D).)

42. D Although Frank has suffered injury and distress, he will probably not be able to recover from Tim on any theory. Both assault and intentional infliction of mental distress require that the plaintiff be aware of the threat to him at the time of the action upon him. The impact upon him must be contemporaneous with the defendant's action. (*See* ELO Ch.2-V(E) and VII(B)(3).) Choices **A** and **C** are therefore incorrect. Choice **B** is incorrect because the tort of battery requires some harmful or offensive contact with the body or personal effects of the plaintiff, and the bullet never touched Frank. The correct answer is Choice **D**.

43. B The law of trespass has been in transition over the last century and most courts no longer impose liability for an involuntary or unintended incursion upon the land of another. So long as the invasion is neither intentional nor negligent, liability will be found only if the defendant carries out an "abnormally dangerous activity." (*See* ELO Ch.3-I(B)(2).) The best answer is Choice **C**. Jack did not intend a trespass on Dan's land. He did not know he was on Dan's land, but honestly believed he was on public land. Choice **A** is incorrect under the modern view which does not impose liability for an unintended accidental inroad on another's property. Choice **B** is incorrect because under the common law, damage was not an essential ingredient of the tort of trespass. Under the modern view, nominal damages can be recovered when the trespass is intentional even when the harm is minimal. Finally, Choice **D** is an incorrect statement of the law. The victim of a trespass does not have to show loss to the market value of his land to recover in trespass, provided the other elements of the tort are proved.

44. A A trespass occurs when the defendant intentionally, negligently, or by engaging in an abnormally dangerous activity, causes an encroachment upon the land of another. When Bill sprayed water on Albert's driveway, he committed an intentional trespass. He caused a tangible object — water — to enter Albert's driveway. (*See* ELO Ch.3-I(G).) Because of the trespass, Bill is liable for any injuries resulting from his acts, including the injury to Albert. Modern courts impose liability even for mental distress which occurs as a result of the trespass. The correct answer is Choice **A**. Choice **B** is incorrect because Bill *intentionally* sprayed the water upon Albert's land. Choice **C** is incorrect. Although trespass and nuisance can sometimes co-exist, that is probably not the case here. A nuisance occurs where the defendant substantially and unreasonably interferes with the plaintiff's use or enjoyment of his land. Here, we are dealing with a single trespassory act, not a continuing interference with use or enjoyment of Albert's land. Finally, Choice **D** is incorrect because it is not necessary for the defendant himself to enter on the plaintiff's land. He is liable if he causes an object to touch or encroach on the land.

45. B   A conversion occurs when the defendant takes possession of the property of another with the intent to interfere with his use or possession of the property. A bona fide purchaser of stolen goods is considered by most courts to be a converter. (In New York and a few other states, a bona fide purchaser is not a converter unless he refuses to give the goods back to the lawful owner.) The correct answer is Choice **B**. (*See* ELO Ch.3-III(E)(1)(a).) Because Jessie purchased the television set from Howard intending to be the legal owner, a conversion occurred. Jessie is liable to Randy for the reasonable value of that item. Choice **A** is incorrect. The tort of conversion is not triggered by causing damage to the property of another but by interfering with its use or possession. Choice **C** is incorrect. As we have stated, in most states even a bona fide purchaser for value would be liable for conversion even if he did not know the goods were stolen. Even in New York, Jessie would be liable on these facts because he refused to return the set to Randy. Finally, Choice **D** is incorrect because it is not supported by the facts we are given, which show no negligence, and, in any event, Randy's failure to exercise reasonable care in protecting the TV set from being stolen is irrelevant to the issue of conversion.

46. C   A merchant who has parted willingly with possession of a product cannot use force to regain it. He must use judicial process instead. Although Exco may have been entitled to repossess the motor home, it could not do so by force. Exco's employee committed both assault and battery upon Owner, and the correct answer is Choice **C**. Choice **D** is incorrect because it does not state the reason which entitles Owner to recover. Whether or not Owner was in default, Exco had no right to attempt repossession by force. Choice **A** is incorrect, again, because Owner's default did not entitle Exco to use force. Finally, Choice **B** is incorrect because assumption of risk is not a defense to an intentional tort.

47. D   One is entitled to use deadly force when threatened with serious bodily harm or death by another person. Because Leo had taken a step toward Anthony with his knife drawn, Anthony was entitled to respond with deadly force. (*See* ELO Ch.4-III(G).) Choice **C** is incorrect because the fact that Anthony was in illegal possession of a firearm does not detract from his right to use it against Leo under these circumstances. Choice **A** is incorrect because Anthony, when he shot Leo, was defending himself (rather than attempting to reclaim the basketball). Finally, Choice **B** is incorrect because (in most jurisdictions) Anthony had no obligation to order Leo to "Stop!" before shooting.

48. B In virtually all jurisdictions, no one can validly consent to conduct which constitutes a crime or a breach of the peace. In a fistfight between two men, each will be allowed to sue the other because their consent to the fight is deemed ineffective. (*See* ELO Ch.4-II(H)(1).) Xavier is liable to Chuck because he participated in the fight. Choice **A** is incorrect. Xavier's qualifications as a boxer are immaterial, as is Chuck's ignorance of these qualifications. Choice **C** is incorrect because Chuck could not validly consent to a public fistfight. Finally, Choice **D** is incorrect because it's immaterial who struck the first blow. Both fighters are liable to each other because neither could legally consent to the fight.

49. C One who is attacked by another may use whatever force is reasonably necessary under the circumstances to prevent serious bodily harm or death to himself. (*See* ELO Ch.4-III(F).) Because Aaron initiated the attack by lunging at Eddie and was 4 inches taller and 22 pounds than Eddie, Eddie was entitled to use reasonable force to repel him (Aaron's height and weight are not as important as the fact that he attacked Eddie, but they are important on the issue of how much force by Eddie was reasonable). Because Eddie was unaware of Aaron's previous operation and only intended to disable him, the force utilized was justified. Choice **D** is incorrect. Whether or not Aaron had the legal right to attack him, Eddie was entitled to use reasonable force to repel the attack. The force utilized by Eddie was justified to prevent Aaron from causing him serious bodily harm. Choice **B** is incorrect since, as discussed above, Eddie's force was reasonable under the circumstances. Finally, Choice **A** is incorrect because comments of this kind would not, under any circumstances, justify Aaron's attack upon Eddie.

50. D If he is attacked, one may use whatever force is reasonably necessary under the circumstances to prevent serious bodily harm or death to himself. (*See* ELO Ch.4-III(F).) Because Darren was attempting to attack Sam with a knife, Sam was entitled to disable Darren. Choice **C** is incorrect because the mere fact that Darren was illegally carrying a knife would not alone permit Sam to injure him. It would be necessary that Darren threaten Sam with the knife. Choice **A** is incorrect because, in most jurisdictions, one has no duty to retreat from his attacker. In this situation, Sam could justifiably assume that Darren might pursue him. (*See* ELO Ch.4-III(H).) Finally, Choice **B** is incorrect because Sam was not obliged to choose the alternative of wresting the knife away from Darren instead of blocking it and punching Darren. Because Darren had attacked with deadly force, Sam was entitled to respond as he did.

51. C   Violation of a statute constitutes negligence *per se*, but only when (1) the conduct prescribed by the statute is clear, (2) the plaintiff is in the group sought to be protected by the statute, and (3) the plaintiff was injured as a consequence of the defendant's failure to comply with the statute. (*See* ELO Ch.5-VIII(A)(1).) Because the entire hallway was engulfed in flames, it cannot be said that The Argyle's failure to have at least two fire exits caused Martha's injuries (*i.e.*, even if The Argyle had had four fire exits on the second floor, Gordon and Martha could not have reached them, as is evidenced by the fact that Gordon had to jump from the window). Choice **D** is incorrect because Martha's apprehension and concerns could reasonably be anticipated in light of her advanced age and disability. Choice **A** is incorrect because, as explained above, there was no causal connection between The Argyle's failure to comply with the statute and Martha's injuries. Finally, Choice **B** is incorrect for the reasons given above.

52. C   In most states, rescue personnel (*i.e.*, fire, police, etc.) cannot recover in negligence for injuries incurred during the performance of their duties. Since Gordon, a fireman, was injured in the course of his duties, he probably will be unable to prevail against The Argyle. In any event, the facts tell us that the fire was an accident and we know that violation of the statute by The Argyle was not the cause of any injuries to Gordon. Choice **D** is incorrect because Gordon probably did not act unreasonably in jumping onto the awning. This would appear to be the only option he had. Choice **A** is incorrect because, as explained in the answer to the previous question, there would be no causal connection between The Argyle's failure to comply with the statute and Gordon's injury. Finally, Choice **B** is incorrect because the lack of fire exits was not the cause of Gordon's injuries and the fire was not the fault of The Argyle. Also, (in most jurisdictions) firemen are precluded from recovering for injuries sustained in the performance of their duties.

53. B   Those who participate in a fight or who commit intentional batteries are liable for any consequence which ensue, even though they may not have intended them. (*See* ELO Ch.2-IV(F).) It is reasonable to anticipate that someone will step in to stop a fight. Zigby can recover from both Paul and John because they both participated in the fight and it would be impossible to determine whether one was more at fault than the other. Zigby can probably recover from Paul. Choice **A** is incorrect on the facts.

It's not clear that Paul was the one who started the fight. At first, all he did was scream at John. It was John who committed the first battery by pushing Paul. Choice **C** is incorrect because, as discussed above, Zigby can recover from both John and Paul. It's immaterial which of them struck the first blow since it cannot be determined which of them actually struck Zigby. Finally, Choice **D** is incorrect because assumption of risk is not a defense to an intentional tort. Also, Zigby did not consent to being struck by trying to stop the fight. .

54. A One cannot ordinarily use force capable of causing death or serious bodily injury in the defense of property. (*See* ELO Ch.4-V(C).) Although John was a trespasser, Louis had no right to shoot at him. There was nothing to indicate to Louis that John had committed a felony or that he was threatening Louis with injury. On the contrary, John was running away when Louis shot at him. Choice **B** is incorrect because, even if John recognized that Louis was a security guard, Louis was not privileged to shoot at him. Choice **C** is incorrect because the force used by Louis was not reasonable under the circumstances. Finally, Choice **D** is incorrect because although the presence of the two men caused John to climb the fence, Louis was still not privileged to shoot at John.

55. D The private necessity doctrine confers a privilege to prevent injury to the person or property of another, even at the risk of damaging private property, if there is no other reasonable way of preventing the harm. Here, for example, the choice for George was between saving eight vintage Cadillacs and driving onto a lawn. However, if the volunteer causes damage to the property of another, he must reimburse him for it. (*See* ELO Ch.4-VIII(D)(2)(a).) Because George trespassed upon Laura's land, he is liable for the damage to her equipment. Choice **C** is factually incorrect. George did act reasonably under the circumstances, especially since he had no way of knowing he was on Laura's land. Choice **A** is incorrect. It doesn't matter that George didn't know he was on Laura's land. It's sufficient that he intended to go onto the lawn which turned out to be on her land. Finally, Choice **B** is incorrect because under the private necessity doctrine the actor is still liable for any injury or damages he actually causes.

56. C There is ordinarily no duty to rescue another or to fail to act to help a person in distress or danger. Exceptions arise in certain circumstances, *e.g.*, when one member of an immediate family is dependent upon another (a father or mother is obliged to rescue their minor children). (*See* ELO Ch.8-II(A)(2).) Additionally, there is a duty of rescue when one is responsible for creating the risk of injury. (*See* ELO Ch.8-

II(B)(3).) Although Anne and Emma were half-sisters, Anne was not legally obliged to rescue Emma's child (even if she could do so without any risk of harm to herself). Choice **D** is incorrect because Anne had no obligation to call the police. In any event, if she had an obligation to intervene at all, calling the police might not be an adequate response to the risk. Choice **A** is incorrect as an unjustified legal conclusion. Anne did not act unreasonably because one is not legally obliged to undertake the rescue of "strangers." Finally, Choice **B** is incorrect because consanguinary relationships — as in this situation — do not necessarily create a duty to attempt a rescue.

57. B One acts in a negligent manner when he fails to act reasonably under all the prevailing circumstances. (*See* ELO Ch.5-IV(A).) Dad should have been more careful in securing the "race car." Because the boy was able to retrieve the vehicle relatively easily, Dad is probably liable to Jane. (*See* ELO Ch.5-IV(B)(6)(d).) Choice **A** is incorrect because the fact that driving the "race car" was an adult-like activity and that a child was engaged in that activity would support Jane's claim. Choice **C** is incorrect because, although a valid statement of the law, the claim here is not based upon strict liability but upon Dad's failure to secure the "race car" so as to prevent its use by the boy. Finally, Choice **D** is incorrect because a defendant ordinarily takes the plaintiff as he finds her, infirmities and all. (*See* ELO Ch.6-III(D)(1).)

58. B A commercial supplier who, in the regular course of business, provides a defective product, is liable to the purchaser or user for personal injury or property damage resulting from the defect, even when the defendant exercised due care in the item's production; Restatement of Torts 2d, § 402A. This is the doctrine of strict products liability. (*See* ELO Ch.14-III(A)(B).) We may conclude that because the blade of the power saw became loose the first time it was utilized, it was in an unreasonably dangerous condition when it left Roo's possession. Thus, Joe can recover against Roo for his injuries under a products liability theory. Choice **A** is incorrect because it is unclear that Bill was negligent in failing to read the instruction booklet. In any event, he was utilizing the power saw properly; nothing he might have read in the book would have prevented the accident; and the accident was caused entirely by a defect in the saw. Choice **C** is incorrect because, in most jurisdictions, even a bystander may recover under a products liability theory. (*See* ELO Ch.14-VI(B)(2).) Finally, Choice **D** is incorrect because The Hardware Store was probably under no duty to inspect the item. In any event, its intervening negligence, if any, in failing to detect the loose blade would not relieve Roo of liability as the manufacturer.

59. A A plaintiff is deemed to have assumed the risk of harm if she knowingly and voluntarily undertakes the activity which may cause the harm. (*See* ELO Ch.11-III(A).) Bill will argue that Mary assumed the risk by accepting the ride and by remaining in the car when he began to drive erratically. However, there are circumstances in which a person cannot really be said to undertake a risk "voluntarily." For example, a person may act under duress or under circumstances which negate free will. (*See* ELO Ch.11-III(D)(3)(c).) Because Bill and Mary were in a rural area of Minnesota at a late hour, Mary was justifiably concerned about being left at the roadside and exposed to the elements. The absence of a "guest" statute in the jurisdiction will assure the success of Mary's lawsuit, although she will probably be able to prove gross negligence by Bill. (*See* ELO Ch.5-VI.) Choice **B** is incorrect because there is no indication that the failure of the backlights had any causal connection with Mary's injuries. Choice **C** is incorrect because, as discussed above, Mary did not assume the risk. Finally, Choice **D** is incorrect, since (given all of the circumstances) Mary was not contributorily negligent by continuing to drive with Bill.

60. B A defendant is not liable for negligence unless there is a causal connection between his conduct and the plaintiff's injury. Although John had been exceeding the speed limit, he was stopped at a light when his vehicle was struck from behind by Harvey. Mary could only prevail in a negligence action against Harvey. Choice **A** is incorrect because John's prior negligence in speeding did not contribute to Mary's injuries. (*See* ELO Ch.6-I(A).) Choice **C** is incorrect because Mary can not be held to have assumed the risk of John's speeding. It would be unreasonable to require a woman to leave a car in the dark if she was afraid to do so. (*See* ELO Ch.11-III(D)(3)(c).) As to Harvey, she obviously did not assume any risk of his supervening negligence. Finally, Choice **D** is incorrect because, even if there is no guest statute, John was not responsible for the accident and Harvey would not be helped by the guest statute — the typical guest statute relieves only the driver of the vehicle in which the guest is seated of negligence, not persons who negligently collide into the car in which the guest is riding. (*See* ELO Ch.5-VI.)

61. D Many courts recognize the shopkeeper's privilege to detain temporarily a person who is reasonably suspected of shoplifting. (*See* ELO Ch.4-VI(C).) On these facts, Art probably had a reasonable basis for his suspicions because Desmond's sweatshirt bulged at several places. Art and Marcy's appear to have exercised the shopkeeper's privilege properly. They did not coerce Desmond into confessing or attempt to restrain him. Choice **A** is incorrect because, even though the incident may have been embarrassing for Desmond, there was no other reasonable way for Art to determine whether Desmond had in fact been shoplifting. Choice **B** is incorrect. A stern voice and an imposing figure are not likely to be construed as "a confinement." A person is "confined" when he is restricted by definite physical boundaries. (*See* ELO Ch.2-VI(D).) Finally, Choice **C** is incorrect because the facts do not tell us that Art did close the door. If he had closed it, and if he had detained Desmond for more than a few minutes, then the shopkeeper's privilege might have been violated and Art and Marcy would be liable.

62. A A druggist who deals with hundreds of prescriptions every day is held to a very high level of care because an error on his part can have grievous consequences. No druggist can reasonably ask a clerk to read a prescription to him. Many drugs have names which are confusingly similar to the names of other drugs. Maxwell's failure to read the prescription himself constituted negligence. Choice **B** is incorrect because there is no indication that either Donatol or Ponatol was defective as a product. Choice **C** is incorrect. The rules which impose strict liability for accidents which occur as a result of abnormally dangerous activities were not meant to cover the pharmaceutical profession. ELO Ch.13-II(C). Otherwise, all druggists would be strictly liable for their mistakes. Instead, they are held to the level of care which is normally practiced by druggists. Finally, Choice **D** is incorrect because, as discussed above, Jane could successfully sue Maxwell for his negligence.

63. D When its product is substantially changed by a subsequent seller (as a consequence of which a subsequent buyer or user is injured or incurs property damage), a manufacturer is relieved of culpability under a products liability theory. (*See* ELO Ch.14-III(H)(4).) Because Buyer's injuries were attributable to Seller's loosening of the seat belt, Buyer will be unable to recover from Fordico. Choice **A** is incorrect because Fordico ceased to be culpable under a products liability theory when Seller refitted the seat belt. Choice **B** is incorrect because there is no indication that Fordico failed to act reasonably in the manufacture of the seat belt or that the seat belt was defective. Finally, Choice **C** is incorrect because there is nothing to indicate that Buyer realized that the strap was too loose to prevent injury if a collision occurred. Under these circumstances, she cannot be said to have assumed any risk.

64. B A retailer who sells a product which is in an unreasonably dangerous condition is liable to the consumer or user for physical harm only if the he was in the regular business of selling that product, and the product is expected to, and does, reach the buyer or user without substantial change from the condition in which it was sold; Restatement of Torts 2d, § 402A. (*See* ELO Ch.14-III(B).) Because the rocking chair collapsed almost immediately after it was purchased, Romo (as a commercial supplier) would be liable under a products liability theory. There is no indication that the chair was intended to be used only by persons of a certain weight. Nor is it reasonable to expect that a chair would be sold to the general public if it was unsafe for a person weighing 162 pounds. Choice **A** is incorrect because, even if Romo had made a careful inspection of the rocking chair, it would still be liable to Melba under a strict products liability theory. Choice **C** is incorrect because foreseeable users (as well as purchasers) can assert a products liability theory. In fact, in most jurisdictions, bystanders can also assert this doctrine. (*See* ELO Ch.14-VI(A).) Finally, Choice **D** is incorrect because Romo is a commercial supplier of chairs. (Romo would presumably have a right of indemnity against Zero.)

65. **C**   A purchaser who voluntarily proceeds to use a product or commodity after he becomes aware of a defect which may result in injury to him may be deemed to have assumed the risk of that injury. (*See* ELO Ch.14-IX (A)(1)(b),(B).) The fact that one of the tires became wobbly when Oscar made a quick stop suggests that it was defectively manufactured, especially because it was brand new. Oscar should have taken the vehicle in for repairs immediately when he was advised to do so by Ajay's mechanic. Choice **A** is incorrect because the chief mechanic at Ajay did not minimize the risk. He advised Oscar to bring the vehicle in "as soon as possible." Choice **C** is incorrect because Oscar's negligence or assumption of risk would preclude a successful products liability action against Ajay. Finally, Choice **D** is an incorrect statement of the rules of products liability. Each commercial supplier of a defective item is liable to the buyer or user under the products liability doctrine.

66. **C**   Although (1) Rusty was a vicious animal, (2) his tendencies were well known to John, and (3) the owner of a vicious dog is strictly liable under the dangerous animal doctrine when the plaintiff is injured by the animal, John will probably not be liable to Ralph on these facts because John was careful to tie the dog up and Rusty did not injure Ralph. *See* ELO Ch.13-I(B). Choice **B** is incorrect because John acted reasonably in bringing Rusty inside his home after seeing the snake and in tying the dog to the kitchen table. Nor did he owe Ralph any duty to warn him. Nothing in these facts indicates that John had given permission to Ralph to enter his house. Choice **D** is incorrect because we do not know whether Ralph was trespassing and there is no general rule which

relieves the owner of a dangerous animal from liability to trespassers. Finally, Choice **A** is incorrect because, as explained above, the "dangerous animal" doctrine is not controlling on these facts.

67. A   Under the products liability doctrine, a manufacturer is strictly liable for damage caused by a defective product distributed by it in commerce. Because the lawn mower was defective — no mower should move when the motor switch is turned off — John can successfully recover from Dynatron. (*See* ELO Ch.14-III(B).) Choice **B** is incorrect. Although it is a general statement of a manufacturer's duty with which no one can argue, it is not dispositive on these facts. The relevant facts are that the mower was sold by Dynotron's customer to John in a defective condition and that liability follows. The essence of strict liability is that the defendant is liable even if due care was exercised. Choice **C** is incorrect. Liability by Dynatron is not limited to personal injury. Property damage resulting from the mower's malfunction is covered as well. Finally, Choice **D** is incorrect because John did not assume the risk of the lawn mower's moving on its own. While it had apparently sputtered on other occasions before shutting down, the facts do not show that the mower had ever moved on its own when it was shut it off. John cannot be held to have assumed a risk he was not aware of.

68. B   Negligence consists of a failure to act reasonably under the applicable circumstances which results in injury or damage to the person or property of another. Except under the most unusual and compelling circumstances, it is not reasonable for a person driving a motor vehicle in traffic to turn his head around. Confronted only by a bad odor, Bill should have pulled over to the curb before inspecting the rear of his car. Choice **C** is incorrect because Joe's conduct was not a superseding cause of the accident. Joe's actions preceded the collision and were intentional. They would not prevent Owner from prevailing against Bill. Choice **A** is incorrect because Bill was not negligent in leaving the back door of his car unlocked. A driver would ordinarily have no reason to foresee that another person would place foul-smelling rags in the back of his car. Finally, Choice **D** is incorrect because, as discussed above, Bill was unreasonable in allowing himself to become distracted under the circumstances and in not pulling over to a stop before turning his head.

69. D   The applicable statute would seem to preclude recovery by Paul against Curtis because no court has ever "adjudged" either or both of them liable. However, we need to know if any court in this jurisdiction has ever construed this statute before we can choose the right answer. For example, is a defendant who has voluntarily settled with the claimant precluded from recovering against his joint tortfeasor? Must both tortfeasors be sued in one action by the plaintiff before the court can "adjudge" whether one or both are liable? These and other questions must be answered. The correct answer is Choice **D**. We must first study and analyze the applicable case law. This is often the case when a statute attempts to define liability. Choice **A** is incorrect because the fact that one defendant is guilty of negligence *per se* does not preclude recovery by him against the other tortfeasor under a contribution theory. Choice **B** is incorrect because we will not know until we study the applicable case law whether a right of contribution exists under these circumstances. Choice **C** is not the best answer, because, again, we cannot know whether this is correct until we study case law or ask a court to determine the question for the first time.

70. C The essence of a claim for defamation is that it have a tendency to harm the reputation of the plaintiff. If the plaintiff belongs to a large class of persons, it is difficult to argue that a remark about that entire class should be construed as a reflection on his own individual reputation. (*See* ELO Ch.17-II(D)(2).) Because Arnold's comments, however defamatory, pertained to lawyers in general, Malcolm will be unable to sustain an action for defamation. Choice **D** is incorrect because it is not always necessary to show monetary damage to support an action for defamation. (*See* ELO Ch.17-II(D)(2)(a).) Choice **A** is incorrect because it is not reasonable to believe that remarks about lawyers in general would apply to a particular lawyer without a fairly clear link. Finally, Choice **B** is incorrect for the reasons discussed above.

71. C Contributory negligence is a complete defense to an action for negligence, except in those states which have adopted some form of comparative negligence, under which the court assesses the relative degree of responsibility by the defendants. Since there is no statement here that comparative negligence applies, the correct answer is Choice **C**. Arthur was clearly negligent in going through the red light and his negligence contributed to the accident. (*See* ELO Ch.11-I(A).) Choice **B** is incorrect because it's immaterial to recovery by Albert that Eddy was not hurt. Choice **D** is incorrect. Eddy did not act reasonably under the circumstances. No one is supposed to increase his speed at an intersection to "beat" a light. Finally, Choice **A** is incorrect, because the last clear chance doctrine does not apply unless the defendant had an *actual* opportunity to avoid the accident at the last moment. (*See* ELO Ch.11-I(I)(4)(a).) On these facts, it cannot be said that Eddy had an opportunity to avoid the accident. He did apply his brakes, but it was too late. It is not even clear that the accident would have been avoided if he had not increased his speed. (It might be mentioned that in a comparative negligence state, the LCC doctrine is completely eliminated. It is simply a factor which is calculated into the determination of each party's proportion of fault.)

72. A   A defamatory statement must be reasonably susceptible of application to the plaintiff to be actionable. Because Joseph's statements were made indiscriminately to an indeterminate number of people at the office and because his remarks were interpreted by the friend as applying to Bill, Bill probably does have a cause of action. The plaintiff in a defamatory action must show that the statement in question was reasonably interpreted by at least one listener as referring to him. (*See* ELO Ch.17-II(D).) Joseph's remarks are clearly defamatory. And they would appear to have been made with a careless disregard for the facts when you consider that Bill did nothing more than ask Josephine to "stop by" if she passed the store. Choice **B** is not the best answer because a false statement about someone does not in itself constitute defamation. It's also necessary that the statement be published and the publication must be done either negligently or deliberately. (*See* ELO Ch.17-I(A).) Choice **C** is incorrect on the facts because a reasonable person — the friend — did associate the statements with Bill. Choice **D** is incorrect on the law. Defamation can be committed verbally.

73. A   The collateral source doctrine provides that the damages that a plaintiff recovers in a tort action will not be reduced by reimbursement she may receive from independent sources (*i.e.*, insurance proceeds, etc.). Although Debbie received an amount equal to her lost income as a consequence of her disability insurance, Karen is not entitled to an offset. (*See* ELO Ch.10-I(E)(1).) The reasoning behind this doctrine is that the plaintiff has paid for these benefits in some way (*e.g.*, by paying the insurance premiums) and that the contrary rule would create a windfall for the negligent defendant. Choice **B** is incorrect, since Debbie is not being indemnified by the insurance company. An indemnity payment results from the shifting of payment from one culpable party to another culpable party. The insurance company was not culpable. (*See* ELO Ch.7-V(A).) Choice **C** is incorrect. It is the very essence of the collateral source doctrine that the plaintiff is able to recover from the defendant as well as collect her contractual benefits (note, however, that the collateral sources doctrine has been criticized because it does provide duplicate recovery to the plaintiff). Choice **D** is an incorrect statement of the existing law in most jurisdictions.

74. A A joint and several tortfeasor who has paid more than his pro-rata share of a judgment ordinarily has a right of contribution from the other tortfeasors who participated in the accident. Because Mark's proportionate share of the joint and several judgment is one-third of $120,000, or $40,000, and he paid the full $120,000, he will be entitled to recover $40,000 each from Bruce and David. (*See* ELO Ch.7-IV(A),(B).) Choice **B** is incorrect because Mark cannot recover from Bruce or David under an indemnity theory. They were all equally culpable in causing the injury to Carl. (*See* ELO Ch.7(V)(A).) Choice **C** is incorrect because this is a contributory negligence jurisdiction, not one that relies on comparative negligence. No allocation of fault is made among the joint and several tortfeasors in a contributory negligence jurisdiction. Finally, Choice **D** is incorrect on the facts, which tell us that the three defendants were adjudged jointly and severally liable. (**Note:** the facts do not indicate what issues were tried before judgment was rendered against the defendants. Under these facts, either Bruce or David might argue that Mark was not entitled to contribution because he acted intentionally by participating in a drag race and violating the statute. However, because all three participated in the drag race, this argument would not be very persuasive.)

75. B Under "straight" or "pure" comparative negligence principles, a plaintiff's recovery is reduced by a proportion equal to his fault in bringing about the occurrence in question (even if he is more than 50% at fault). In calculating Veronica's recovery, we take the total loss suffered by both ($40,000) and multiply that by the percentage (60%) of responsibility attributable to Veronica, resulting in $24,000. We then subtract that number from Veronica's damage ($30,000) to get $6,000, which is the correct answer. [Note that Betty will be forced to swallow her entire loss of $10,000 in addition to her payment to Veronica under this formula: $40,000 x 40% =$16,000 - $10,000 = $6,000 (Betty's responsibility)].Choice **A** is incorrect because it fails to take the value of Betty's counterclaim into consideration. Choice **C** is incorrect because Veronica was 60% at fault and the amount is miscalculated. Finally, Choice **D** is incorrect. The facts tell us this is a straight or pure comparative negligence jurisdiction. In a partial or modified comparative negligence jurisdiction, a party more than 50% at fault (*e.g.*, Veronica) would not be entitled to recover.

76. B Computers are almost always sold by retailers in their original cartons. There is no way for the retailer to determine whether or not the computer is defective or will cause injury. Under these circumstances, especially because the retailer is strictly liable to the consumer for injuries caused by the defective products, it is only logical and fair to permit the retailer to secure indemnity against the manufacturer. (*See* ELO Ch.7-V(B)(2).) Because MiddleManCo also received the computer in its original carton from Compco and, presumably, did not alter the computer in any manner, The Computer Warehouse is entitled to indemnity only from Compco. Choice **A** is incorrect because there is no right of indemnity against MiddleManCo. Choice **C** is incorrect because the retailer ordinarily has a right to indemnity only against the manufacturer of the item unless the distributor has altered it in some manner. Finally, Choice **D** is incorrect. On these facts, The Computer Warehouse should be able to obtain indemnity from Compco.

77. C   The facts tell us that Kim and Stacy were equally culpable. Unless we are told otherwise, we can assume we are in a contributory negligence jurisdiction instead of one which utilizes comparative negligence. Because Stacey and Kim were joint tortfeasors, they are required to share the loss. (*See* ELO Ch.7-IV(B).) Choice **A** is incorrect because it states the reverse of the applicable rule. Choice **B** is incorrect because it doesn't matter who struck Patti. Both contributed to the accident. Choice **D** is incorrect. First of all, we have no basis in the facts for applying comparative negligence principles. Secondly, except in some states, in the states which use comparative negligence, the relative liability would be apportioned even if one of the two tortfeasors was more than 50% at fault. (*See* ELO Ch.11-II(D).)

78. D   Although one who engages in an abnormally dangerous activity is ordinarily liable to those suffering personal injury or property damage as a consequence of the peculiar risk associated with that conduct, he will not be liable if either (1) the harm is not that which can reasonably be anticipated from that conduct or (2) a supervening cause is actually responsible for the damage or injury. The peculiar risk associated with fumigation is the escape of noxious gas. It is not an explosion caused by a stranger who recklessly lights a match. (*See* ELO Ch.13-II(B).) Choice **A** is incorrect because the peculiar risk associated with fumigation is the escape of a noxious gas, not the flammability of that gas. Choice **B** is incorrect because although the fumes may have been a contributing cause, Kevin's reckless conduct was a superseding cause. Finally, Choice **C** is incorrect because both the abnormally dangerous activity doctrine and the principles of negligence allow an aggrieved plaintiff to recover for property damage as well as personal injury.

79. A The owner of a dangerous animal is strictly liable for injuries or property damages caused to others as a consequence of the propensities of the animal. Breeding poisonous snakes in a residential area probably constitutes this type of strict liability activity. This being the case, Amy could successfully sue Jocelyn, despite her own probable negligence in firing the rifle in a makeshift range in her backyard. (*See* ELO Ch.13-I(B).) Choice **C** is incorrect because contributory negligence by the plaintiff is not normally a defense to an action based on strict liability. Also, Amy could probably not be reasonably expected to foresee that Jocelyn was keeping a poisonous snake. Choice **B** is not the best answer because contributory negligence can be asserted as a defense even when the plaintiff is guilty of negligence *per se*. (*See* ELO Ch.5-VIII((D)(5).) Finally, Choice **D** is incorrect because a warning by Jocelyn after the snake had escaped would not remove her liability. Amy could not reasonably have been required to adopt any measures which would prevented the snake from biting her.

80. B A contractor which engages in an abnormally dangerous activity is liable to those suffering personal injury or property damage as a consequence of the peculiar risk associated with that activity, even if the defendant acted with due care. Since Danco was involved in an abnormally dangerous activity (blasting alongside a highway), it would be strictly liable for Carl's injuries. (*See* ELO Ch.13-II(C).) Contributory negligence by the plaintiff is not normally a defense in a strict liability claim, especially when the plaintiff's negligence consisted of inattentiveness. (*See* ELO Ch.13-III(C).) The fact that Carl may have been negligent in failing to notice the sign does not relieve Danco of liability. It's usual for people who blast to place flagman on the road to warn motorists under these circumstances. Choice **A** is incorrect because Danco's liability arises from the strict liability placed upon those who work with explosives, not from negligence or lack of care. Choice **C** is incorrect because one cannot assume a risk without having actual knowledge of it. Because he failed to notice the sign, Carl cannot have had any knowledge of the danger posed by the blasting. Finally, Choice **D** is incorrect because, even if Carl was contributorily negligent, he could nevertheless recover against Danco under strict liability principles.

81. A The owner of a domestic animal which has not previously exhibited dangerous or violent propensities is not strictly liable if that animal unexpectedly causes harm to another. (*See* ELO Ch.13-I(B)(1)(a).) Because Froo-Froo was obviously accustomed to the presence of people and Susan had no reason to suspect that she would ever bite anyone, Cindy can not recover from Susan. Choice **B** is incorrect because it states the wrong reason for precluding recovery by Cindy. The fact that she may have been engaged in an improper act is not a defense *per se* in a case involving the dangerous propensities of an animal. Choice **C** is incorrect because dogs are not considered dangerous animals unless and until they exhibit dangerous tendencies. Finally, Choice **D** is incorrect, because Susan's failure to obtain a license does not constitute negligence *per se*. There was no direct link between the lack of a license and the bite. There must be a nexus between the failure to comply with a law and the plaintiff's injury. (*See* ELO Ch.5-VIII(A)(2).)

82. **C**   Because the power saw malfunctioned in use and was defective for its purpose, Steve is able to recover in strict product liability. Any commercial supplier who, in the regular course of business, provides a defective product, is liable to the purchaser or user for personal injury or property damage resulting from the defect, even when that supplier has exercised due care; Restatement 2d of Torts 2d § 402A. (*See* ELO Ch.14-III(B).) Because Wecut Company, The Marx Brothers and Tom's Hardware Store are all commercial suppliers in the chain of delivery to Blue, they are all liable to Stephen under a products liability theory. Choices **A** and **B** are incorrect because they fail to recognize that liability extends to each level of the chain of supply. Finally, Choice **D** is incorrect because the facts specifically recite that there is no evidence that the power saw was negligently manufactured and the law does not require proof of negligence because Wecut is strictly liable for its defective product.

83. **D**   Strict liability for defects in products is applied only to sellers who are regularly engaged in the business of selling the product at issue. Restatement of Torts 2d § 402A(i)(a). (*See* ELO Ch.14-III(B).) Because Andrew was not a commercial supplier of cars, it is unlikely that Charles will recover from him under a products liability theory. Choice **B** is therefore incorrect. Choice **C** is wrong on the facts. There is nothing to indicate that Andrew was negligent in any way. He drove the car without problems for an entire week. Finally, Choice **A** is incorrect because only a ***merchant with respect to goods of that kind*** can be liable for breach of the implied warranty of merchantability. UCC § 2-314(1). Also, the warranty is not usually extended to used goods and the car had been used by Andrew when he sold it to Charles. (*See* ELO Ch.14-II(C)(1)(b),(c).)

84. **B**   A commercial supplier who, in the regular course of business, provides a defective product, is liable to the purchaser or user for personal injury or property damage resulting from the defect, even when the defendant has exercised due care in the item's production; Restatement of Torts 2d, § 402A. *See* ELO Ch.14-III(B) Although Drugco provided the pills to Dr.

Frank gratuitously, it did so with the intent that Dr. Frank should in turn offer them to her patients, not that she should put them in a glass case. Drugco's purpose was to encourage commerce in its product. Although the courts are sometimes more reluctant to apply strict products liability in the case of prescription drugs (*See* ELO Ch.14-III(D)(1)(a)), especially when the drugs have FDA approval, the injury here seems so severe and unforeseeable that strict liability should be imposed, especially because there is no evidence that the FDA had approved. Choice **A** is incorrect because Dr. Frank regularly provides services, rather than products. She is not a supplier of drugs in the normal chain of supply. Choice **C** is incorrect because Dr. Frank is not a merchant (someone who ordinarily deals in items of this type), and therefore would not come within the purview of UCC § 2-314. Finally, Choice **D** is incorrect because Alex can probably recover against Drugco for implied warranty of merchantantability in most courts. The doctrine of privity is now rarely applied to prevent recovery by a customer against the manufacturer of a defective product. (*See* ELO Ch.14-II(C)(3).)

85. B This question puts at issue the liability of a merchant for injuries to a stranger who is neither the purchaser nor a member of the family of potential users. It also requires examination of the difference between strict products liability and liability for implied warranty of merchantability. The correct answer is Choice **B**. Even though Margaret was a bystander, she was a foreseeable user. The product in question was a toy to be played with by children. Children often play with other children, who use their toys. Even though Jolson's Toy Store sold the toy rocket to Brett, it was intended for use by James and his friends. Margaret's guardian can successfully sue Jolson's under a products liability theory. (*See* ELO Ch.14-VI(B).) Choice **A** is incorrect because there is no evidence that James' parents were negligent. James had been utilizing the toy rocket without incident for a whole month. Choice **C** is incorrect because the lack of privity is no longer regarded in most courts as an obstacle to recovery for breach of the implied warranty of merchantability. (*See* ELO Ch.14-(C)(3)(d).) Finally, Choice **D** is incorrect because, as explained above, although Margaret may have no claim against Brett, it is likely that Margaret can successfully sue Jolson's Toy Store in products liability.

86. A An eight-seat airplane is obviously intended to be used by eight passengers. Because they are all foreseeable users, their executors will all be able to recover in strict product liability against the merchant who sold the plane to John if the plane was defective and the defect caused the plane to crash. Because the plane's engine malfunctioned on its first flight, it was clearly defective and Equinox will be liable to their executors. (*See* ELO Ch.14-VII(A).) Choice **B** is incorrect because, even if the evidence shows that the pilot performed his duties in a negligent manner, his negligence will probably not overcome the strict liability of Equinox. (*See* ELO Ch.14-IX(A).) Choice **C** is incorrect because, although Equinox did not ordinarily sell aircraft, it still provided planes to lessees or buyers on a regular basis. It was in the business of dealing in airplanes. Its liability for defects in its planes extended equally to planes it sold and planes it leased. Finally, Choice **D** is incorrect because even if it exercised due care, Equinox will still be liable in products liability.

87. B   A product is "defective" when, in light of its anticipated use, it is in an unreasonably dangerous condition. All the firms in the chain of distribution of Mountain High should have recognized that their warning was not adequate to prevent the ingestion of the product by a child. Nor did it describe adequately the extent of the risk involved. Mouthwash is meant to be placed in the mouth. There is no guarantee that it will not be swallowed. An adequate warning under all these circumstances would have told of the risk of death to a child who swallowed the mouthwash. (*See* ELO Ch.14-V(C)(2).) In addition to a more precise warning, a difficult-to-remove twist-off top could have been used. Because Acme Supermarket is a commercial supplier, it is liable to Margaret in strict product liability. Choice **A** is incorrect. It's immaterial whether or not Marlene could reasonably foresee that her child might ingest the mouthwash. The choice raises the issue of Margaret's contributory negligence. Contributory negligence is not normally a defense to a claim based on strict product liability. Choice **C** is incorrect because, again, Marlene's negligence does not relieve Acme of liability. Finally, Choice **D** is incorrect because Acme is a commercial supplier. It would have a right of indemnity from the distributor or manufacturer of Mountain High.

88. A   The key to answering this question correctly is to recognize that the claim is one for battery. Battery is an intentional tort in which the actor either intends the consequences of his acts or is charged with knowledge that the consequences are substantially certain to flow from his acts. (*See* ELO Ch.2-I(A),(B).) Once the manufacturer had recalled the vehicle, Floyd's should have recognized that an injury to a customer was substantially certain to occur and should have made certain that no salesperson would offer the car. Choice **B** is incorrect because the choice sounds in negligence and in product liability, neither of which is the basis for Mrs. Boom's complaint. Her claim is for battery. Choice **C** is incorrect. The salesperson's intent is irrelevant. The injury to Mrs. Boom was substantially certain to occur as a consequence of Floyd's conduct in failing to quarantine the car. Finally, Choice **D** is incorrect. because, even if Mrs. Boom was negligent in her operation of the car, her negligence would not relieve Floyd's of liability for battery.

89. A   An essential element of the torts dealing with injury to a person's reputation is that a statement made by the defendant about the plaintiff be communicated to at least one person other than the plaintiff. In other words, the statement must be "published." (*See* ELO Ch.17-V(A), Ch.18-I(E).) This is true both of defamation and of false light. Since Josh's remark was made only to Peter it would not be actionable. The fact that Peter re-told Josh's comment to several of his co-workers is not pertinent. The "publication" was not by Josh but by Peter. Choice **B** is irrelevant since no tort has occurred, and, in any event, an apology would not preclude liability if defamation had occurred. Choice **C** is incorrect because both defamation and false light, by their very nature, require publication. Finally, Choice **D** is incorrect because there has been no public disclosure of objectionable private facts. The "public disclosure" or "invasion of privacy" element of this tort is missing.

90. A   The tort called invasion of privacy is actually four distinct torts. The one relevant to this question is the tort of publicity of private life. This tort occurs when someone publicizes the details of a plaintiff's private life. If the plaintiff is to succeed, he must show that the disclosures would be highly offensive to a reasonable person. He must also show that the facts disclosed are truly private and, probably, that they are not of legitimate public concern. (*See* ELO Ch.18-I(D); Rest. 2d of Torts § 652D(b).) These facts present a dilemma. Is a wedding by its nature so public that it cannot ever be considered "private." And is news about a wedding ever offensive? As between Arnie and the Ranka family, there has probably been an invasion of privacy. This is because Arnie was specifically told that the wedding was private and that the press was excluded. The answer might be different if a reporter for Exposed had succeeded in invading the wedding without being invited. Choice **C** is incorrect because Exposed did not itself cover the event but obtained the tape from its joint tortfeasor. Choice **B is** incorrect only because it does not go far enough. Arnie not only taped the wedding, he sold the tape to Exposed. Choice **D** is incorrect. Not all weddings are social and public events. People often have good reason to arrange very private weddings.

91. D   A commercial supplier who, in the regular course of business, provides a defective product, is liable to the purchaser or user for personal injury or property damage resulting from the defect, even when the defendant has exercised due care with respect to the item; Restatement 2d of Torts

§402A. (*See* ELO Ch.14-III(B).) The injured plaintiff many sue any or all of the firms which have been a part of the chain of distribution — manufacturer, distributor or retailer. If she recovers against one, the defendant may be entitled to indemnity from another firm in the chain. Yattle is liable to John under the products liability doctrine, but can obtain indemnity from Xavier, the manufacturer, which is more directly culpable than the distributor. The correct answer is Choice **D**. Choice **C** is incorrect because the retailer is not more directly culpable than Yattle (the distributor). Choice **B** is incorrect because (1) John was probably a foreseeable user (rather than a mere bystander), and (2) even bystanders are, in most jurisdictions, permitted to recover under a products liability theory. (*See* ELO Ch.14-VI(B).) Finally, Choice **A** is incorrect because products liability is a strict liability theory. Yattle is liable under this theory even if it exercised due care in handling the set.

Index

References are to the number of the question raising the issue.
"E" indicates an Essay Question; "M" indicates a Multiple-Choice Question